Paul Hattaway, a nat[illegible] Asia for most of his li[illegible] the author of *The Heav[illegible], An Asian Harvest, Operation China*, and many other books. He and his wife, Joy, are the founders of Asia Harvest (www.asiaharvest.org) which supports hundreds of indigenous missionaries and has provided millions of Bibles to spiritually hungry Christians throughout Asia.

Also by Paul Hattaway:

The Heavenly Man

An Asian Harvest

Operation China

China's Book of Martyrs

The China Chronicles 1: Shandong

The China Chronicles 2: Guizhou

The China Chronicles 3: Zhejiang

The China Chronicles 4: Tibet

The China Chronicles 5: Henan

The China Chronicles 6: Xinjiang

SHAANXI

The Cradle of Chinese Civilization

Paul Hattaway

PIQUANT editions

Asia Harvest

First published in 2023 by Piquant Editions in the UK
Also published in 2023 by Asia Harvest, **www.asiaharvest.org**

Piquant Editions
www.piquanteditions.com

ISBNs
978-1-80329-009-6 Print
978-1-80329-010-2 Mobi

British Library Cataloguing-in-Publication Data
A catalogue record of this book is available in the UK from the British Library.

ISBN 978-1-80329-009-6

Cover and Book Design: projectluz.com

Shaanxi

陕西

"West of the Mountain Passes"

Map of China showing Shaanxi

Pronounced:	Shahn-shee		
Old Spelling:	Shen-si		
Population:	35,365,072 (2000)		
	37,327,379 (2010)		
	39,528,999 (2020)		
Area:	79,500 sq. miles (205,800 sq. km)		
Population Density:	484 people per sq. mile (192 per sq. km)		
Highest Elevation:	Mt. Taibai – 12,360 feet (3,767 meters)		
Capital City:	Xi'an	5,206,253	
Other Cities:	Baoji	871,940	
(2010 – the most	Xianyang	730,704	
recent census with	Tongchuan	463,866	
specific city data)	Yulin	429,189	
	Ankang	379,707	
	Hanzhong	350,167	
	Weinan	347,484	
Administrative	Prefectures	10	
Divisions:	Counties	107	
	Towns	1,745	
			Percent
Major Ethnic Groups:	Han Chinese	35,188,651	99.5
(2000 – the most	Hui	139,232	0.4
recent census with	Manchu	15,801	0.1
specific ethnic data)	Mongol	6,060	0.1

Contents

Foreword

Over many years and generations, the followers of Jesus in China have set their hearts to be the witnesses of Christ to the nation. Many have paid a great price for their ministry, and the brutal persecutions they have endured for the faith have often been unimaginable.

The Bible commands all believers to "Go into all the world and preach the gospel to all creation" (Mark 16:15). Many foreign missionaries responded to this command in the past, traveling to China to proclaim the Word of God. They blessed the land with their message of new life in Christ, and suffered greatly when the darkness clashed with God's light. Their faithful service despite great hardship was a beautiful example for Chinese believers to emulate as they served God.

China today still urgently needs more servants and laborers to take the gospel throughout the land. God is looking for people who will stand up and declare, "Lord, here am I. Please send me!"

The Day of our Lord is near. May your hearts be encouraged by the testimonies of what the Lord Jesus Christ has done in China, to the praise of His glorious Name!

May the Lord raise up more testimonies that will glorify His Name in our generation, the next generation, and forever more!

Lord, You are the victorious King. Blessed are those who follow you to the end!

A humble servant of Christ,
*Moses Xie (1918–2011)**

---

* The late Moses Xie wrote this Foreword for The China Chronicles prior to his death in 2011. He was a highly respected Chinese house church leader who spent 23 years of his life in prison for the Name of Jesus Christ.

Reactions to China Chronicles Books from Christians in China

The book you have in your hands is part of The China Chronicles, which the author is primarily writing to bless and encourage the persecuted Church in China. Each book in the series is being translated into Chinese, and thousands of copies are being distributed free of charge throughout China's house church networks.

The Communist authorities in China have blocked the publication of most Christian books, especially those that deal with revival and persecution. Consequently, these China Chronicles books have been like living water to the thirsty Chinese believers who eagerly desire to read about the mighty acts God has performed in their nation. Here are just a few reactions from house church Christians:

> We never had a good understanding of how the Lord established His kingdom in our midst, but thanks to these precious books, now we know how God has achieved great and amazing works through His servants in each province. We continue to pray that more life-giving books will flow to us!
>
> (Brother Yang, Chongqing)

> We believe the revival fires of the Holy Spirit will again be lit in our generation, and the mighty power of the Lord will sweep millions of our countrymen and women into the family of God. These are really amazing books. Please send more!
>
> (Brother Jiang, Hubei Province)

It is very important for the children of God to understand the history of the Church in different parts of China. After all, history is His Story. These are precious books, offering us in-depth accounts of the history of the body of Christ. We eagerly await each book in the series, as they will give us a more comprehensive understanding of God's glorious work in China.

(Brother Zhai, Beijing)

My husband and I read your book together, and we shared many thoughts and tears as we discovered testimonies we have never heard before. Our spiritual lives have been deeply enriched and encouraged. We hope to receive new books in the series as soon as they are available.

(Sister Xu, Shanghai)

We live in Wuhan and read your book while our city was going through its unprecedented trial. As we read how the Lord established and empowered His Church, we realized that He has been in control in the past, He is in control in the present, and He will continue to be in control in the future. Thank you for sharing these priceless nuggets of gold with us!

(Brother Cai, Hubei Province)

I shared your book with my fellow brothers and sisters in our Bible study group. We all loved it. Such living and relevant Christian history is nowhere to be found in our country, and we treasure it. We beg you to send more of these books.

(Brother Zhou, Zhejiang Province)

I gave your book to my son, who is a college student. He studies history, but said that none of the textbooks in his school teach anything like this. It is eye-opening and refreshing to our souls.

(Sister Ping, Jiangxi Province)

As the sovereignty of our Lord Jesus Christ was revealed to us through all the incidents in history, we grew acutely aware that He is in complete control, and we have nothing to fear. As a result, we now have more confidence and faith in Him, knowing that He cares for us and that the Spirit of God is at work behind the scenes, weaving together a beautiful narrative as His salvation spreads throughout our nation.

(Brother Gong, Sichuan Province)

The China Chronicles Overview

Many people are aware of the extraordinary explosion of Christianity throughout China in recent decades, with the church now numbering in excess of one million members. Few, however, know how this miracle has occurred. The China Chronicles are an ambitious project to document the advance of Christianity in each province of China from the time the gospel was first introduced to the present day.

The genesis for this project came at a meeting I attended in the year 2000 in which leaders of the Chinese house church movements expressed the need for their members to understand how God established His kingdom throughout China. As a result, it is planned that these books will be translated into Chinese and distributed widely among both the church in China and overseas. Millions of Chinese Christians know little of their spiritual heritage, and my prayer is that multitudes would be strengthened, edified, and challenged by these books to carry the torch of the Holy Spirit to their generation.

My intention is not to present readers with a dry list of names and dates, but to bring alive the marvelous stories of how God has caused His kingdom to take root and flourish in the world's most populated country. I consider it a great honor to write these books, especially as I have been entrusted, through hundreds of hours of interviews conducted throughout China, with many precious testimonies that have never previously been shared in public.

Another reason for compiling The China Chronicles is to have a record of God's mighty acts in China. As a new believer in the 1980s, I recall reading many reports from the Soviet Union of how Christian men and women were being brutally persecuted, yet the kingdom of God was growing rapidly, with many people meeting Jesus Christ. By the time the Soviet empire collapsed in the early 1990s, no one had systematically recorded the glorious deeds of the Holy Spirit during the Communist era. Tragically, the body of Christ has largely forgotten the miracles God performed in those decades behind the Iron Curtain, and we are much the poorer for it. Consequently, I am determined to preserve a record of God's work in China so that future generations of believers can learn about the wonderful events that have transformed tens of millions of lives there.

At the back of each volume will appear a detailed statistical analysis estimating the number of Christians living within each province of China. This is the first comprehensive survey of the number of believers in China—in every one of its more than 2,800 cities, districts, and counties—in nearly a century. Such a huge undertaking would be impossible without the cooperation and assistance of numerous organizations and individuals.

I appreciate mission organizations such as the International Mission Board, Overseas Missionary Fellowship, Revival Chinese Ministries International, and many others who graciously allowed me to access their archives, libraries, photographs, collections, and personal records. I am indebted to the many believers whose generosity exemplified Jesus' command: "Freely you have received; freely give" (Matt. 10:8).

Many Chinese believers, too numerous to list, have lovingly assisted in this endeavor. For example, I fondly recall the aged house church evangelist Elder Fu, who required two young men to assist him up the stairs to my hotel room because he was eager to be interviewed for this series. Although he had spent many years in prison for the gospel, this saint desperately wanted to testify of God's great works so that believers around the world could be inspired and encouraged to live a more consecrated life.

Finally, it would be remiss not to thank the Lord Jesus Christ. As you read these books, my prayer is that He will emerge from the pages not merely as an historical figure, but as Someone ever present, longing to seek and to save the lost by displaying His power and transformative grace.

Today, the church in China is one of the strongest in the world, both spiritually and numerically. Yet little more than a century ago, China was considered one of the most difficult mission fields. The great Welsh missionary Griffith John once wrote,

> The good news is moving but very slowly. The people are as hard as steel. They are eaten up both soul and body by the world, and do not seem to feel that there can be reality in anything beyond sense. To them our doctrine is foolishness, our talk jargon. We discuss and beat them in argument. We reason them into silence and shame; but the whole effort falls upon them like showers upon a sandy desert.[1]

How things have changed! When it is all said and done, no person in China will be able to take credit for the amazing revival that has occurred. It will be clear that this great accomplishment is the handiwork of none other than the Lord Jesus Christ. We will stand in awe and declare:

> The Lord has done this,
>   and it is marvelous in our eyes.
> The Lord has done it this very day;
>   let us rejoice and be glad. (Ps 118:23–24)

Paul Hattaway

Publisher's Note: In The China Chronicles, we have avoided specific information such as individuals' names or details that could directly lead to the identification of house church workers. The exception to this rule is when a leader has already become so well-known around the world that there is little point concealing that person's identity in these books. This same principle applies to the use of photographs.

Several different systems for writing the sounds of Chinese characters in English have been used over the years, the main ones being the Wade-Giles system, introduced in 1912, and Pinyin, literally "spelling sounds" which has been the accepted form in China since 1979. In The China Chronicles, all names of people and places are given in their Pinyin form. This means that the places formerly spelled Chung-king, Shantung, and Tientsin are now respectively Chongqing, Shandong, and Tianjin; Mao Tse-tung becomes Mao Zedong, and so on. The only times we have retained the old spelling of names is when they are part of the title of a published book or article listed in the notes or bibliography.

The term "Evangelical" has various meanings to different people, and in some parts of the world in recent decades has come to define those with a political agenda. In The China Chronicles, the term "Evangelical" is used to describe all Christians in China who are not Catholic or Orthodox Christians.

Introduction

The Chess Pavilion in the Hua Mountains of Shaanxi
Imagine China – Tuchong

West of the mountain passes

The first thing the non-Chinese ought to know about Shaanxi Province in north China is that it is not the same as the similarly named Shanxi Province which borders it to the east. The Zhongtiao Mountain Range and the Yellow River, the sixth longest river in the world, form the border between the two northern provinces.

Shaanxi (陕西) means "west of the mountain passes," while neighboring Shanxi (山西) means "west of the mountains." In spoken Chinese, the names of the two provinces differ only by tone. In Pinyin, the method of spelling Mandarin words with Roman letters, Shānxī and Shǎnxī would normally be spelled the same, with only the tone markers to distinguish them. To avoid confusion, the Pinyin system made an exception by doubling the first vowel in Shaanxi—thus the spelling was adjusted to avoid confusion in the rest of the world. In the pre-Communist era, the Western world usually differentiated the two provinces of Shaanxi and Shanxi by spelling them Shensi and Shansi, respectively.

The similarities between Shaanxi and Shanxi are not limited to their names. The provinces are also similar in size, terrain, language, and ethnic composition. They share an almost identical population, with Shaanxi home to 39.2 million people in 2020, compared to Shanxi's 38.9 million.

However in China, Shaanxi holds a very distinct position in history. Scholar Leo Moser remarks,

> Nomadic incursions often isolated the people of Shaanxi and the other western provinces from the remainder of the Sinitic peoples. The very fact that the current name of the province, Shaanxi, means 'west of the passes' implies that the perceived center of the Han world had moved toward the east.[1]

Today, Shaanxi Province's 39 million people inhabit an area of 79,500 square miles (205,000 sq. km), which is almost identical in size to the US state of Minnesota, although Shaanxi is home to seven times as many people as the North Star State. For another comparison, Shaanxi is slightly smaller yet contains two-thirds more people as England and Scotland combined.

Three markedly different regions

Geographically, Shaanxi can be divided into three regions. The north of the province is where Chinese civilization first began and is today a plateau covered with a thick layer of wind-blown loess soil. Life is difficult for those who try to eke out a living there, and winters are bitterly cold whenever icy winds sweep down from the Mongolian grasslands north of the Great Wall. At times, dust storms roll down from the steppes, suffocating entire towns.

Most people in Shaanxi live in the central areas where the industrial and agricultural heartland of the province is located. The densely populated Xi'an Plain has seen waves of people migrate from other parts of China during the past century, particularly from Shandong, Shanxi, and Henan Provinces. The people of the Plain are cut off from southern Shaanxi by the rugged Qinling Mountains, which rise to 12,360 feet (3,767 meters) above sea level. The Qinling Range divides the river and weather systems of the province in much the same way the Rockies do in the United States.

For thousands of years, the people of southern Shaanxi have been isolated by the formidable mountain barriers which historically had just three passes spanning their entire length. As a result, many natives of Xi'an consider themselves to be "pure" Shaanxi people, and they tend to look down at those from outlying parts of the province.

Even the cuisine differs on each side of the mountains. In the south, the food has a sour and spicy flavor like that of neighboring Sichuan, whereas food in northern Shaanxi emphasizes savory flavors and uses condiments such as salt, garlic, onions, and vinegar. Noodles, rather than rice, form the staple of Shaanxi cuisine, while centuries of Muslim influence in the province is reflected in its many lamb and mutton dishes.

The south, which borders six different provinces, is comparatively lush and enjoys a milder climate that the rest of Shaanxi, with much of the region still covered by dense forests. A small number of China's beloved giant panda dwell in bamboo forests there, along with exotic animals including golden snub-nose monkeys, red pandas, and golden leopards.

The great inventions

An entire book would scarcely do justice to the remarkably rich history of Shaanxi, and thus it seems inadequate to include just a short summary here. The province has been the seat for what the Chinese call the "Four Great Inventions" that changed the world—the compass, paper, printing, and gunpowder.

The Chinese were using the compass to navigate approximately one thousand years before Christ, and they used gunpowder during the Tang Dynasty (618–907), at least three centuries before the first mention of it in the West. Similarly, printing in China dates to the eighth century AD, some 700 years before it was seen in Europe. By the time of the Northern Song Dynasty (960–1127), texts were being widely printed and distributed across north China. Apart from the Four Great Inventions, a vast array of lesser inventions emanated from China including,

> Steel, the blast furnace… the crossbow, the horse collar and stirrups, scissors, the abacus, chopsticks, fireworks, and porcelain. Wheelbarrows were invented to facilitate the moving of loads; playing cards were made to pass the time; matches were developed to provide fire, and waxed umbrellas to keep off rain and the sun's rays.[2]

Centuries of famine and flood

The people of Shaanxi have encountered many obstacles over the course of history with drought, famines, wars, and floods bringing great distress upon the besieged population. As the ground in Shaanxi is typically rocky, for centuries people have found the lush plains of other provinces tempting, especially during times of famine. Between AD 281 and 290, severe drought caused millions of people to flee Shaanxi, with many settling in

Henan Province. In some areas, according to a Chinese account, less than two out of ten families remained.

The frequent mass exoduses of people have kept the population of Shaanxi moderate by Chinese standards, with its 39 million people today significantly less than two of its similarly sized neighboring provinces: Henan (97 million) and Hubei (55 million).

Marco Polo in Shaanxi

The extraordinary travels of Marco Polo took him and his uncle Maffeo through Shaanxi in the thirteenth century, although they did not spend much time there. They entered China by the western arm of the Silk Road and reached a terminus in the city of Chang'an, which was later renamed Xi'an.

Xi'an served as the capital and greatest city of China for 1,200 years, but it lost that honor to Beijing just seven years before Polo visited Shaanxi. Xi'an remained an important city, however, and one of Kublai Khan's sons ruled the province from a magnificent palace, which Polo detailed in his description of the city:

> In old times it was a noble, rich, and powerful realm, and had many great and wealthy kings.... It is a city of great trade and industry. They have great abundance of silk, from which they weave cloths of silk and gold of divers kinds, and they also manufacture all sorts of equipment for the army. They have every necessity of life very cheap.... The people are idolaters, and outside the city is the palace of the Prince Mangalai, crowned king, and son of the Great Khan.
>
> A fine palace stands in a great plain abounding in lakes and streams and springs of water. Round about it is a massive and lofty wall, five miles in compass, well built, and all garnished with battlements.... The king's palace is so great and fine that no one could imagine a finer one. There are in it many great and splendid halls, and many chambers, all painted and embellished with work

> in beaten gold. Mangalai rules his realm well with justice and equity and is much beloved by his people.[3]

In a single sentence that fascinated Christians in Europe at the time, Polo reported on the religious practices of the people he observed: "The inhabitants in general worship idols, but there are also found here Nestorian Christians, Turks, and Saracens [Arabs]."[4]

When the account of Marco Polo's travels was published in Europe years later, many mocked his descriptions, saying it was impossible for a palace to have a five-mile-long wall and causing some critics to question the veracity of his writings.

We know now, however, that Marco Polo's account was accurate. Today, tourists can visit the Weiyang (never ending) Palace, which was first constructed in 200 BC. It remains the largest palace in history, covering 1,200 acres, making it almost seven times the size of the Forbidden City in Beijing, and eleven times larger than the Vatican City.

Traumatic events

For centuries, Xi'an vied with Rome and Constantinople for the title of the greatest city in the world, but over time Xi'an's glory faded. Regular floods and famines plagued the province, and a massive earthquake in 1556 is believed to have killed 830,000 people, making it one of the deadliest earthquakes in China.[5] The quake affected people in 97 counties across a 520 mile (840 km) area. Rebellions have also caused huge societal upheavals and the deaths of millions of people in Shaanxi.

The Great Mosque, which serves as the spiritual base for Muslims not only in Xi'an but throughout north China, was first built in 742 and is the largest mosque in China today. Although it now serves as a tourist attraction, the mosque was the center of many conflicts and uprisings over the centuries. One rebellion devastated the province from 1340 to 1368 and helped usher in the Ming Dynasty, and a later uprising from 1620 to 1644 resulted in the overthrow of the Ming and the establishment of the Qing (Manchu) Dynasty, which ruled China until 1911.

A widespread Muslim rebellion between 1862 and 1877 resulted in the slaughter of a massive number of people. One summary of what is now known as the Dungan Revolt indicates the remarkable impact the conflict had on the people of Shaanxi and neighboring Gansu:

> The conflict led to a population loss of 20.77 million people in Shaanxi and Gansu due to migration and war-related death. It was started by riots of the Hui and massacres of the Han Chinese, accompanied by the revenge killing of Hui by the Han. At least four million Hui were in Shaanxi before the revolt, but only 20,000 remained while the rest were all killed in massacres and reprisals by government and militia forces, or were deported out of the province....
>
> 700,000 to 800,000 Hui in Shaanxi who were deported to Gansu were massacred along the way by the militia carrying out the deportations, until only a few thousand of them remained alive. Many also died from thirst and starvation on the journey.[6]

In another time of tragedy, at least five million people perished in a famine from 1876 to 1878, when starving people resorted to cannibalism. Later famines in the 1910s and 1920s claimed millions more lives.

The traumatic events that have shaped Shaanxi throughout its long history resulted in sharp demographic rises and falls. A massive influx of immigrants from other provinces caused the population of Shaanxi to more than double between 1947 and 1964, as the following table shows:

POPULATION OF SHAANXI (1912–2010)		
Year	**Population**	**Percent change**
1912	9,364,000	—
1928	11,802,000	+26.0
1937	9,780,000	−17.1
1947	10,011,000	+2.4
1954	15,881,281	+58.6
1964	20,766,915	+30.8
1982	28,904,423	+39.2
1990	32,882,403	+13.8
2000	35,365,072	+7.6
2010	37,327,378	+5.5
2020	39,528,999	+5.9

Mao Zedong riding a horse during the Long March, which concluded in Shaanxi in 1935 and helped the Communists win the civil war

The heart of Chinese Communism

The grinding poverty and dismal conditions in Shaanxi during the first half of the twentieth century contributed to the appeal and rise of the Communists. They enjoyed strong support for their civil war against the Guomindang (Nationalists), which Mao directed from his base at Yan'an in northern Shaanxi from 1936 to 1947.

One of the greatest heroes of the Communist Revolution was Xi Zhongxun, a native of Fuping County in Shaanxi. He was recognized for his bravery and was part of the first generation of Communist leaders.

In 1953, Xi's wife Qi Xin gave birth to a son, whom they named Jinping. He grew up in Shaanxi, and even lived in a cave house in the north of the province for a time. The young man applied to join the Communist Party nine times but was rejected on each occasion before his tenth attempt finally succeeded in 1974.

Five-year-old Xi Jinping (left) with his brother and father in 1958

After gradually rising through the ranks, Xi Jinping came to power as the president of China in 2013, and he quickly eliminated his detractors and consolidated his authority. In 2018, term limits were removed, effectively making Xi "president for life." A personality cult soon grew up around this son of Shaanxi who in all but name and title could be considered the latest in a long lineage of emperors dating back to the start of Chinese history.

The people of Shaanxi today

Shaanxi is recognized as the cradle of Chinese civilization and the center of the Han people. Its population is overwhelmingly Han, with few ethnic minorities found in the province. According to a Chinese census taken in 2000 that included specific ethnicity data, some 99.5 percent of the population in Shaanxi is Han, with only the 200,000 Hui (Chinese Muslims) making any noticeable variant to the demographic composition. Small communities of Mongols are also found in northern Shaanxi.

Although a large majority of Han people in Shaanxi speak Mandarin, more than four million people living in northern parts of the province speak the Jin language, which is used by more than 50 million Chinese throughout north China. Visitors from other parts of China are often baffled when they hear Jin being spoken, as it is markedly different from Mandarin.

The Shaanxi economy

Almost all of Shaanxi is rugged and mountainous, leaving only 1.6 percent of its land able to be farmed. Wheat, maize, and linseed are common crops, while the province ranks third in China for the production of coal, natural gas, and oil.

Shaanxi is also acknowledged as the country's leading aircraft and aerospace manufacturer. Textiles and electronics are other major industries, and in the past twenty years the government has attempted to transform Shaanxi's economy by creating many high-tech industrial and software zones. While higher paying jobs have attracted skilled workers to the province, most people outside the major cities remain poorly educated and financially impoverished.

Christianity in Shaanxi

Each volume in *The China Chronicles* has a different emphasis. Volumes on some provinces highlight the extraordinary revival that has swept millions into God's kingdom in the past several decades. Other books focus on the rich missions history of that province, detailing how the church was established by waves of dedicated missionaries before the mantle was handed over to Chinese Christians.

This book on Christianity in Shaanxi has a unique emphasis. Although it covers both the missions history and current explosive growth of the Chinese church, the province stands alone in that many readers will find the ancient history of Shaanxi the most fascinating part of the book—with some events that pre-date Christianity having shaped Chinese culture to the present day.

After a painstakingly slow and difficult start in the nineteenth and early twentieth centuries, Evangelical Christianity in Shaanxi has flourished in recent decades. Although there are provinces in China with many more Christians, Shaanxi has been part of the great revival of Christianity under Communism. Today an estimated 3.4 million Christians live in the province—about 8.6 percent of the population. This book details the story of how the Spirit of God breathed life into the Shaanxi church and caused it to flourish during the past forty years.

The Cradle of Chinese Civilization

Huang Di and the beginning of Chinese identity

From the very beginning of recorded history, Shaanxi has been considered to be the cradle of Chinese civilization. It was the home of the fabled "Yellow Emperor," Huang Di, who appeared so long ago that historians aren't sure how much of the accounts of his life are myth or fact.

A seventeenth-century Jesuit priest Martino Martini, after carefully studying the Chinese histories and classics, estimated that Huang Di ruled from 2698 to 2598 BC. The Chinese accepted Martini's research, and it is still used today.[1]

According to some Bible scholars, these dates would place Huang Di's reign in the century following the dispersion of humans after Noah's flood, and within decades of people being scattered around the globe following the Tower of Babel.[2] The Bible states, "Now the whole world had one language and a common speech. As people moved eastward, they found a plain in Shinar and settled there" (Gen. 11:1–2), and: "From there the LORD scattered them over the face of the whole earth" (Gen. 11:9). Although it's impossible to prove dates from so long ago, it is startling that the Chinese chronologies so closely match the earliest biblical records of the dispersion of mankind.

Huang Di is said to have introduced basic arts and sciences to China and is credited with inventing the calendar, boats, and pottery. As a result, he has traditionally been considered to be the first emperor of the Chinese people. The Han today still regard

Huang Di as the father of the Chinese race in much the same way that Abraham is the father of the Jews.

A cataclysmic flood

If the first inhabitants of Shaanxi Province arrived soon after the biblical flood recorded in Genesis, it would be natural to assume that they would have possessed accounts of the flood that wiped out almost the entire human race. Incredibly, at least a dozen ethnic minority groups in China have retained oral accounts of a global flood. The earliest Han Chinese records also tell of a

A woodcut depiction of Huang Di by an artist during the Tang Dynasty (AD 618–907)

cataclysmic flood, which modern scholars have tried to explain as merely a major flood of the Yellow River. In the *Shu Jing* (Classic of History), Emperor Yao (*c.* 2356–2255 BC) described the epic event in these words: "Like endless boiling water, the flood is pouring forth destruction. Boundless and overwhelming, it overtops hills and mountains. Rising and ever rising, it threatens the very heavens. How the people must be groaning and suffering!"[3]

Another ancient Chinese account says, "Great waters overspread the universe, and men were reduced to the condition of fishes."[4] The Evangelical missionary Samuel Clarke, who labored among the tribes of southwest China for more than thirty years, translated into English several flood stories that were handed down orally from generation to generation. He writes,

> According to Chinese mythology, Pan-ku was the first man, but Fuxi was also the first man of another epoch, and it is worthy of note that there were ten generations between Pan-ku and Fuxi (the same number of generations as between Adam and Noah). The time of Fuxi is given as 2852 BC. Evidently for these reasons some writers have spoken of Fuxi as the Chinese Noah.[5]

Emperor Shun

Emperor Shun lived from approximately 2317 to 2208 BC and was the last ruler of China's legendary Three Sovereigns and Five Emperors period. As documented in the *Shu Jing*, Emperor Yao offered the throne to Shun after he proved worthy by being a moral and upright leader. Shun, who was 53 years old at the time, had sought to appoint someone more virtuous than himself, but Emperor Yao could find no such person.

According to many Bible scholars, Shun lived at the same time as Abraham, and remarkably the two patriarchs, thousands of miles apart, shared some of the same characteristics in the way they sought to honor the true God. In a crucial decision that was to have major ramifications in China for countless generations, after ascending the throne, Emperor Shun offered sacrifices to the Heavenly Emperor, Shangdi—which is the name used for God in the Chinese Bible today.

The attributes of Shangdi include that He is the Creator of the universe, is all-knowing and all-powerful, and cannot be represented by any image, and He controls all the affairs of mankind. Some have suggested that the ancient Chinese must have heard of the sacrificial rites revealed by God to the Israelites, but Emperor Shun lived centuries before the law of Moses was given.

A depiction of Emperor Yao by a thirteenth-century artist

Three ancient songs

The earliest Chinese rulers offered their sacrifices to Shangdi atop a circular mound during a ceremony consisting of nine stages. Upon reaching the altar,

> with his face to the floor, China's emperor—the most powerful man in the most powerful nation of the world at the time—humbled himself to worship and burn incense to Huang Tian Shangdi, meaning "Supreme Lord of the Great Heaven". He accorded Shangdi the highest honor by kneeling three times and koutouing [prostrating himself with his forehead touching the ground] three times with each kneeling, for a total of nine koutous.[6]

During the annual Border Sacrifice, musicians played tunes, and ancient lyrics were sung which told of events in history dating back to God's creation. Just when these songs were composed, and how the ancient Chinese knew the information contained in them, has baffled historians. One song, the "Zhonghe Zhiqu" (Song of Central Peace) says,

> In the beginning, there was great chaos, without form and dark. The five planets had not begun to revolve, nor the two lights to shine. In the midst of it there existed neither matter nor sound. You, O Spiritual Sovereign, came forth in Your sovereignty, and first did separate the impure from the pure. You made heaven; you made earth; You made man. All things became alive with reproducing power.[7]

A second song, "Yuanhe Zhiqu" (Song of Beginning Peace), begins,

> Lord, when You separated the heavens and the earth, Your creative work had begun. You did produce, O Spirit, the seven elements. Their beautiful and brilliant lights lit up the sky and the earth. All

> things were good. I, Your servant, thank You fearfully, and while I worship, present this memorial to You, calling you Sovereign.[8]

While this worship was conducted, the emperor of China prostrated himself on the ground in sub-zero temperatures before Shangdi. In a third song, the emperor of China proclaims God's love and the greatness of His Name:

> You have promised to hear us, for You are our Father. I, Your child, dull and unenlightened, am unable to show forth my dutiful feelings. I thank You, that You have accepted our pronouncement. Honorable is your great Name.... As swallows rejoice in the spring, we praise Your abundant love.[9]

An altar mound discovered in Xi'an in 1999 is believed to be at least one of the places where emperors met with Shangdi to offer annual sacrifices. An online archaeological report says,

> Constructed of rammed earth and composed of four circular platforms that originally rose 26 feet (7.9 meters) high, the altar was

This circular altar, discovered in the suburbs of Xi'an in 1999, is where emperors are believed to have offered annual sacrifices to the God of Heaven

> uncovered a half-mile (800 meters) southeast of Xian's southern gate, confirming references to it in ancient historical sources such as The Old History of the Tang Dynasty and The History of the Sui Dynasty. The sides and the surfaces of the altar's platforms were covered with a layer of yellow clay and topped off with a quarter-inch thick layer of gray-white paste, made from seed husks and straw, that gave the altar a white appearance.[10]

Chinese Christian scholar Chen Kei Thong enthuses: "Xi'an was the imperial capital for at least five different dynasties. It is therefore not surprising that such an altar, central to the worship of Shangdi, was found there."[11]

By offering an annual sacrifice, the emperor of China sought God's favor on the nation, and His blessing on their crops. Many centuries later, after China's capital was moved to Beijing, the emperors of the Ming Dynasty rekindled the annual sacrifice at the Temple of Heaven, observing rituals based on ancient records that stemmed from the time of Emperor Shun and his successors.

The Shimao Kingdom

In recent years, archaeologists have begun to examine the ruins of the Shimao Pyramid which lies within Shenmu County in the northernmost part of Shaanxi Province. The ruins are located between the northern edge of the Loess Plateau and the southern edge of the Ordos Desert which spreads far into neighboring Inner Mongolia. The lifeblood of the region, the Yellow River, is situated nearby.

Whereas many of the earliest records of Chinese civilization teeter between the realms of myth and fact, the Shimao site provides one of the earliest and most concrete evidences of life in Shaanxi prior to the first dynastical rule.

In 2022, a team of archaeologists reportedly found a portrait of a king carved into the foot of the huge Shimao Pyramid, which they have dated to approximately 2200 BC. A report on their findings says,

> At more than 70 meters (230 feet), Shimao is about half the height of the Giza pyramids that were built around the same time in Egypt. But unlike other ancient pyramid structures, which mostly served religious purposes, Shimao had a practical use: at the top of it stood a palace spanning more than 80,000 sq. meters [20 acres]—about the size of ten soccer fields.
>
> Archaeologists have uncovered complex structures in the palace including a garden pool where crocodiles were kept. It overlooked a vast walled city—50 times bigger than the palace—with courtyards, streets and public squares all built with stone.[12]

Other excavations revealed that the Shimao city was surrounded by inner and outer stone walls, which were an average of 8 feet (2.4 meters) thick. The outer wall had a perimeter of 3.5 miles (5.7 km) and featured gates, watchtowers, and turrets. The size of the city suggests it could have contained tens of thousands of residents.

On a sobering note, approximately eighty human skulls have been found buried beneath the city gate, mostly of young girls.[13] This practice was common when new cities were constructed in the ancient world, with virgins being ritually sacrificed and their bodies incorporated into the foundations of the city gate in a bid to procure the blessing of the spirit world on the new endeavor.

The archaeological report went on to say,

> The identity of its ruling class remains a mystery since the ancient civilization appears to have vanished suddenly 3,800 years ago, and there are no known mentions of it in any historical texts…
>
> In recent years, more than 70 stone carvings have been discovered at the foot of the pyramid, including human faces, mythical beasts, and animals. These stone carvings—some of them still attached to the pyramid walls—are most likely related to the

> Shimao people's spiritual beliefs, and that they might have hoped to protect the palace with images of kings and nobles....
>
> The Shimao pyramid, built before the founding of the Xia Dynasty—the first in ancient China—could have a connection to other extinct civilizations from around the globe.[14]

Just how the Shimao Kingdom relates to the Xia Dynasty which rose to power at around the same time remains a mystery, although if the scientific research is accurate, the demise of Shimao society occurred about two centuries before the Xia Dynasty collapsed and was replaced by the Shang.

The Xia Dynasty (c. 2205–1600 BC)

Emperor Yu founded the Xia Dynasty which ruled China for more than six centuries from approximately 2205 to 1600 BC.[15] This period parallels a biblical timeline from Abraham to about a century before the birth of Moses.

Yu is credited as being a leader who was determined to honor Shangdi. He believed that having the blessing of the Heavenly Emperor was more important than anything else, and he searched for a successor who would place God first in all things. Later Xia rulers, however, decided that China's emperors should be appointed by hereditary succession, and the throne began to be passed down from father to son.

As Han culture developed, people under its influence formed a cohesive identity, while they considered the tribes outside their realm to be uncivilized barbarians. This worldview has persisted in various forms to the present day. Although Huang Di and his successors are shrouded in the mists of antiquity, most scholars agree that during the Xia Dynasty, bronze casting became highly refined, with the Wei River Valley in Shaanxi emerging as a main hub of skilled bronze craftsmen.

The Shang Dynasty (c. 1600–1046 BC)

During the Shang Dynasty which ruled for more than five centuries, the supreme Creator, Shangdi, continued to be worshipped by the emperors, as they believed He controlled the weather and harvests and was the judge of all mankind.[16]

The ruling base of the Shang emperors was the Yellow River basin. The Evangelical missionary John Ross—who carefully studied the ancient Chinese classics—explained the religious belief system that prevailed at the time:

> The relation between the Supreme God and inferior deities is practically the same as that which existed in Canaan in the time

Emperor Cheng Tang, the first ruler of the Shang Dynasty

> of Abraham. During those [first] twelve centuries the religiosity of the Chinese was most pronounced. They appear to have lived under the unceasing consciousness and interference of an all-ruling Power, and under the protecting care of an intelligent, just, all-knowing, benevolent, and almighty Providence.[17]

The Shang continued to rule northern China until 1046 BC, which corresponds to the reign of King David in Israel. The Shang Dynasty therefore spanned the approximate biblical period from Moses to David. During the Shang period, the Sinitic language developed many of its key characteristics. The earliest forms of writing are found on tortoise shells and animal bones from the later part of the dynasty.

Alas, after more than a millennium of China's rulers seeking the blessing of Shangdi, Emperor Wu Yi (reign 1147–1112 BC) was a corrupt man who introduced idolatry into Chinese culture. According to the great historian Sima Qian, Wu Yi made a wooden idol of Shangdi. He would play a gambling game with the idol, with someone else playing on behalf of the image. When the idol of Shangdi lost a game, the wicked emperor would mock the image. He hung a leather bag filled with pig blood around the idol's neck and would shoot the bag with an arrow, causing the blood to splatter everywhere.

One day, while he was hunting between the Rivers Ho and Wei, Emperor Wu Yi was suddenly struck dead by lightning from heaven. Many people believed the Living God had taken the emperor's life for the wicked deeds and disrespect he had shown by making an image of the omnipotent God.

Toward the end of the Shang Dynasty, a dramatic story is recorded in the *Historical Records*. As the Zhou armies were gaining ascendency, the Prince of Wei, who was the elder brother of the last Shang emperor, Di Xin (reign 1075–1046 BC), went into hiding. When news reached him that his brother had been defeated and the dynasty was overthrown,

> The Prince of Wei emerged from hiding and literally offered himself as a living sacrifice to the new king. He approached King Wu's camp with his upper body stripped and his wrists bound together, dragging a lamb and accompanied by an attendant carrying sacrificial vessels. This was to show that he was ready and willing to be used as a sacrifice, like a lamb, at the conqueror's whim.[18]

The new ruler, touched by the prince's humility, personally untied his wrists and restored to him all the honors he had enjoyed as the brother of the fallen emperor.

The Zhou Dynasty (1046–256 BC)

The Shang Dynasty collapsed and was replaced by the Zhou Dynasty—which ruled for nearly eight centuries until 256 BC, making it the longest dynastic regime in Chinese history. The Western Zhou rulers built their capital on the banks of the Fen

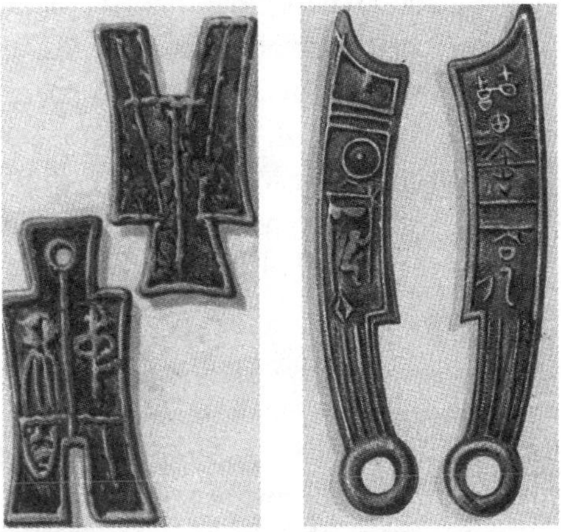

Some of the earliest money in world history was used in China during the Zhou Dynasty, including the cloth "bubi" coins (left) used about 700 BC, and bronze "dao" (sword) money (right), used for trade around 300 BC

River near today's Xi'an. They were the first emperors to rule from the capital city of Shaanxi Province, starting a practice that continued for many centuries.

The Zhou period is considered to be one of the golden ages of Chinese civilization when philosophers such as Confucius, Mencius, and Laozi formulated ideas that have deeply impacted every subsequent generation of Chinese. In the fifth century BC, the military strategist Sun Zi (traditionally spelled Sun Tzu) wrote his famous book *The Art of War*, which is still studied in military academies around the world today.

Various Zhou emperors began construction of a "Great Wall" to prevent barbarian tribes from invading their realm. At the same time, to encourage commerce within the empire, work commenced on the Grand Canal, linking north and south China through a network of canals stretching 1,104 miles (1,788 km).

The Mandate of Heaven

It was during the Zhou Dynasty that the "Mandate of Heaven" was first adopted. Political rulers were believed to have been granted their position by heaven itself, and corrupt or inept emperors would be overthrown if they displeased the powers above. The great philosopher Mencius (372–289 BC) wrote, "They who accord with Heaven are preserved, and they who rebel against Heaven perish."[19] The British historian Jonathan Fenby remarks,

> The doctrine had two great advantages. It explained why things on earth could go wrong despite the omniscient divine power; this was the fault of rulers who fell short of the Mandate. It also provided for changes of regime without any questioning of the fundamental basis of belief. The ultimate power of the divine was thus not brought into jeopardy, as men were blamed for their own failings.[20]

Historian Leo Moser further explains how the Mandate of Heaven has deeply affected the worldview of every Chinese, Japanese, and Korean generation to the present, and he provides clues into how oppressive Communist regimes in China and North Korea are able to rule with little dissension from their populations:

> Philosophers and historians envisioned a concentric world. The emperor was at its center, the sovereign world of Zhongguo—the central kingdom—the one legitimate state under heaven, inhabited by the civilized people of the world. As the Son of Heaven, he performed the rites needed to keep earth in harmony with heaven....
>
> The Mandate of Heaven required all the world be ruled by the emperor who held that mandate and performed the rites necessary to maintain it.... As there was but one heaven, there could only be one emperor and one state with legitimacy in the world.[21]

It was no coincidence that when Mao's forces concluded their Long March in northern Shaanxi in 1935, they paid homage at the tomb of China's first emperor. This act gave the Communists credibility in the eyes of millions of people and made Mao a legitimate heir to the Mandate of Heaven and the seat of Chinese power. Later when the current hardline President Xi Jinping rose to power in 2013, his credentials were boosted by the fact he had spent part of his childhood living in a cave in Shaanxi Province, not far from the cultural and historical seat of imperial power in China.

Because of the deep level of fear and respect that ancient Chinese society held toward the Creator God, on more than a few occasions corrupt rulers were overthrown because the people believed heaven was displeased with them. When the ruler of the State of Hu (based in Shaanxi Province) made changes to the ritual sacrificial ceremonies and changed the dates of the seasons, the people were outraged, saying the seasons were fixed by God and not by any ruler. Not even the emperor had the right to alter them. His actions were viewed as rebellion against heaven, and he was overthrown and put to death for attempting to usurp God's order.

Interestingly, it was also during the Zhou Dynasty that in Babylon, thousands of miles to the west, the Jews were taken into captivity, and King Nebuchadnezzar was humbled by God. In response, Nebuchadnezzar released his own "Mandate of Heaven," declaring, "the Most High is sovereign over all kingdoms on earth and gives them to anyone he wishes and sets over them the lowliest of people" (Dan. 4:17).

The belief in the Mandate of Heaven also helped restrain some of China's emperors from wicked behavior, as the Mandate gave them a sense of humility. The Heavenly Emperor, Shangdi, was the final judge of all human beings, and their role as emperor was a temporal one: to faithfully carry out His order and justice. A Shunzhi emperor who ruled China in the seventeenth century stated,

> He who attempts to cheat Heaven above, or the spirits in the dark, cannot escape. What is done in the light, men can reward. Heaven rewards what is done in the darkness. For what men do in secret, Heaven hears as though it were the roar of thunder; and when they sin against their conscience in the darkness of their room, the offence is seen by the spirits as by a lightning flash. Say not then that Heaven is high and remote and cannot see the acts of men. Heaven is just overhead and cannot be deceived. To Him, everything is brilliantly clear.[22]

The Mandate of Heaven philosophy has served as a cornerstone of Chinese society for more than 2,000 years. Anyone who seeks to understand Chinese culture and worldview needs to first understand the mindset toward leadership that has prevailed in China for more than two millennia.

Although officially there have been no emperors in China since 1911, an insight into the total power that emperors wielded can be seen in the demonstrations of the reigns of terror of the Chinese Communist Party in the last century. The word of men like Mao and Xi is law and cannot be challenged, and any who fall foul of them and their policies are likely to end up dead or in prison for many years.

A clash of cultures

A prime example of the power that the Mandate of Heaven holds in the mindsets of China's rulers took place in 1793. The government of Great Britain sent a delegation of one hundred diplomats and merchants to meet the Qianlong emperor to request a relaxation of trade rules and give Britain more access to Chinese markets.

The meeting went ahead on September 25, 1793, but Lord George Macartney and his team refused to *koutou* (also spelled kowtow) before the aged emperor, which was expected of all who met the "Son of Heaven." The custom required people to go down before the emperor on both knees before leaning forward with their forehead touching the ground in utter reverence. A person was usually required to *koutou* three times before the emperor, but sometimes nine prostrations were necessary before a suitable level of deference had been given.

Macartney was notified of this custom before he met the Qianlong emperor. But he regarded the act as humiliating, and he considered Britain to be the most powerful nation on the earth, not China. Macartney sent a message to the court officials notifying them that he intended only to show the emperor the same level of deference that he would give a British monarch, and no more.

After several speeches and presentations, the insulted Qianlong emperor rejected all the British requests and sent the delegation home. The long letter sent by the Chinese emperor to

King George III reveals just how far apart the two cultures were. The start of the letter says,

> You, O King, from afar have yearned after the blessings of our civilization, and in your eagerness to come into touch with our converting influence have sent an Embassy across the sea bearing a memorial. I have already taken note of your respectful spirit of submission, have treated your mission with extreme favor and loaded it with gifts, besides issuing a mandate to you, O King, and honoring you at the bestowal of valuable presents. Thus has my indulgence been manifested....
>
> Our Celestial Empire possesses all things in prolific abundance and lacks no product within its own borders. There is therefore no need to import the manufactures of outside barbarians in exchange for our own produce.[23]

As if this initial humiliation was not enough, the emperor went on to patronize the king of Great Britain:

> Our dynasty, swaying the myriad races of the globe, extends the same benevolence towards all.... Nevertheless, I do not forget the lonely remoteness of your island, cut off from the world by intervening wastes of sea, nor do I overlook your excusable ignorance of the usages of our Celestial Empire. I have consequently commanded my ministers to enlighten your ambassador on the subject, and have ordered the departure of the mission.[24]

Finally, the Qianlong emperor concluded his letter with a warning and piece of advice for the "barbarian" king of England:

> Should your vessels touch our shore, your merchants will assuredly never be permitted to land or to reside there, but will be subject to instant expulsion. In that event your barbarian merchants will have had a long journey for nothing. Do not say that you were not warned in due time! Tremblingly obey and show no negligence! A special mandate![25]

The Qin Dynasty (221–206 BC)

Although it lasted a mere fifteen years, from 221 to 206 BC, the Qin Dynasty constituted the first unified Chinese empire. The brief reign of Emperor Qin Shihuang was marked by ghastly acts of cruelty and torture of innocent people. Some scholars have identified Qin's reign as a spiritual turning point in Chinese history, as he turned his back on the ancient worship and sacrifices to Shangdi and introduced a host of deities. It was around that time that Chinese documents began referring to the Mandate of Heaven as instituted by "the gods," rather than by the one Creator and all-knowing God, Shangdi.

In an incident in 213 BC that has often been repeated down through the centuries, Emperor Qin issued an order to "burn the books" because he despised Confucian philosophy and wanted to control the thoughts of his subjects. The Chinese classics were almost lost. But copies of the writings were preserved for later

Emperor Qin Shihuang, from whom the English name for China is derived

generations; otherwise records of the early worship of Shangdi would have been erased from history.

Emperor Qin also greatly increased the length of the Great Wall. Under his rule, it stretched from Gansu in northwest China to Liaoning in the northeast—a distance of more than 3,100 miles (5,000 km). By comparison, that distance is further than from Los Angeles to New York or from London to Moscow and back again. Millions of soldiers and prisoners were forced to labor on the wall, and an estimated 400,000 men died in the process. Many were buried within the wall itself.

Qin also left his mark in other ways, including beginning nearly two thousand years of strong, centralized government. China's script and currency were standardized for the first time, and Qin organized the country into provinces that remarkably reflect the provincial borders still used today. Europeans also adopted the name Qin (pronounced Chin) as the name of China.

Qin Shihuang was also the first Chinese monarch to use the title Huangdi (Emperor) rather than Wang (King) to reflect his belief that he was a greater ruler than all who had ruled before him. Qin proclaimed that his dynasty would last 10,000 generations. In a bid to fulfill his great ambition and cement his legacy, he ordered the construction of more than 8,000 life-sized warriors, horses, and chariots to represent a vigilant army in battle formation to guard his tomb located near Xi'an, the capital of Shaanxi Province.

The Historical Records written by Sima Qian, a famous historian from the first century BC, provide a glimpse into the incredible opulence and detail of Qin's tomb, which has yet to be excavated and probably never will be.[26] Sima Qian wrote,

The famous Terracotta Army in Shaanxi, which dates from 200 BC
IMB

> The tomb contains palaces and pavilions filled with rare gems and other treasures and is equipped with crossbows which automatically shoot intruders. The ceiling was inlaid with pearls to simulate the sun, stars, and moon. Gold and silver cast in the form of wild geese and ducks were arranged on the floor, and precious stones were carved into pines.... At the end of the internment rites, the artisans who worked inside and the palace maids who had no children are said to have been forced to remain in the underground palace—buried alive so that none of its secrets could be revealed.[27]

The world knew nothing of Emperor Qin's extraordinary initiative until March 29, 1974, when farmers in Lintong County near Xi'an unearthed part of a statue as they were digging a well. The

Chinese authorities immediately shut off the area and began an extensive excavation, uncovering the thousands of soldiers that make the Terracotta Army one of the wonders of the world. Archaeologists have found that the statues were constructed with incredible detail, with each soldier having unique characteristics and facial features.

Toward the end of his life, Qin grew increasingly paranoid and sent emissaries throughout the empire in a bid to find the elixir of life so he could live forever. When news arrived at the palace that a large meteor had fallen from heaven inscribed with the words, "The emperor will die, and his empire will be divided," Qin immediately dispatched soldiers to investigate. But when the soldiers couldn't identify who had written the inscription, all the people living in the vicinity of where the meteor had fallen were slaughtered, and the rock was ground into dust.

Emperor Qin died at the age of 49. It is believed that he consumed mercury in his bid to gain immortality. Tragically, he perished before he had the chance to hear of the true elixir of life, Jesus Christ, who was born several thousand miles to the west during the next dynasty just a few centuries later.

The next thousand years

The Chinese consider the Han Dynasty (206 BC–AD 220) to be one of their greatest periods in history. Paper was invented by a court eunuch named Cai Lun, and for the first time, China extended its borders through military campaigns. Foreign lands were connected to China via several Silk Roads that led from Xi'an to Central Asia, the Middle East, and ultimately to Europe and Africa.

As history crossed the line between BC and AD, the Chinese gradually lost touch with their spiritual roots, and idolatry filled the land. Subsequent generations of Chinese worshipped a myriad of deities, and the once pure practice of the emperor making sacrifices to the God of Heaven was corrupted. The Chinese Christian scholar Chan Kei Thong reflected on the early centuries of Chinese civilization and determined the key role their belief in the Creator God played:

> Among all the beings that the Chinese worshipped over a period of several thousand years, there was One who stood out—One who was so preeminent in His attributes that we today can recognize Him as the same God revealed in the Bible. Incredibly, the Chinese people did not attempt to make an image of this One whom they worshipped. Although many idols can be found in Chinese society, nowhere is there a single image or physical form of this Supreme Being. God in the Hebrew Scriptures proscribed such images; the Chinese evidently adhered to the same ban.[28]

Most of China continued to function as a cohesive ethnic and political entity during the first millennia of the Christian era. The empire was ruled for the most part from the royal palace at Chang'an (meaning Long Peace), just two miles northwest of today's Xi'an, the capital of Shaanxi. The fate of this capital city ebbed and flowed markedly with the rise and fall of dynasties. The low point was reached in the early fourth century AD when military defeats and natural disasters caused a severe decline in population: "not more than 100 families lived in Chang'an, with just four carts between them, while weeds and thorns grew as thickly as in a forest."[29]

The former glories of Chang'an were soon revived, however, with the high-water mark of Chinese civilization occurring during the Sui (581–618) and the early part of the Tang (618–906) Dynasties. It has been said that,

> Under the Tang, Chang'an became the largest city in Asia, if not the world. At the height of Tang power Chang'an was a cosmopolitan city of courtiers, merchants, foreign traders, soldiers,

A view at dusk from atop the massive Xi'an City wall
Chuyuss

> artists, entertainers, priests, and bureaucrats, with a million people within the city walls and perhaps another million outside. The thriving metropolis of commerce, administration, religion, and culture was the political hub of the empire and the center of a brilliant period of creativity.[30]

A few centuries later, the fortunes of the Shaanxi capital once again turned, and in 881, Xi'an was overrun by 600,000 rebels. An orgy of looting, murder, and cannibalism ensued, leaving the city in such ruin that one Chinese historian wrote, "thorns and brambles filled the city, foxes and hares ran everywhere."[31]

Today, Xi'an retains the massive wall that was first constructed over twenty-two centuries ago in 194 BC during the Qin Dynasty.[32] This wall forms a rectangular shape in the city and has a circumference of nearly 9 miles (14 km). The wall stands 39 feet (12 meters) high and has a similar width at the top, which allowed multiple chariots to navigate from tower to tower.

With such a remarkably rich history, the people of Shaanxi have long regarded themselves as the true guardians of Han culture. Although the capital of China moved to Beijing more than seven hundred years ago, "the inhabitants of Xi'an look down on Beijing as a recent development and one built by aliens (the Mongols) at that. The people of Xi'an have no doubt that the true heart of China's Great Tradition lies in Shaanxi."[33]

The Bible Revealed in Chinese Writing

The first thing many non-Chinese people notice about China is their unique writing system, but few realize that the origins of Chinese characters date back thousands of years. Each word, or character, is made up of small pictographs, or radicals, that have individual meaning. In recent decades, scholars have examined many of these characters and have found uncanny parallels with events recorded in the Bible.

The Catholic priest Jean-Francois Foucquet collected thousands of Chinese books during his twenty-three year stay in China from 1699 to 1722. He wrote,

> It was 23 years ago that I began to study spoken and written Chinese, with the intense desire of finding some way to get inside the written relics of that nation. The style of those books, the ideographs in which they are written, their great age, the subjects that they deal with, all of these are things of which we have no other examples even among the most learned nations elsewhere in the world. All of this piqued my already lively curiosity, and I can assure you I omitted no means that might enable me to satisfy it.
>
> After many years of incessant study, I began to see a sure way to enter these mysterious depths, which for so long had seemed to me inaccessible. The more I advanced the more I discovered their true marvels, and at last I became convinced that these written relics are like a sanctuary of the most venerable antiquity, yet one unknown in Europe until this present time.[1]

We have already discussed how recorded Chinese history began less than a century after the dispersion of people groups from the Tower of Babel. So catastrophic was the flood and subsequent events, it's natural to assume that the earliest people to reach China would have brought the story of God's creation and mankind's fall with them, to be handed down as a warning to future generations.

The apostles Paul and Barnabas stated, "We are bringing you good news, telling you to turn from these worthless things to the Living God, who made the heavens and the earth and the sea and everything in them. In the past, he let all nations go their own way. Yet he has not left himself without testimony" (Acts 14:15–17).

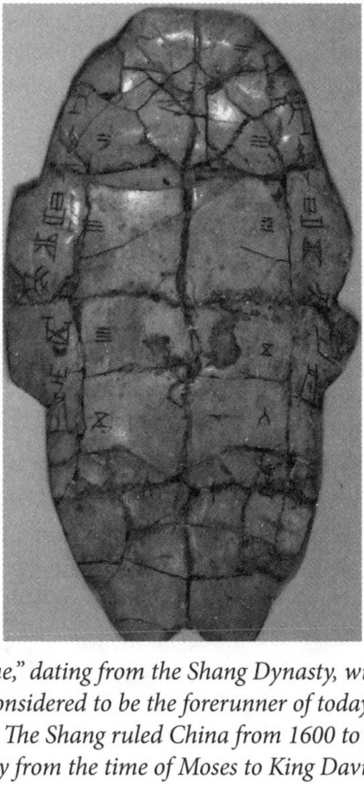

An "oracle bone," dating from the Shang Dynasty, with pictographs that are considered to be the forerunner of today's Chinese characters. The Shang ruled China from 1600 to 1046 BC—approximately from the time of Moses to King David in the Bible

Could it be that God, in His infinite wisdom, chose to preserve a testimony of His great deeds by retaining knowledge of these stories within the very structure of the Chinese language?

Although several recent books have deconstructed various Chinese characters to show parallels with biblical events and doctrine,[2] we will examine just five Chinese characters to understand this unique concept.

造 To Create

The character meaning "to create" consists of several radicals: dust or mud 土 ; speech 告 ; and walking 辶 . Furthermore, the radical meaning "speech" (告) is constructed from the characters 生 meaning "life" and 口 meaning "mouth." It is surely more than coincidence that the ancient Chinese combined these components together in such a way that the character resembles the account of the creation of Adam found in Genesis 2:7: "Then the LORD God formed a man from the dust of the ground and breathed into his nostrils the breath of life, and the man became a living being."

鬼 The Devil

Adam and Eve enjoyed a time of perfect peace and harmony in the garden of Eden until the devil tempted them to sin, and their relationship with God was ruined. The Chinese character for "the devil" or "tempter" includes these three components: man 儿 ; garden or field 田 ; and secret or private 厶 . Thus, the ancient character for "devil" includes a man in a private garden, again reflecting the account in Genesis, this time chapters 2 and 3 which describe how Adam and Eve were placed in a private garden before the devil tempted them to rebel against God.

船 Boat

The traumatic global flood that wiped out all human beings except eight survivors would have been fresh in the minds of the earliest Chinese, and flood accounts persist to the present day among many of China's ethnic groups. The full Chinese character for "boat" consists of three interesting components, with the character for mouth also used to signify people: vessel 舟 ; eight 八 ; and mouth 口 . The book of Genesis records that only Noah and his family survived the cataclysmic flood in a boat that God instructed Noah to build (Gen. 6:9–8:22). Elsewhere the Bible says, "he did not spare the ancient world when he brought the flood on its ungodly people, but protected Noah, a preacher of righteousness, and seven others" (2 Pet. 2:5).

Although some modern academics have mocked Christian claims that many Chinese characters reflect stories from the Bible, they fail to offer any explanation for why words like "boat" are comprised of specific components that so closely reflect the biblical flood account.

義 Righteousness

Finally, the concept of sin being atoned for by animal sacrifice has been imbedded in many cultures from ancient times. The earliest records in the Bible are when the Lord killed animals to clothe Adam and Eve after they had sinned (Gen. 3:21) and when Abel "brought an offering—fat portions from some of the firstborn of his flock. The Lord looked with favor on Abel and his offering" (Gen. 4:4). Both instances could be interpreted as making atonement for sin.

Later, God delivered the Israelites from the oppressive power of the Egyptians and from the angel of death by commanding them to sacrifice a lamb and apply the blood to the doorposts of their homes (Exod. 12:1–13). Then in the wilderness of Sinai,

He gave them instructions for sacrificing animals to atone for sin (see Lev. 16:15–16). This concept of atonement appears to have come into the Chinese language as the traditional character for "righteousness" consists of these four components: sheep 羊 ; I or me 我 ; hand 手 ; and spear 戈 . According to this ancient concept, righteousness is obtained by a person being covered by a sheep (or lamb) that has been slain by their own hand.

來 Come

Many Chinese believers have used the origins of their ancient characters as a bridge to share the gospel with non-Christians. A favorite witnessing tool is the Chinese character for the word meaning "come." The character consists of a cross 十 along with a person 人 on that cross. Fascinatingly, as well as the person on the cross, there are two other people (人人) present. In Chinese, when the character for person is written twice, the meaning changes to "everyone," which is significant because Jesus died on the cross with two thieves on either side of Him. By piecing these different radicals together for meaning, a person may see the example of Christ dying on a cross between two guilty thieves as a sacrifice for everyone who will believe and come to Him.

Over the years, many Chinese people have come to faith in Jesus Christ after the composition of this one character has been explained to them. Believers are not generally dogmatic when presenting this topic to their fellow citizens. Rather they explain that while the origins of ancient characters are not certain, one explanation is that the earliest Chinese had knowledge of the God of the Bible and His righteous requirements. This approach often piques the interest of unbelievers and enables Christians to share more of the gospel with them. They explain that Christ's invitation to "come" to Him for salvation is freely available to everyone. But at the crucifixion, one of the thieves believed in

Jesus, and the other rejected Him. Evangelists may then pivot the conversation to ask the hearer, "Which one are you?"

There are dozens of other examples of Chinese characters that Christians say reflect the biblical text. It appears that God surely did leave a witness for the Chinese people both in their ancient written language and by His provision for righteousness which was fulfilled by the perfect sacrifice of the Lamb of God, Jesus Christ.

China's First Christian Influence

Shaanxi Province is widely acknowledged as the gateway through which Christianity first entered China. Xi'an was the capital city of China at the time of Christ and was strategically positioned at the southern terminus of the famous Silk Road. According to Chinese historical annals, the first contact China had with "barbarian nations" occurred in 128 BC when Emperor Wudi sent Zhang Qian—a man nicknamed "the road opener"—to negotiate alliances with the Yuezhi tribes in the region that spans part of today's Afghanistan, Kazakhstan, and Uzbekistan. The Yuezhi rejected the offer, saying they were satisfied with their lives and had no need to associate with the Chinese. Zhang returned to Shaanxi two years later, after being captured and imprisoned by the Huns on his homeward journey.

Nevertheless, Zhang's stories about the vast western regions fascinated the emperor, and additional envoys were dispatched to

This map shows the several ancient land and sea routes that linked China to the rest of the world at the time of Christ

other nations, with some making it as far as the Roman Empire and North Africa. Historian Samuel Moffett remarks,

> The Chinese, alert and impatient for trade with the newly discovered West, flung open a road across the top of the world for caravans to come from as far away as the Indus River valley in southern Asia and the still farther borders of Greco-Roman Syria. For the first time in history Asia took on a semblance of continental unity, tied together at last by the long, thin thread of the Old Silk Road.[1]

A few decades later in 91 BC, another embassy was sent along the Silk Road from Xi'an to Anxi, a hub of the Parthian Empire in modern-day Iran. The king of Parthia dispatched a large army of 20,000 soldiers to meet the travelers on the eastern frontier. Trade discussions were held, and silk was bought and sold. The Parthians were fascinated by their Chinese visitors and their wares, and a reciprocal embassy was arranged after the Chinese invited their hosts to come and see the greatness and extent of their empire. When the Parthians arrived in Xi'an, they offered gifts to the emperor that included large birds' eggs, while skilled musicians and jugglers entertained the court.

Brisk trade between China and the Middle East continued until the seventh century when silk moth eggs were secretly smuggled out of China to Syria inside a bamboo cane. The Syrians and Persians soon began to manufacture their own silk, and China no longer had a monopoly on the much sought after product.

While AD 635 is commonly regarded as the year the gospel first reached China, several fascinating stories exist which—although many academics do not put much weight in them—are nonetheless worth mentioning. If true, these stories date the first Chinese contact with Christ to the very first moments of the Savior's life!

Liu Xiang

The missing astronomer

The Gospel of Matthew records, "After Jesus was born in Bethlehem in Judea, during the time of King Herod, Magi from the east came to Jerusalem and asked, 'Where is the one who has been born king of the Jews? We saw his star when it rose and have come to worship him" (Matt. 2:1–2). Several ancient nations surrounding Israel including Babylon, Persia, Sheba, Arabia, and India passed down traditions of their astrologers traveling to Judea in response to a special star that appeared in the west. However, few are aware that the same tradition exists in historical accounts from China.

The Chinese were using the compass one thousand years before the birth of Jesus, and maps dating from two millennia ago have been found which show a clear land passage from China to the Mediterranean Sea. At around the time of the birth of Jesus, one of the chief Chinese astrologers at the imperial court in Xi'an was a high-ranking official named Liu Xiang.[2] Liu mysteriously disappeared from China for over two years at the time of Christ's birth after astronomers there discovered a star which they called the "King Star." The brilliant nineteenth-century Scottish missionary-scholar James Legge first alerted the Western world to the possibility of Chinese Magi when he translated some of the Chinese classics and ancient histories. It was said that a king was born whenever this special star appeared, and records showed that this star was at its most brilliant peak during the Han Dynasty (202 BC–AD 220).

Liu Xiang is believed to have lived from 77 BC to 6 BC. At first glance those dates would appear to place him outside the span of Jesus' birth. But many Bible scholars point out that due to differences in calendars, Jesus was probably actually born between 6 BC and 4 BC according to today's widely used Gregorian calendar.

At the time, a journey along the Silk Road from Xi'an to Judea took from between one to two years, depending on the quality of mounts used by the traveler. If Liu had been granted permission by the emperor to undertake the journey, it is likely he would have been allowed use of the finest horses and camels. Also being a high official, he was likely accompanied by a large group of soldiers for protection.

Liu Xiang's many roles in Chinese society have been described as "astronomer, mathematician, historian, librarian, and politician."[3] A brilliant man, he is credited with improving the calculation of pi to 3.1547. To honor Liu Xiang's contribution to science, a crater on Mars has been named after him.

It is unclear if Liu Xiang ever completed the return journey to China. He may have died en route, or as he was almost 70 years old, he may have found the journey too demanding to undertake. Some have suggested that his son Liu Xin, who lived from 50 BC to AD 23, is more likely to have been the one who completed the long journey and paid homage to the newborn King of the Jews.[4]

The belief that the Chinese were represented among the Magi who traveled to Bethlehem persisted, and in the eighth century a Nestorian church leader claimed, "The Magi, returning from Bethlehem, brought the first news of the Savior to China."[5]

When considering the possibility that Chinese were among the Magi, it is important to reflect on the Gospel accounts, as many people have become so familiar with the story that they miss some of its subtleties. For example, the Bible never says there were three wise men. This commonly held belief likely exists because the Gospel of Matthew mentions that three kinds of gifts—gold, frankincense, and myrrh—were offered to Jesus (Matt. 2:11). This assumption has been reinforced over the centuries by popular Christian culture through Christmas carols, cards, nativity scenes, and movies which invariably depict three Magi at the manger. There is nothing at all in the Bible that limits the number to three. If there had been five, ten, fifty, or any other number of Magi, the Gospel account would not be affected.

Revealingly, when the wise men first arrived in Jerusalem and asked where they could find the newborn king, Matthew records, "When King Herod heard this he was disturbed, and all Jerusalem with him" (Matt. 2:3). It's unlikely the whole city would have been disturbed if just three men had arrived in Jerusalem which continually had merchants from many countries passing through it. If a large group had turned up together, however, along with hundreds of soldiers and bodyguards—some from as far afield as China—their arrival would have caused quite a stir, leading to the wicked king attempting to annihilate all competition to his throne.

A recent book,[6] citing a 1,700-year-old Syriac document in the Vatican archives, tells of twelve Magi, not three, and in other parts "a group the size of a small army"[7] that traveled to Bethlehem.

Notably the Bible says, "Then Herod called the Magi secretly and found out from them the exact time the star had appeared" (Matt. 2:7). Afterward, they returned home via an unexpected route. "When Herod realized that he had been outwitted by the Magi, he was furious, and he gave orders to kill all the boys in Bethlehem and its vicinity who were two years old and under, in accordance with the time he had learned from the Magi" (Matt. 2:16). A two-year lapse between the time the star had first appeared and the birth of Jesus aligns well with the length of time historians say it took someone to travel the length of the Silk Road from Shaanxi Province to Judea.

Perhaps God in His wisdom chose to honor the birth of His Son by sending dignitaries from across the ancient world to mark the momentous event. Many Chinese Christians today are thrilled to think that their race may have been among the first worshippers of Jesus Christ.

Modern research

In 2010 Brent Landau, an expert in ancient Bible languages and literature, published the findings of his seven-year project translating and analyzing an ancient Syriac document in the Vatican archives and its 1927-published Syriac text.[8] Landau describes it as "an incredibly grand story … most detailed apocryphon" in which the Magi, a mystical sect, "are descendants of Adam and Eve's third son, Seth. They live in this far eastern land. The text calls the land 'Shir,' and from other ancient texts, it seems like the place it had in mind is the land of China,"[9] a place "located in the extreme east of the world, at the shore of the Great Ocean … a place where silk comes from."[10]

Although most historians might dismiss claims of a Chinese presence at the birth of Christ as wild speculation, the account of Chinese Magi persists to the current time. *ABC News* in the United States even produced a report on the possibility just before Christmas in 2010.[11]

Contemporary Chinese scholar and author Chan Kei Thong remarks,

> It is not surprising that the Magi were the ones who noticed this unusual star. It must truly have been an extraordinary astronomic occurrence to have caused them to embark on a long journey all the way to Jerusalem to seek the source and the reason for it....
>
> The astronomers in far-off China saw the same star! Like their counterparts in the Near East, Chinese emperors were served by imperial astronomers who kept careful watch of the skies for signs from heaven. This imperial office consisted of 14 night-time observers and three daytime observers who were on duty in shifts.... And so it happened that Chinese astronomers observed and recorded several unusual astronomic phenomena around the time of the birth of Jesus.[12]

Chan goes on to cite an entry in the *Astronomy Records of the Book of the Han Dynasty*, from the second year of Emperor Ai, who reigned from 7 to 1 BC.[13] At that time, a special comet appeared for seventy days. Comets were believed to signify important change. Incredibly, the date given for the appearance of the comet was

> the second month of the second year of [the reign of Emperor Ai], which correlates to March 9 to April 6, in the year 5 BC. This timeframe is highly significant because most experts place the birth of Jesus at 5 to 4 BC....
>
> Although the Chinese did not know about the birth of Jesus, they were so convinced of the "great importance" surrounding the comet's appearance and its association with a new beginning that ... some imperial ministers proposed changing the name of that

> year from the "Second Year of Jian Ping" to "The First Year of Tai Chu," which literally means "Genesis" or "the Grand Beginning." The change was adopted and lasted until the eighth month when the original reign title of Jian Ping was restored.[14]

That is not all, however. A second event was recorded when a unique star appeared on the third day of the third month of Jian Ping. According to Chan Kei Thong,

> That would be April 24, 4 BC. The more significant fact that this historical record reveals is that the time elapsed between the appearance of the first star and the second star was approximately 13 months. This suggests the Magi were on the road for about a year, which is roughly how long a journey of that distance would have taken at the time. More significantly, it explains why Herod ordered all male infants in Bethlehem under the age of two killed. He wanted to be absolutely certain of killing the one who would be King of the Jews, who he thought would take his throne.[15]

"Man from heaven died"

After the remarkable events surrounding the birth of Jesus and the fascinating account of the Magi, additional signs in the heavens were recorded approximately thirty-four years later which may align with the crucifixion of Christ. The Bible records that when Jesus died, darkness fell upon the land for three hours (Matt 27:45; Mark 15:33). This total eclipse is recorded in Roman histories, and according to the Chinese classic *History of the Latter Han Dynasty*, "In the summer, fourth month of the year, on the day of Ren Wu.... Yin and Yang have mistakenly switched, and the sun and moon were eclipsed. The sins of all people are now on one man. [The emperor] now proclaims pardon to all under heaven."[16]

Chan Kei Thong further notes,

> The emperor's reaction to this solar eclipse is both highly significant and astonishing. Eclipses were not uncommon events, but this was a prolonged eclipse that fell on a special day, and the Chinese understood that it signified something of extraordinary import. The emperor was convicted of his sins and expressed deep remorse. He even proclaimed his sinfulness and took responsibility for it. This act alone was virtually unheard of in all Chinese history. Even more significantly, he knew that the sins of all the people were laid on One Person!
>
> Incredibly, a comment in the Record of the Latter Han Dynasty said simply: "Eclipse on the day of Gui Hai, Man from heaven died."
>
> The Man from heaven died! Could there be a more apt description or a more accurate understanding of the Crucifixion? We do not know how the ancient Chinese arrived at this interpretation, but it is an interpretation that certainly fits the monumental event of that day: the ultimate sacrifice made by a God of both justice and love for the sake of mankind.[17]

Just how the Chinese, living thousands of miles from Jerusalem, could have made a connection between a special eclipse and a "man from heaven dying" is beyond the realms of human knowledge. It may have been a supernatural revelation by the Spirit of God and the fulfillment of a prophecy given by Isaiah seven hundred years earlier when he spoke of the day that the Messiah would suffer and die:

> Just as there were many who were appalled at him—
> his appearance was so disfigured beyond that of any human being
> and his form marred beyond human likeness—
> so he will sprinkle many nations,
> and kings will shut their mouths because of him.
> For what they were not told, they will see,
> and what they have not heard, they will understand.
> (Isa. 52:14–15)

A startling discovery

Most historians believe the first Christian presence in China dates to the arrival of the Nestorians in 635. Yet at the start of the twenty-first century, a Christian professor named Wang Weifan greatly surprised the academic world when he presented evidence of stone carvings from the Eastern Han Dynasty (AD 25–220) which are held in the Museum of Xuzhou Han Stone Carvings in Jiangsu Province. The stones and some bronze basins, according to Wang, depict Bible stories, designs, and creation symbols from the early Christian era, including fish, phoenix (representing resurrection), cherubim, the garden of Eden, and the miracle of Jesus multiplying the loaves and fish.

Wang was able to precisely date a tomb in which these carvings were found, for to the left of one carving was written: "The seventh day of the third month in the year of Yuanhe."[18] This date equates to AD 86. In an article published in the influential *China Daily*, Wang further explains,

> The Bible stories were told on the stones in a kind of time sequence. One of the reliefs showed the sun, the moon, living creatures in the seas, birds of heaven, wild animals, and reptiles—images linked to the creation story in Genesis. Another one depicted a woman taking fruit from the "tree of knowledge of good and evil" and a snake biting her right sleeve. It also included the angel sent by God to guard the tree.[19]

A first-century Han Dynasty engraving with Christian symbols

A bronze container from the Eastern Han Dynasty (AD25–220) depicting the story of the loaves and fishes

In response to Wang's findings, the Communist authorities appear to have discouraged further examination of these artifacts because such an early date for the arrival of Christianity in China undermines their efforts to eradicate the faith and to label it as a tool of Western imperialism. Consequently, Lin Xixiang, the director of archaeology at the National Museum of China, scornfully dismissed Wang's claims, saying, "Fancy those stones having anything to do with Christianity! I cannot imagine their telling the Bible stories. It's impossible."[20] Other historians doubt that the gospel could have spread east along the Silk Road in the earliest years of the church. Widespread unrest closed the region to travelers in AD 16. But by about AD 80, a measure of calm had returned to Central Asia, and the Silk Road reopened for trade.

Other claims of first-century Christians traveling to China include several fascinating stories that cannot be proven today. One of them says,

> In AD 64, the Chinese emperor Mingdi had a dream that caused him to send messengers along one of the roads that led to the west. They were to find out who the great prophet was who had arisen in the western lands. On the way, the messengers met two missionaries who were on their way to the emperor's court. They all returned to the court together, and the missionaries remained there until they died six years later.[21]

Wang Weifan, who was a much-loved preacher and theologian within the registered Three-Self Church, died in 2015 at the age of 88. His startling discoveries have not been widely accepted or explained by the academic community. But they leave us with physical evidence and a strong suggestion that God was at work in China centuries earlier than previously thought.

Nestorians in Shaanxi

Until recently, almost all Christian and secular scholars have held to the start date for Christianity in China of AD 635. In that year, Nestorian missionaries from Central Asia and the Middle East traveled down the Silk Road to Xi'an, the capital of both Shaanxi Province and China at the time. However, the

The Nestorian Stone before it was moved to a museum in Xi'an

information about artifacts presented in the previous chapter of this book suggest that Christians were in China as early as the first century. Also, the Tibet volume of *The China Chronicles* reveals that the Nestorians were active in Tibetan areas of China in 549, almost a century earlier than China's commonly accepted date for the first Christian presence.[1]

The Nestorian Stone—a large, black limestone tablet standing over 9 feet high, 3 feet wide, and a foot thick—was unearthed by people digging foundations for a house near Xi'an in 1625. In part, the inscription states that the imperial court approved of the message being shared by the foreign guests:

> Bishop Alopen of the Kingdom of Ta'chin, bringing with him the sutras and images, has come from afar and presented them at our Capital. Having carefully examined the scope of his teaching, we find it to be mysteriously spiritual, and of silent operation. Having observed its principal and most essential points, we reached the conclusion that they cover all that is most important in life.... This teaching is helpful to all creatures and beneficial to all men, so let it have free course throughout the Empire.[2]

The large characters at the top of the Nestorian Stone

The Nestorian Stone has images of two creatures, perhaps cherubim, carved over the top edge, a small Nestorian-style cross near the center of the top, and nine large Chinese characters beneath it which translate into English as "A Monument Commemorating the Propagation of the Ta'chin Luminous Religion in the Middle Kingdom." A portion of the stone's inscription states that it was made by a Persian Christian named Adam and erected on January 7, 781. The names of seventy Nestorian missionaries are written in Chinese and Syriac at the conclusion of the 2,000-word inscription. This stone can be viewed today at the Forest of Stone Steles Museum in Xi'an. It was moved there in 1907 after the Chinese authorities were informed that a Danish adventurer was meeting with local officials, seeking to purchase the relic and ship it back to Europe.

Correcting falsehoods

While many Christians throughout history have been quick to dismiss the Nestorians, who were officially called the Church of the East, as a heretical sect, the truth is not so clear-cut. Rather the available evidence indicates that Nestorian Christianity was a powerful force for good, especially in the early centuries when countless thousands of lives were radically transformed by the gospel of Jesus Christ. For many centuries the Catholics labeled Nestorians as heretics in regard to the person and deity of Christ. But in 1539, the German reformer Martin Luther wrote that the charges against the Nestorians were unclear, and he suspected that the accusations had been fabricated by jealous Catholics. Luther wrote,

> For a while I could not understand just what Nestorius' error was; in any event, I thought that Nestorius had denied the divinity of Christ and had regarded Christ as no more than a mere man, as the papal decretals and all papal writers say. But their own words,

when I really looked at them, made me change my mind.... Their writing is so confused they still do not know today how and why they condemned Nestorius....

It appears that the Pope and his followers put the words into Nestorius' mouth that he viewed Christ as a mere man and not also God, and that he took Christ to be two persons or two Christs. This appears (I say) not only from their histories, but also from the very words and documents of the popes and their writers.[3]

Alopen

Little else is known about Alopen except that he and the other Nestorian monks are believed to have been Syriac-speaking Persians. Some have speculated that the name "Alopen" was a Chinese transliteration of Abraham. The emperor, who was a man of great learning, seems to have been attracted to the new

A painting dated 641 of Alopen (third figure from the left) translating for Emperor Taizong

faith. He "brought Alopen into the imperial library and ordered him to begin translation of his sacred books."[4]

Although Alopen remains a mysterious figure who has gone down in history as the leader of the first gospel mission to China, the historian Samuel Moffett notes,

> Alopen was probably not the first Christian in China. Sassanid Persia had opened trade connections with China in the fifth century, and Nestorians were numerous in the merchant class of those times. The earliest recorded reference to a Nestorian Christian in China proper is the mention of a Mar Sergis as head of an important immigrant family from the western lands; who settled in 578 in Lintao, about 300 miles [486 km] west of Xi'an in Gansu, along the Old Silk Road.[5]

Under Alopen's leadership, a total of twenty-one Persian monks commenced work in China, and in 638, the first church building was constructed in the western suburb of modern-day Xi'an. This Chinese capital was reputedly the largest city in the world at the time and "drew people from many countries, mostly for trade. There were approximately one million residents, with half living

Emperor Taizong (reign 627–649) and Gaozong (650–683) who extended favor to the Nestorians and helped them establish the faith in China

inside the city walls. This included about 300,000 foreigners who were concentrated around the international trade market or Western Market in the city."[6]

Evidence exists that the gospel was spread far and wide by the Nestorians so that by the late seventh century, a Christian presence was also found in Japan and on the Korean Peninsula. The beams of an ancient temple dating from that period are housed in the Tokyo National Museum, and these beams have crosses and inscriptions in ancient Syriac carved into them. A large seventh-century tomb known as "the tomb of Jesus" has also been found in northwest Japan. The tomb was likely that of a Nestorian Christian who preached the gospel among the Japanese people.

The oldest church building in China

The imperial palace had an atmosphere of goodwill and tolerance at the time, with Emperor Taizong personally ordering the construction of the first church building, and paying for it from his own treasury. The first Nestorian monastery and church building were built in Shaanxi Province in 638, just three years after the arrival of the first missionaries. It was called Daqin—which was the ancient Chinese name for the Roman Empire, and

The Daqin Pagoda is a Christian structure dating from the eighth century

occasionally for the Persian and Syrian empires. Later when Nestorianism had gained favor among the population, the faith was referred to as Jing Jiao, meaning the "brilliant" or "admirable" religion.

In the 1930s, a Japanese scholar named P. Y. Saeki discovered a Nestorian site in Zhouzhi County, about 50 miles (81 km) south of Xi'an City. In 1998, in an adventure reminiscent of an Indiana Jones movie, the British researcher Martin Palmer used Saeki's hand-drawn map and found a seven-story pagoda which many people assumed to be Daoist because it is located near a prominent Daoist monastery. An elderly nun told Palmer that although the pagoda had been taken over by the Daoists, it was originally built by "monks who came from the West and believed in one God."[7]

Palmer returned a year later and was given permission to enter the pagoda. Using a flashlight, he examined two damaged statues. He soon recognized that one statue was of Mary holding the baby Jesus, and the other was Jonah preaching in Nineveh, which was in the Nestorian homeland. Palmer recalled his excitement when he realized the terrace that had been cut out of the hill to hold the pagoda ran from east to west as Nestorian structures always do, whereas all Buddhist and Daoist temples are oriented north to south:

> I ran down the hillside shouting to everyone. A Buddhist nun wanted to know what this was all about. When I told her that I thought this was an ancient Christian site, she looked completely astonished and said: "Well of course it is. This was the greatest Christian monastery in China. We all know that!"
>
> To my astonishment I discovered that the local people all knew of the Christian history of the site. Lost to the wider world for over a millennium, the local people had retained memory of the five monks from the West.[8]

The Daqin Pagoda still stands, although it has a dangerous lean like the famous Tower of Pisa. The pagoda was probably damaged and abandoned after the massive earthquake of 1556. Locals say that a church building had stood next to the pagoda for centuries but had been destroyed by Red Guards during the Cultural Revolution in the 1960s.

Other Chinese and foreign scholars have visited and examined the pagoda in recent decades and have backed Palmer's claims. However the Chinese authorities have not been keen on opening the site to tourists due to its isolated location and unsound structure.

The first Nestorian persecution

Taizong was succeeded as emperor by his son Gaozong, who is said to have established "illustrious monasteries" for the Nestorians "in every prefecture."[9] Things started to go wrong for the young monarch, however, when he took one of his deceased father's concubines into his own ménage. The concubine, Wu Zetian—who was also known as Wu Hou—schemed her way to the top. She bore the emperor a son and then murdered the boy to cast blame on the empress. She eventually overthrew the empress, chopping off her rival's hands and feet and letting her bleed to death. Historian Samuel Moffett, who called Wu "the wicked witch of traditional Chinese history," noted, "The new queen completely dominated the government for the remaining 27 years of his reign. When he died in 683, the first days of growth for the Christian church in China ended, and under the Buddhist empress dowager, the ruthless Wu Hou, the days of persecution began."[10]

Another historian summarized her rule of terror this way:

> China's only female emperor and the founder of her own dynasty, Wu Zetian was the most extraordinary woman to appear in

> the centuries of imperial rule. Melding ruthlessness and great acumen, superstition, and quick-wittedness, she was a unique figure. Her deadly treatment of opponents struck fear into those who opposed her. She employed an army of spies.
>
> As she grew older, she was said to have become addicted to aphrodisiacs, which made her grow additional teeth and eyebrows. She conferred too much authority on two brothers who were her lovers, and was dethroned in 705, dying a broken old woman a year later at the age of 80.[11]

When Wu Zetian had established herself in full control of the country, she adopted Buddhism as the state religion, and encouraged persecution of Christians. Mobs destroyed the Nestorian church at Luoyang in 698, and by 712, the violence had spread to Xi'an, where a hostile crowd was permitted to demolish the oldest Nestorian church in the city.

A wall painting, dating from 683 to 770, of a Palm Sunday procession in China with Nestorian monks holding palm branches

One hundred and fifty years of success

The persecution did not destroy the Nestorian enterprise, however. By the early ninth century, the Church of the East was able to look back on a fruitful century and a half in China. The Nestorian historian George Malech wrote this magnificent summary of the eight groups of missionaries who traveled down the Silk Road and gave their lives to reach China:

> Syrian missionaries went to China, and for 150 years this mission was very active ... sending missionaries to China, and from time to time a number of missionaries went out to continue the work which their brethren had begun and carried on with so many sacrifices until death had claimed them.
>
> 109 Syrian missionaries worked in China during 150 years of the Chinese mission. Among them were bishops, priests, monks, and deacons. It is said about these men—the messengers of the King of Kings—that they were as gentle as lambs and unassuming, but courageous and fearless with the hearts of lions. They sacrificed life and health in the unknown land and did their work among the heathen with faith and trust in God.
>
> They went out from Beth Nahrin, the birthplace of Abraham, the father of all the believers. The missionaries traveled on foot; they had sandals on their feet, and a staff in their hands, and carried a basket on their backs, and in the basket was the Holy Writ and the cross.
>
> They took the road around the Persian Gulf; went over deep rivers and high mountains, thousands of miles. On their way they met many heathen nations and preached to them the gospel of Christ. The heathen who worshipped idols were told about the Savior, who would take their sins upon Himself and save them. They sowed the good seed in the field, worked zealously and won many souls among the heathen nations.
>
> The work of the mission became a blessing to the nations, and the missionaries influenced greatly those among whom they worked; they brought many from sin and idol worship to

> God; they went to the palaces of the kings and to the cottages of the poor.
>
> Kings and princes heard about the love of Christ, and they believed; the subjects followed their princes, and with their own hands they destroyed the temples of their idols; those that they had worshipped and hoped to get help and comfort from.
>
> Great gifts were given to the missionaries, but they distributed everything given them in the best way to serve the spreading of the words of Christ, and many souls were won. The missionaries themselves always remained poor, denying themselves everything; many of them became martyrs for their faith; but they were followed by others who took up their work, built churches and schools in the foreign countries, and thus the mission went on for 150 years.[12]

The Nestorian work continued to expand until 845. Then everything suddenly came to a halt when the emperor issued an edict against religion. This edict was intended to target Buddhists, but the Nestorians were also caught up in the persecution. The edict resulted in the destruction of 4,600 Buddhist monasteries throughout China and forced 265,000 monks and nuns into secular work. The destruction of Nestorian churches and monasteries, coupled with the approximately 2,000 Christian monks and nuns who were forced to abandon their spiritual vocation, dealt a serious blow to the fledgling church in China at the time.

The second persecution and spiritual decay

The remnant of Nestorian Christianity that survived the persecutions of 845 had a much lower profile for most of the next four centuries. But God preserved a small number of believers who secretly continued to worship Him. They were truly the first "underground" church in China.

Finally, after almost four hundred years, this hidden root of the body of Christ in China resurfaced. By 1271—when the Mongols had conquered all of China and established the Yuan Dynasty—Christianity again rose to prominence. When Marco Polo arrived in China in the late thirteenth century, he found Nestorian churches in many locations. Another medieval explorer described the Nestorians as having "very handsome and devoutly ordered churches with crosses and images in honor of God and the saints. They hold sundry offices under the emperor and have great privileges from him."[13]

Tragically, the religious freedoms the Nestorians enjoyed came at a cost to their spiritual lives. Their light gradually dimmed, and their moral demise caused them to become a stench to those they sought to reach. The French Franciscan William of Rubruck, who arrived in China in 1254, had nothing positive to say about the Nestorians. One account of William's visit lamented,

> He complained that they did not know the language of their sacred books, that they chanted like the ignorant monks of Europe, were usurers, drunkards and polygamists. He said that the bishop came only once in 80 years and that when he made his visit all the male children were ordained priests. The Nestorians were, he declared, worse than the pagans around them.[14]

Alarmingly, William of Rubruck also noted that Nestorian priests not only failed to condemn sorcery and divination, but "many practiced it themselves, giving charms to their followers and claiming to heal the sick with ashes."[15]

The once powerful Church of the East had also declined because of theological compromise. James Legge, an expert on ancient China, speculated that the movement had become "swamped by Confucian, Daoist and Buddhist ideas; a certain degenerate, nominal Christianity."[16]

Many prominent Nestorians were on friendly terms with the Mongol leaders, some of whom were known to have embraced Christianity. Their political alliances helped the Nestorians survive until 1368, when the Mongol empire fractured from internal strife, and the Yuan Dynasty came crashing down. For more than a century the Han Chinese had been oppressed by the Mongols, so when a chance for revenge presented itself there was no holding back. Hundreds of thousands of Mongols were slaughtered throughout the nation. Nestorian Christians were also targeted because of their connection to the Mongol leaders. What exactly happened in the Second Nestorian Persecution following the overthrow of the Yuan Dynasty is not clear. What is known is that the Nestorian church disappeared from China, leaving almost no trace of its existence. Samuel Moffet remarks,

> With the defeat of the Mongols, China turned Chinese in religion also, but there is little evidence of direct religious persecution.... It is likely that Nestorians and foreigners were killed indiscriminately in the pursuit of the Mongols, and that without foreign support a Church that had become dependent upon it withered away. And because its withering was so undramatic, China lost even the memory of its passing.
>
> This was the second disappearance of Christianity from China, and when it returned 200 years later, the next wave of Christians seemed largely unaware that there had ever been Christians there before them.[17]

Early Catholics in Shaanxi

The Franciscan priest John of Montecorvino is thought to have been the first Catholic missionary to reside in China. He arrived in Beijing in 1294, and within five years had built a "magnificent cathedral." The Nestorians were still active in China at this time. However by then they had lost their spiritual fervor, and their leadership was said to be wracked with immorality and drunkenness.

The jealous Nestorians called John a "spy, magician, and deceiver of men," and they did all they could to stall his progress. By 1305, however, John had won 6,000 converts and was granted permission to build a second church directly opposite the imperial palace. He lamented, "If not for the above-named slanders I should have baptized more than 30,000."[1]

The St. Francis Cathedral in Xi'an, built in 1716

Reflecting on John of Montecorvino's effective ministry, the renowned Christian historian Latourette writes, "Almost single-handedly he established the Roman Catholic faith in the capital of the mightiest empire of his time."[2] By the time of John's death in 1328, there were an estimated 100,000 Catholic converts throughout China.[3]

The great missionary Matteo Ricci arrived in China in 1582 and labored tirelessly in Beijing until his death in 1610 at the age of 57. Ricci met a Chinese Jew named Ai Tian who told him of surviving Jewish communities scattered throughout the empire. One day, Ai brought a man named Chang to meet the missionaries. Chang was visiting from Shaanxi Province and claimed to be a Christian, although Ricci was unable to ascertain the source of his belief.[4]

The most famous Catholic to dwell in Shaanxi Province during this period was the German Jesuit Adam Schall.[5] He had been

The famous Adam Schall lived in Shaanxi from 1627 to 1630

prominent at the emperor's court in Beijing, where he helped reform the Chinese calendar. A brilliant mathematician and astronomer upon whom the emperor bestowed several honorary titles, Schall was assigned to Xi'an in Shaanxi from 1627 to 1630. There he studied Chinese and built a new church. Then he returned to Beijing and remained there until his death in 1666, using his high position to protect Christians throughout China. At that time, a significant number of believers were scattered throughout Shaanxi, although most histories state that Catholic work in the province officially commenced in 1625 and had grown to 24,000 church members by 1663.[6]

The eighteenth century proved difficult for Catholics in Shaanxi, with persecution breaking out at regular intervals against both the foreign priests and their Chinese converts. The hardships caused the number of believers to rise and fall, and by 1703, the number of church members in Shaanxi had decreased to only 9,000.[7] Despite the struggles, the large St. Francis Cathedral was constructed in Xi'an in 1716. By 1765, the number of Catholics in Shaanxi had fallen further to just 6,000.[8] The large drop from 24,000 a century earlier shows the difficulty believers faced as many of them were relentlessly hunted down and persecuted by the authorities.

Martyrs in Shaanxi

Although Xi'an had lost its privileged position as the nation's capital centuries earlier, Shaanxi remained a place of pride and stubborn resistance toward outsiders. People in the province viewed themselves as the guardians of Chinese culture and history, and Christianity was shunned as an unwelcome foreign intrusion. Tensions sometimes spilled over into violence, and the Italian missionaries Francesco Magni and Antonio Sacconi were martyred in 1785. Magni had served as the Bishop of Shaanxi until 1777, when Sacconi succeeded him.

In December 1784, officials in the far north of Shaanxi arrested a group of Christians and held them in prison under horrific conditions. A vigorous search was launched for missionaries throughout the province, and some of the believers, under the duress of torture, provided the names of several foreign priests who had been hiding in the province for years. When Bishop Sacconi heard that the government had arrested a group of Chinese believers in order to lure him out of his secret location,

> He decided to leave his hiding place and to give himself up to the authorities. On the day before Christmas 1784, he prepared a little bundle of personal belongings and went alone to the city to present himself to the governor.... The bishop said that only his love of the Chinese people had prompted him to leave his native country and come to China, where he had lived for many years teaching others the way of salvation and exhorting them to embrace a religion in which they could hope to gain eternal happiness.[9]

Sacconi, who spoke and read Chinese fluently, told his accusers, "I am ready to suffer any punishment, but ask that the Chinese Christians be set free since they have committed no crime."[10] The authorities ignored his request, and by the end of March 1785, a total of sixty-five Chinese believers were in prison awaiting sentence. At the hearing, the provincial governor explained that he did not have the power to release the men because the order for their arrest had come from the emperor in Beijing, and to disobey his orders would result in his own death.

The unhygienic conditions and brutal torture took its toll on the prisoners, and many perished before they had the chance to stand trial. The two Italian bishops were sent on the long overland journey to Beijing for trial. After weeks of traveling over bumpy roads, confined inside cages like wild animals and jeered at and reviled by crowds at each town they passed through, Magni and Sacconi arrived at the nation's capital. They were thrown into a filthy dungeon along with fifty-one other Catholic leaders who had been rounded up throughout the country. Their condition was described as "wretched and pitiful. As a result of the unhygienic state of the prisons and the lack of food, most of them fell sick. Before the trial was completed, 10 of the 53 prisoners had died."[11] Among the ten who went to their eternal reward were the two Shaanxi bishops, Magni and Sacconi. Sacconi died during the night of February 5, 1785, with Magni following him a week later on February 12.

The next decade saw more harsh persecutions of Catholics in Shaanxi. On August 1, 1795, a French Lazarist missionary named Raymond Aubin was arrested at the provincial border while on his way to visit the Vicar Apostolic of Shaanxi. Aubin was taken to prison in Xi'an, where he died shortly after.[12] After nearly two centuries, the Catholic Church in Shaanxi was battered and bruised and tiny in number. They remained the only representatives of Christ in Shaanxi, as a further eighty years passed before the first Evangelical missionaries arrived in the province.

1870s

The Evangelicals arrive

Catholic work in Shaanxi had officially commenced in 1625, but a staggering 251 years elapsed before the first Evangelical (Protestant) presence missionaries in the province. By 1873, Catholic churches in Shaanxi and the neighboring Gansu Province had grown to a combined 21,000 believers,[1] although the work was scattered over a wide area and had struggled to advance among the population.

The first Evangelicals in Shaanxi walked into a red-hot cauldron, for a widespread uprising by Hui Muslims against the Chinese authorities had resulted in what is now known as the Dungan Revolt which raged from 1862 to 1877. This summary indicates the enormous impact the conflict had on the population in Shaanxi:

> At least four million Hui were in Shaanxi before the revolt, but only 20,000 remained in the province while the rest of the Hui were all killed in massacres and reprisals by government and militia forces or were deported out of the province. 700,000 to 800,000 Hui in Shaanxi who were deported to Gansu were massacred along the way by the militia carrying out the deportations, until only a few thousand of them remained alive. Many of them also died from thirst and starvation on the journey.[2]

As was common with many of China's more inaccessible provinces, the first Evangelical pioneers in Shaanxi were members of Hudson Taylor's China Inland Mission (CIM). In August 1876, British missionaries Frederick Baller and George King took a two-month trip north into Shaanxi from Hubei Province. The duo were surprising choices to win the honor of being the first Evangelicals to visit the province. Baller at the time was 33 years old and had been in China less than three years, while King was a young man of just 19 years of age who had arrived in China the previous year.

Baller wrote a report of their groundbreaking journey detailing how they sold and gave away gospel literature to all who were interested. After entering Shaanxi from the south, they made their way as far as Ankang after visiting several key cities. But they did not make it to Xi'an. They encountered Catholic influence in many places which they believed had generally closed people's hearts and minds to the true gospel. Baller wrote,

> We arrived at Yuenchang and spent the remainder of the day preaching and selling Gospels. We had excellent congregations, the people listening with marked attention. We also sold a good many books. The [magistrate] of the place sent four soldiers to

Frederick Baller and 19-year-old George King—the first two Evangelical missionaries in Shaanxi

> protect us, and to explain to the people that our object was to sell books and to preach....
>
> On Friday we stayed at a small village. The people were very averse to hearing anything about the gospel. One man sitting at his shop door refused to buy a copy of the Gospel as he was a Roman Catholic. On inquiring how long he had been one, he replied "from birth". His ancestors were Romanists and not merely his parents; therefore, he was one too. In a good many small places we found the same thing; men professed to be Catholics because their parents had been....
>
> We arrived at Baihe, the second city inside Shaanxi. We preached before dusk, but found the people reserved and suspicious; they only bought a few books and did not care to listen to the truth. On the Lord's Day, however, we had some good congregations both inside and outside the city.... One of the men asked many intelligent questions about the Lord Jesus and got a good understanding of all the leading facts of the gospel.[3]

During their initial foray into Shaanxi, Baller and King exposed thousands of local people to the claims of Christ for the first time, and they also witnessed to Hui Muslims who were scattered throughout the province. Baller wrote,

> We met with many Muslims, who listened with great attention. One of the things that seemed to strike them much was the fact of the resurrection of the Lord Jesus. As I pointed out the superiority of a living Christ over all the sages who had long since passed away, many seemed impressed with the novelty of the idea. May they be led to seek Him who sits on the right hand of the Majesty on High!
>
> On returning to the boat, I met with a young Muslim and had a long talk with him about the gospel. He appeared to understand and showed a spirit of inquiry which was pleasing and encouraging.
>
> The journey had been more expensive and tedious than we had expected, and our money was now getting low. We set out on

> our return. A pleasant voyage down the river brought us safely to Wuhan, after having been absent more than two months. May the work done be followed by God's blessing, and the information gathered be helpful in future journeys to these regions beyond.[4]

Subsequent visits

The teenage George King was touched by the needs in Shaanxi, and just three months later he returned to the province after recruiting five fellow missionaries and two Chinese Christians from Shanghai. For five months the group traveled throughout Shaanxi, visiting the famous city of Xi'an while researching strategic locations in which to base future work. In December 1877, King again returned to Shaanxi, this time accompanied by Charles Budd, George Parker, and George Easton. The two Georges traveled on to Gansu Province, while Budd filed this report on his time in Xi'an and in towns along the Wei River:

> We spent nearly a week in the capital, daily preaching and selling books. The people were not greatly astonished, but, overall, were polite and well-disposed. Like the rest of the Chinese, they are much given to idolatry, having no higher idea of God than heaven; or, as it seems to me, a misty recognition of an overruling Providence....
>
> We spent a day at Weinan preaching and selling books. I met a man who appeared more interested than the rest, so (with a few others) we sat down on a piece of wood and we read a Catechism through together, which I explained as well as able. He seemed to understand it. May we meet him among the redeemed ones![5]

Missionary James Cameron, who walked or rode thousands of miles across previously unchartered territory in remote parts of China, passed through Shaanxi in the late 1870s and encountered strong opposition because of the distasteful influence of Catholics in the area. Cameron reported,

One day, about noon, we put up in a small market town, but were not allowed to stay, for which I was sorry, as it was market day. The headman of the village came to the inn and looked at my books. Supposing they were Catholic, as they had the Name of Jesus in them, he sent out the town-crier to warn the people against buying any.

I visited him to inquire his reason for so doing, but he would not appear, and his son and others became quite angry and threatened to give me a beating. I went on to the street with my books, nevertheless, and sold a few; but most people were afraid to buy. I soon returned to the inn, where I found the poor innkeeper so frightened by the bully, that he had ordered my man to depart without even providing food for us.[6]

Tragedy and triumph in Hanzhong

George King married Emily Snow in 1879, and the young newlyweds were able to establish the first Evangelical mission in Shaanxi. Emily had only been in China six months when she married George. Instead of sending them to the famous city

Emily King was the first Western woman to live in Shaanxi

of Xi'an, the China Inland Mission appointed the Kings to the remote town of Hanzhong, which duly became the first CIM mission base in the province.

Situated in southern Shaanxi at the headwaters of the Han River, Hanzhong was 185 miles (300 km) southwest of Xi'an. The work in Hanzhong blossomed in subsequent years, and due to its proximity and shared culture with people across the border in Sichuan and Gansu, the gospel also spread into those provinces.

Emily King (neé Snow) is regarded as the first Western woman to ever reside in Shaanxi. It was said of her, "By the time Emily gave birth to her first child the following winter, she had seen 18 Chinese women baptized, and the church was growing fast. It was a heavy blow to all of them when she was struck down with typhoid in the spring of 1881 and failed to recover."[7] George was deeply shaken by the sudden loss of his wife of just two years, as they had dreams of spreading the gospel westward into unevangelized regions.

George King went on to serve in China many years. He married Harriette Black, who was one of five sisters to offer their lives to serve Christ in China. Their son, George Edwin King, became a renowned missionary-doctor. He established the Borden Memorial Hospital in Gansu Province in 1915, before his life was cut short when he accidentally drowned in the Yellow River.

A Buddhist convert

In 1881, George Easton returned to Hanzhong after an absence of four years. He was delighted to meet many of the local believers and reported,

> I had the pleasure of seeing several of the new converts baptized by Mr. King.... The first man to be baptized was a man named He, a native of Sichuan Province. He is a short, square man, grave

and reticent in manner, with very little that is attractive or interesting about him.... He is an educated man but has no literary degree; I believe he has sometimes practiced as a doctor; but the greater part of his life has been spent studying and propagating the stricter forms of the Buddhist religion.

He was no mere nominal Buddhist, but one who was as sincere about error as I believe he now is about truth. A prominent member of a large and influential society of vegetarians, he travelled throughout Sichuan, Gansu, and Shaanxi provinces, earnestly seeking to induce the people to become vegetarians and devout Buddhists, and instructing those who were already of their number....

God had better things in store for him. He has a naturally inquisitive mind, given to investigation, and so was led to go and hear the foreigners preach about religion. He drank in all that was said, and thought much about it, too. He continued to attend the preaching and sought private instruction in conversation with Mr. King. The Holy Spirit enlightened him, he was convinced, and immediately acted upon his convictions, believing that he had at last found the truth that he had been groping for all his life.... He was eventually baptized and came to live on the mission premises to give his time to the study of the truth.[8]

Other new Christians in Hanzhong included a 24-year-old baker named Xie, while others lived in villages within walking distance of the city. Easton wrote about some of the trials these young believers faced:

Some of the young believers at Hanzhong have met with persecution and have needed all the grace and strength supplied to enable them to stand firm. Mr. Liu lives at a village a days' journey from Hanzhong, and so is not often able to meet with us. His neighbors have sorely tried him, and even threatened to pull his house down, but by his consistent life and gentle expostulations Liu has lived all such feeling down, and the ringleader of the persecuting party is now an enquirer....

> There is also a young tailor who constantly attends the meetings, and whom we have looked on as a sincere and earnest believer for some time. He desires to be baptized but is kept from joining us by the cruel severity of his father, who beats him repeatedly, sometimes taking him away in the middle of service and thrashing him. He is compelled by his father, for whom he works, to work on Sundays, though he generally manages to get away to the meetings.[9]

From these days of small beginnings, today the whole of Hanzhong Prefecture encompasses ten counties and one district, with a combined population of 3.4 million people. Of these, an estimated 138,000 are Evangelical Christians,[10] worshipping in both registered Three-Self churches and unregistered house church fellowships. From those humble beginnings, a mighty harvest has emerged in unfashionable Hanzhong, and the light of the gospel has gone out from there into the surrounding provinces.

1880s

Single women

Some of the first Evangelical Christians in Shaanxi

In an era when single women serving God was generally frowned upon, the CIM welcomed a steady flow of single ladies to work in Shaanxi, which helped propel the kingdom of God forward. In February 1880, two single ladies set off on a 1,000-mile (1,620 km) journey across China to join the work at Hanzhong. Elizabeth Wilson from the English town of Kendal was 50 years old at the time and was described as "well past middle life."[1] Although she tried hard to learn Chinese, Wilson never reached the fluency that her younger colleagues did. Her lack of linguistic ability, however, was more than made up for by her grey hair which won the respect of the Chinese people. They frequently listened to her message more intently than they did when the younger missionaries spoke.

Wilson was joined by Annie Faussett. Although many experienced missionaries expressed alarm at two single women traveling around the countryside by themselves, the duo prayed and came up with a strategy that had them traveling by boat and speaking at towns along the riverbanks. This way when hostility rose against them, they could retreat to their boat and escape downstream. The ladies encountered few problems, and people came in great numbers to witness the sight of two foreign women sharing a strange message about a God who died for them.

Another single lady, Annie Harrison of New Zealand,[2] wrote from her mission station at Xixiang:

> We found the young converts of last year very bright and eager to be taught more perfectly the way of God; and we also had the joy of seeing several more turn to the Lord. Though it rained during the greater part of the time we were there, we had numbers of visitors, who listened with much attention and interest to the gospel.[3]

A spiritual void in Xi'an

During the 1880s, a strange dichotomy developed among the Evangelical churches in Shaanxi. The pioneer missionaries were concentrated in Hanzhong, the south of the province, and often had to explain to people living on the populated Xi'an Plain where Hanzhong was located, for many had never heard of it.

The gospel took hold in the southern city, with the medical missions work of Dr. William Wilson and his wife proving effective at spreading the message of Christ.[4] George King filed this report from Hanzhong in 1881: "Eighteen have been baptized, and we are very thankful, but not satisfied.... May we be kept in a receptive attitude of soul ready for the great things our God is willing to do. With the Christians from other places there are 21 and there are other inquirers who may soon be baptized."[5]

Further north, however, the capital city remained almost totally devoid of spiritual light. So King decided to hand the reins in Hanzhong over to his co-workers, and he relocated to Xi'an. On Easter Sunday, he attended the Catholic cathedral there which caused him to lament that while he had stood among more than one thousand Catholic worshippers that morning, "there is not one Protestant convert in the city."[6]

In August 1883, King wrote to a friend highlighting the differences between work in the two places:

> In my former station in this province, Hanzhong, 70 or 80 persons have professed faith, and some give us joy. It is the day of small things in this great city—the former capital of China, the center of Nestorian missionary effort some 1,200 years ago, and the present capital of Shaanxi. Yet I will wait and hope until God's

The CIM mission station at Chenggu was a cave carved out of the soft loess (clay) terrain

time comes, and an open door is set before us that we may enter in the Name of the Lord.[7]

The missionaries who remained in Hanzhong continued to feel buoyed by the success they were having. Reports told of schoolgirls being convicted of their sins and finding new life in Jesus Christ, and idols being destroyed by families who had been touched by the power of God. Mrs. Easton wrote to Hudson Taylor's wife in 1884,

> Progress has been most marked. Many of the books put in circulation have proved useful; some readers have become inquirers, some inquirers candidates, some candidates church members, and some of them have become instructors of others....
>
> I love my Chinese sisters much more than I ever thought it possible, and it is very pleasant to have their love, as I believe I have. Two months ago, we had another baptismal service, when three men and seven women were baptized. Two of the latter were members of my weekly class, one a widow and the other a middle-aged woman, whose husband was baptized at the same time. These two women had been coming to the meetings for nearly two years.... When I first began the class there were only five or six who came, now 15 or 16 regularly attend, and some of them we hope to receive next baptism. I am looking for great blessing this year.[8]

While not all converts in Hanzhong remained in the faith, many stirring testimonies emerged of believers who stood strong in Christ despite persecution from their family members and communities. In November 1895, missionary Arthur Polhill-Turner was delighted to report from a church conference in Hanzhong:

> Our members numbered over 100. The subject was "Christians are the light of the world." On Saturday morning, from 11 till 2 p.m., many of the natives spoke, and great interest was manifested. The words of one, a tailor, are worthy of record. He said:

> "I once had a house and it was most unhealthy; my wife and child got ill, and everything went wrong; the reason was that we didn't have enough of the light of heaven inside.... When I was converted, I thought it was good news for all my friends and neighbors; but they only opposed it and I made little impression. I felt that I didn't have enough of the heavenly light within, so I prayed to God for more."

Ever since his conversion he has been praying for his wife.... Well, on Saturday he had the joy of seeing her baptized with 15 others, a sight which gladdened all our hearts.[9]

The differences between the work in Hanzhong compared to Xi'an continued throughout the decade. A 1888 survey found that the southern city had nine resident missionaries and 173 baptized Christians since the commencement of the work nine years earlier.[10] In Xi'an, however, the three missionaries serving in the city did not have a single Christian convert between them.[11] Eight more years passed, and in 1896, the CIM listed just six church members (all men) in Xi'an—a remarkably low figure considering that twenty years had elapsed since the first CIM missionary had visited the city. The same year, Hanzhong had a thriving church with 106 believers, and a further 92 at Chenggu and 80 at Xixiang.[12]

Xi Shengmo and the Xi'an refuge

Xi'an and the massive surrounding plain remained an elusive target for the gospel. The city leaders were proud, academic men who made a pact to keep the foreigners and their religion out of the ancient capital. A missionary described the frustration many felt at the lack of progress in Xi'an:

> There, walled about in proud exclusiveness, lay the ancient city, once capital of China.... All around Xi'an stretched the vast plain,

> fertile, populous, unreached: 12,000 square miles of country; with 21 walled cities, 60 market towns, and countless villages crowded with people, among whom no witnesses for Christ had ever been able to gain a footing.[13]

However, God the Master strategist had a powerful plan to reach the masses of Xi'an. He raised up a Chinese firebrand who was able to touch lives for Jesus Christ like no foreigner could. Xi Shengmo was born in 1836 and became one of the greatest Chinese Christian leaders of the nineteenth century. Hailing from neighboring Shanxi Province, Xi was a Confucian scholar who had become addicted to opium before the Lord wonderfully saved and delivered him from the drug. In little more than a decade, Xi started about thirty medical clinics to help opium

Xi Shengmo

addicts. In addition to healing human bodies, Xi and his co-workers always ministered to the souls of those they helped by proclaiming the gospel.[14]

In 1888, the Lord first gave Xi Shengmo a burden for the people of Xi'an. He left his home province and traversed the mountains. Many tried to dissuade Xi from entering Xi'an, saying that the local officials would never allow him to settle there once they discovered his reasons for coming. Xi was not a timid man and had taken the first name "Shengmo," which means "conqueror of demons." He prayed and trusted the Lord to open a way for him.

On the journey to Shaanxi, Xi met a Hui Muslim who was traveling home. This man had a great deal of influence with the leaders of Xi'an. When he learned that Xi was a doctor intending to open a clinic for opium addicts, he confessed that he was hooked on the drug and asked Xi to help cure him. He also promised Xi that he would obtain suitable premises for his work and that Xi would not be hindered by the city leaders. Then they arrived in the city. God had answered Xi Shengmo's prayers!

After being delivered from his addiction, the Muslim directed many of his friends to the clinic in the hope that they too would find a way to overcome the cursed drug. Soon, many of the leading academics of the city were coming to Xi and hearing the good news that Jesus Christ could transform their lives. One man, Chang, was the first new believer baptized in Xi'an. When several others gave up their idolatry and confessed faith in Christ, the first Evangelical church in Xi'an was established.

Most of Xi's effective ministry took place in his home province of Shanxi, and he returned there in the latter part of his life before he died in 1896 at the age of 60. His commitment to Christ is still honored today by Chinese Christians who love to read his testimony.

Christian immigrants

The fledgling Evangelical movement in Shaanxi was given a huge boost by the unexpected arrival of Chinese Christians from other provinces who were often fleeing famine and turmoil. Missionary Erik Folke recalls how God orchestrated events in the late 1880s: "One of our first baptized Christians rushed into my room one day, saying, 'I have just met a traveler who told me that a great number of immigrants from Shandong have settled in Shaanxi. Many of them are baptized Christians, but they have no one caring for their souls."[15]

Folke soon met the immigrants, and over the next several years, the missionaries helped them in various ways. Meeting places were built in several towns, and schools were opened. The work was later handed over to the English Baptist Mission, and the influx of Christians proved to be a great blessing for the churches of Shaanxi.

Baptist missionary Henry Paynme with Christian women from Shandong who had migrated to Shaanxi

1890s

The Scandinavian invasion

In the early 1890s, the Evangelical movement in Shaanxi started to gain momentum. The total number of baptized believers in the province had grown from just 159 to 277 in the three years between 1888 and 1891.[1] The trajectory was upward, and new towns were constantly being entered for the first time. By contrast, Catholics in Shaanxi numbered 21,300 church members in 105 churches, a total nearly 80 times more than all Evangelical believers in the province.[2]

Evangelical work in Shaanxi received a boost with the arrival of two new Scandinavian mission organizations. The Scandinavian Alliance Mission (SAM)—consisting mostly of Swedes and Americans of Scandinavian descent—commenced work in the province in 1891. After meeting Hudson Taylor in

Scandinavian Alliance missionaries at Xi'an in 1895

Shaanxi, it was decided SAM should take responsibility for a field extending 350 miles (567 km) in length and 150 miles (243 km) in breadth which encapsulated most of the cities and towns on the Xi'an Plain. Their first two bases were located north of Xi'an, with the Swedish duo of August Berg and Axel Hahne located at Sanyuan, and Alex Tjader at Tongchuan.[3]

Two years later the Swedish China Mission also joined the work in Shaanxi, occupying three centers on the Xi'an Plain. Six more cities were occupied in the following years. Both new mission groups served as associate ministries of the China Inland Mission. This arrangement helped them become established in the province, and their workers enjoyed rich fellowship with the other missionaries while attending annual conferences and other meetings.

Frederik Fransen

The Scandinavian Christians' boost of interest in China was not accidental. Bold challenges by missionary statesman Frederik Fransen roused many believers to action, resulting in more than 100 new missionaries giving their lives to serve God in north China and Mongolia.

Fransen was born in Sweden in 1852 but moved to Nebraska as a teenager and studied evangelism under the famous D. L. Moody in Chicago. He returned to Europe for nine years where he preached powerfully to thousands of people.[4] During those years,

> He preached before the Queen of Sweden and was imprisoned in Denmark for sedition, before making his way to Turkey. He came in touch with Hudson Taylor in 1884, when he sent two Norwegian women to the China Inland Mission.... When Taylor issued his appeal for 1,000 missionaries in 1890, Fransen took the

challenge personally and dispatched so many missionaries they were known as "Fransen's floods."[5]

During a trip to Shaanxi, Fransen visited the small town of Sangjiachuang where there were no Chinese Christians at all. The place was known for lawlessness and violence, with men being killed regularly during skirmishes. However, the Swedish pioneer was able to see into the future through eyes of faith. He pointed to a plot of land and told the local missionaries who were ready to give up that a chapel would be built on that site. When the missionaries asked who would pay for it, Fransen replied, "The Chinese themselves will give."

Several years passed, and the first Chinese converts in the town emerged. The spiritual atmosphere was transformed. There was less fighting, and the townspeople enjoyed a more harmonious existence.

One day a rich man came to the mission's opium refuge for treatment, but his expensive mule was stolen while he was there. He demanded the missionaries lodge a case with the magistrate,

Frederik Fransen, the great Swedish pioneer

but they refused, saying they would pray with him for the return of the beast. After initially mocking the missionaries, the rich man allowed them to pray, and three days later the mule was returned. The man was also delivered from his drug addiction and declared that he wanted to serve the Living God who answered prayer. This report summarizes how God orchestrated the breakthrough at Sangjiachuang:

> The man continued to come to the meetings and became truly converted. Soon after, he gave a fine piece of ground on which to build a chapel. This was the very location that Mr. Fransen had pointed out as a healthy place for us to build. This man also helped in building mission premises.... Many of the people provided free labor, and we got our premises according to Mr. Fransen's prayer. From that time God has blessed the work, and it has gone steadily forward. Quite a number have been converted, and there are now over 40 Christians.[6]

The intensely proud leaders of Xi'an, however, remained determined to keep Christianity out of the ancient city. Undeterred, a zealous young Norwegian, Peder Holman,[7] simply turned up in Xi'an and found himself a place to live! The favor of the Holy Spirit rested on Holman. When he was confronted by indignant local officials and scholars, instead of arguing,

> He made no objection but welcomed them as honored guests, entertained them with the best he could provide, and asked if they were fond of music and would like to hear his guitar.
>
> This was too much for their curiosity! They had never heard foreign music and begged him to play the instrument. Inwardly crying out to God for protection, Holman sang hymn after hymn to simple Swedish melodies, until somehow prejudice was disarmed, and his enemies were listening to the gospel.... Half-interested and half-amused, his would-be opponents went away, won to neutrality if not friendship. Thus, the Swedish mission station in the capital was established.[8]

The China Inland Mission, meanwhile, continued to dominate Evangelical work in other parts of Shaanxi. Many breakthroughs occurred throughout the decade as new bases were established, and a trickle of recruits arrived to help advance the kingdom of God. Medical mission work proved particularly effective. A 1892 report noted that in the town of Chenggu in southern Shaanxi,

> Large blessing continues to rest on the work and workers in the city. Thirty-nine have been added to the church by baptism.... The Sunday congregation eventually had to meet in the open air, until suitable premises were obtained—largely through the contributions of the native Christians themselves, with a little help (one-third) from the missionaries....
>
> From February to December (1891) we had at the dispensary 3,546 visits, of which number about 1,500 came for the first time.... The gospel has been carried into hundreds of homes where otherwise it might never have entered.[9]

The English Baptist Mission

The English Baptist Mission was one of the first Evangelical groups in Shandong Province,[10] but their early attempts at establishing a solid foundation there were wracked with failure and doctrinal squabbles between its members. Amid this dysfunctional and failing mission, Timothy Richard emerged and became not only a key proponent of the gospel both in Shandong but also across much of north China, including Shaanxi. Born in Wales, Richard had been converted to Christ during the great Welsh Revival of 1858 to 1860.

A terrible famine across north China in the early 1890s resulted in approximately 15 million people starving to death. The situation became so dire that after trying to find sustenance by eating tree bark and weeds, many people resorted to cannibalism. Timothy Richard responded with a coordinated relief program across north China which opened the hearts of many people to the gospel. In 1894, a Shaanxi missionary detailed some of the church growth that resulted from the relief work:

> We are in the midst of a remarkable movement. 240 villages in Gaoling District have declared for "the doctrine" and established worship at 27 centers.... Eight magistrates are going around threatening the people if they continue to worship and interact with us. For six weeks now the stir has been going on, and still the interest increases.[11]

As they expanded their work throughout Shaanxi, the English Baptists employed multiple strategies to reach people. Medical work, opium refuges, schools, orphanages, and church planting were all features of their outreach. As a result, the English Baptist Mission grew quickly, and their work was boosted by a steady

A group of twelve new missionary arrivals at Ankang in 1895

supply of Chinese evangelists and pastors from provinces where the harvest was already mature.

As their work expanded, the Baptists often found their progress thwarted by the Catholics who strongly opposed them and offered money to church members who were willing to leave the movement and pledge their allegiance to the Catholic Church. The ploy largely failed, however, and in 1894, the English Baptist Mission was able to report,

> Our work is now extended over a large area, embracing eight counties, radiating from the provincial capital Xi'an and the important town of Sanyuan. In the spring there were 21 organized stations with about 1,000 regular worshippers. Famine has reduced the number of stations to 11 that can be regarded as on a firm basis, and the number of regular worshippers to about 500.[12]

Riots and robbers

The steady growth of the church in Shaanxi caused friction in the spiritual realm, and in October 1892, a riot erupted at the mission base in Chenggu. The premises were destroyed, and all the missionaries' possessions were plundered. Despite much opposition, the fire of the gospel continued to spread, reaching even to remote Mongol communities in barren north Shaanxi. In 1898, Swedish missionary August Karlsson reported,

> I spent two months visiting all the villages in a large district. I made a map, stayed in each village for a week, and from there visited the places all round while preaching and selling Gospels and tracts. There are no inns in that part, and the people, mostly poor farmers, do not use money, so I carried beside my bag of books another bag into which I put the flour, or eggs, or potatoes, with which they paid me.
>
> On one occasion I came across as many as 16 wolves together. These wolves often attack people. I cried out to God, and they did

not touch me. The weather was bitterly cold. My books were all sold out, so I sent two men to fetch some more; and while they were gone, I helped the farmer I was staying with in threshing. Some 15 of us slept in a room together, and I preached to them.

On Christmas morning the farmer and his men were frightened, for they heard that a band of 80 robbers, who had been going about devastating villages, were only two miles away. My friend was comparatively rich, and he employed 40 or 50 men. He told them to arm themselves quickly that they might go out to meet the robbers. Some got sticks, and others had spears or knives.

"Mr. Karlsson," he asked, "have you a gun?" "No," I said, "I have a sword—my Bible; let us first kneel down and pray to the true God, who has all power to protect us." We all knelt and prayed, and while we were doing so, the leader of the robber band came up. I received him kindly, told him that I was a foreigner, that I was extremely poor and had no money, but that I had come here to preach about the true God.

As I told the man the gospel he wept, and I asked him to kneel and join me in prayer. After this I asked him to stay and have a meal with us, and though my own clothes were poor his were poorer, so I offered him a garment before he left.

"Your God is a very great God," the farmer said. "Teach us to pray." So, I stayed another week, and we had large meetings. Since I left, several from that village have gone to different places to hear more of the gospel.[13]

Capistran Goette

In 1895 an American Franciscan missionary, Capistran Goette, was viciously attacked by bandits and almost killed. Capistran was the third Goette brother to become a missionary to China. Born in 1859, he arrived in Shaanxi in 1884, and four years later he was joined in the work by Francis Engbring, the first Native American missionary to China.[14]

Capistran's brother and fellow missionary Athanasius Goette described the incident:

> In October 1895, while taking a walk not far from his mission, he was attacked by a number of pagans and mistreated in a cruel manner. The mob threw him on the ground, and, using his cue as a rope, dragged him almost a mile to the little town of Dazuang. On the way they gave him countless kicks and blows. When the pagans noticed him whispering prayers, they took handfuls of dust from the road and stuffed them into his mouth. He almost died of suffocation.[15]

At Dazuang, the mob tied Goette by his hair to the "criminal's post" in the middle of the town, so high that only the tips of his toes could touch the ground, causing him excruciating pain and anguish. A gun was produced and aimed at the defenseless priest, but it failed to discharge correctly. Otherwise it would have ended his life. Enraged by their misfiring weapon, the mob began to beat Goette with clubs and the handles of their swords. One large man

> hit him violently over the head with an iron rod, so that Capistran became unconscious. Disjointing of the fingers and other tortures, however, soon restored him to his senses. Then they untied him and were on the point of piercing him to death like one slaughters a hog. But one of the authorities of the village, fearing the consequences, hindered the outrage....
>
> The ruffians dragged Capistran to a well, intending to drown him.

Capistran Goette, martyred in Shaanxi

> They were on the point of shoving him into it, when he succeeded in grasping with his hand a little tree growing at the edge of the well. Though they struck his hand with the flat blade of knives and with sticks, he held fast to it. At the moment when he again lost consciousness, help arrived. The pagans fled, and Capistran was carried back to his mission more dead than alive.[16]

For the next three days, Goette walked in the shadow of the valley of death. He fell in and out of consciousness, and his injuries were so severe that his blood-soaked clothing had to be carefully cut into tiny pieces to be removed from his body. Forty-seven serious wounds were counted.

Goette slowly recovered from his injuries, aided by the healing touch of the Living God. In many ways the American was never the same again, however, and a painful headache afflicted him for the rest of his life. He rejected the temptation to move back to his homeland after the vicious attack, believing that as long as he had breath, he should fulfill the call of God on his life. He continued to labor selflessly for the salvation of souls in Shaanxi until August 1919, when he finally succumbed to his injuries.

Of Capistran Goette's sixty years, thirty-five were devoted to missionary work in China. The years after the attack were the most fruitful of his career. During that time five new churches were constructed, and thousands of men, women, and children were introduced to the gospel for the first time.

Steady progress in southern Shaanxi

The southern city of Hanzhong continued to be the hub of Evangelical activity in Shaanxi. When missionary W. G. Lagerquist visited in 1894, he was delighted by what he saw in Hanzhong:

> We stayed five days and had the joy of seeing several workers coming back from different places, with beaming faces and hearts

> full of joy and praise, bringing the names of enquirers from different districts. Some brought nine or ten, others 15, others 20, etc. A great deal of seed has been sown in these places for ten years or more with comparatively little results, but now one can truly see that it has not been sown in vain.... It was a great privilege to see the native Christians, and to hear their songs of praise and thanksgiving.[17]

As the nineteenth century ended, the Evangelical enterprise in Shaanxi was still minuscule compared to the Catholics, but the seed of God's Word was being sown throughout the province, and the first signs of a bountiful harvest were beginning to appear. After many trials and setbacks, the China Inland Mission

Elder Liu, pastor of the Hanzhong church in 1897

succeeded in planting churches in many areas of Shaanxi during the 1890s. Their statistics reveal an increase of mission stations from just three at the start of the decade to 21 by the end; the number of CIM missionaries rose from 15 to 77; and the total CIM church membership in the province nearly tripled from 143 believers to 396.[18]

In the 1890s several other mission organizations arrived in Shaanxi, and the overall Evangelical progress was encouraging, as outlined in this chart of work between 1885 and 1899:

Evangelical Christians in Shaanxi (1885–1899)[19]		
Year	**Baptisms**	**Cumulative**
1885	20	131
1888	13	159
1891	39	277
1896	61	492
1899	41	638

The 1900s

At the dawn of the twentieth century, the body of Christ in Shaanxi was cautiously optimistic. The 1900s promised much for the church, but first it would have to endure a very dark period when violence threatened to sweep away all the hard-earned gains.

Christian influence in Shaanxi during the first decade of the new century was dominated by the Roman Catholics. A 1907 survey found that there were 35,811 members in 259 Catholic churches throughout the province.[1] By comparison, the new Evangelicals numbered just 954 church members in 1904,[2] meaning the Catholics were numerically almost 40 times larger than their Evangelical counterparts at the time.

A group of armed Boxer rebels

The Evangelical community was on the move, however, and both missionaries and Chinese church leaders held high hopes that the gospel would flourish in unprecedented ways throughout the thousands of villages, towns, and cities of Shaanxi. The spiritual fortress of Xi'an also started to show cracks. Swedish missionary V. L. Nordlund wrote this encouraging report:

> It is a great joy for me to tell you of our Chinese conference.... The Holy Spirit moved the hearts of many, and from 13 candidates, seven men were received into the Church by baptism. The work is very encouraging at present, and our Sunday services are well attended. God is working mightily among the people, and many have given in their names as enquirers.[3]

Instead of a big breakthrough, however, the church in Shaanxi had to first endure a time when death and destruction came knocking at the door. For years, anti-foreign sentiment had been simmering throughout north China. All foreign influence was despised, and both missionaries and their Chinese converts were seen as tools of foreign imperialism that had to be eliminated. In 1899, a terrible flood of the Yellow River inundated a vast area of several provinces, and millions of people were drowned or made homeless. Coming on the back of decades of severe drought and humiliation at the hands of foreign powers, this flood was a turning point. The religious leaders of the day declared that the woes were being heaped upon the nation because the spiritual balance had been upset, and the only way to placate the spirits was to rid China of foreign influences.

A secret group known as the White Lotus Society had been active in north China for decades. A subgroup of the Society, the Yi He Quan, literally "righteous harmony fists," came to be known in the English-speaking world as "Boxers" because of their practice of using boxing drills for physical training. The Boxers quickly became the agents of horrific slaughter. This summary gives background on the volcano which erupted in the summer of 1900:

> Early in 1900 the storm clouds of the Boxer Uprising began to darken the horizon. All the forces of conservation, of superstition and reaction gathered for the final effort to resist the advancing tide of progress and of foreign influence. Many were the grievances which China had suffered.
>
> France had seized Vietnam; Belgium had outwitted China; Spain had butchered 20,000 Chinese in cold blood in the Philippines; England held Hong Kong and Weihai; Russia had seized half a million square miles of Chinese territory; the Germans held Jiaozhou and were pressing into sacred Shandong; Portugal had long before taken Macau. The foreign religion was making rapid advances, and the Chinese deeply resented the political influence which the Roman Catholics were bringing to bear in the courts and at provincial capitals.[4]

On June 21, 1900, the Empress Dowager Cixi issued this edict from the imperial palace in Beijing:

> The foreigners have been aggressive towards us, infringed upon our territorial integrity, and trampled our people under their feet. They oppress our people and blaspheme our gods. The common people suffer greatly at their hands and each one of them is vengeful. Thus it is that the brave followers of the Boxers have been burning churches and killing Christians.[5]

With the support of the empress, the Boxers knew the Chinese imperial troops would aid them in the slaughter. The historian Kenneth Scott Latourette notes,

> Protestants, being much more recently arrived in China than the Roman Catholics, and having been in North China, the centre of the Boxer upheaval, for only 40 years, had a much smaller body of converts to undergo persecution. Among the Chinese Christians, therefore, fewer Protestants than Roman Catholics

> were killed. On the other hand, more Protestant than Roman Catholic missionaries perished.[6]

Christians were martyred in a myriad of cruel ways. Hundreds were burned alive, buried alive, or dismembered. Most were decapitated by the long, curved swords carried by the Boxers. In many cases, the persecutors held distorted ideas of gospel truths, such as the resurrection. Sometimes a martyr's body was not allowed to be buried for three days, "with the idea that, like their Lord, they might in that time be restored to life. In other cases the poor remains were burned and the bones ground to powder, to prevent any resurrection."[7]

The carnage began in Shandong and then spread to other provinces. The worst slaughters took place in Shanxi Province where more than 150 Evangelical missionaries were put to death. The China Inland Mission alone lost 136 missionaries and 53 children. More than half of their force in Shanxi was wiped out. However, the greatest toll was of Chinese Christians. Approximately 30,000 are believed to have been killed by the Boxers.

The Boxer onslaught did not become a nationwide rebellion but was mostly confined to the northern provinces. In some parts of the country, sympathetic governors and magistrates chose to ignore the imperial edict. Or they delayed sufficiently to allow the missionaries to escape to the coast and the Chinese Christians to go into hiding. While thousands of Christians were killed in neighboring Shanxi Province, not a single Evangelical missionary perished in Shaanxi because the governor, Duan Fang, had befriended several of the foreign believers. He not only refused to publish the imperial edict to kill missionaries and their Chinese converts, but he also offered protection and assistance to safeguard their well-being.

Before it was confirmed that no foreign missionaries had been killed in Shaanxi, however, many sleepless nights were endured by family members and loved ones in their home countries. Nerves were frayed when the influential *Chinese Recorder* magazine wrongly stated in September 1900, "Of the 154 missionaries stationed in Shaanxi only some 45 are known to have escaped."[8]

While the foreign Evangelicals escaped the Boxer fury, many Chinese Christians in Shaanxi suffered terribly. While most experienced the loss of their possessions and homes, at least twenty-six Chinese believers laid down their lives in the summer of 1900. A Chinese pastor wrote from Xi'an,

> The Mission premises at Huiyi have been looted, some of the houses of the natives have also been looted and others burned. The chapel at Xincheng has been burned and the hospital looted.... The Mission premises and the homes of over 20 Christian families at Huanglong, have been burned, and over ten of the Christians killed.
>
> There are still many other families of which I have no reliable details, but together a total of 26 persons have been killed. Very many of the Christians have been without food and clothing since the commencement of the persecution, and at the present time (September 19th), rain has not yet fallen. The Christians are helpless, and those who have not been killed by Boxers will die of famine and cold.[9]

Albericus Crescitelli

While no Evangelical missionaries were killed in Shaanxi, the Catholics suffered much loss of life. Many Chinese believers were beheaded, while others died by being thrown into wells. Still more suffered prolonged hardship as they fled into remote mountains where they died from exhaustion and starvation while trying to evade their bloodthirsty pursuers.

The most prominent Catholic killed in Shaanxi in the summer of 1900 was the 37-year-old Italian Albericus Crescitelli.[10] After his father and sister were killed in a violent earthquake in 1883, Crescitelli dedicated himself to the service of God and traveled to north China in 1888. After 132 days at sea from Marseille to Shanghai, he endured another five months of grueling travel as his boat slowly inched up the Han River to his new home in Shaanxi. Soon after arriving in the province, Crescitelli won respect as a hard worker and a servant of all. He wrote home,

> Any place where you can bless and console a soul, where the people are poorest, where there is much pain and suffering … is a place of honor for a minister of the church…. My heart tells me that I am where I belong, where God wants me, and I am happy.[11]

Although he was responsible for the spiritual well-being of one thousand believers living in seven villages, Crescitelli had the heart of an evangelist and longed for more Chinese to hear the good news. In 1900, he was transferred to the remote county of Ningqiang, a wild place located high up in the mountains. Because of its isolation, Ningqiang had become a nest of Boxer

Albericus Criscitelli

activity. Crescitelli sensed the danger, but in a letter to his loved ones he told how he was prepared to face whatever would come his way:

> Who knows how it will go in this distant district. At any rate, life and death are both in the hands of God: not a leaf drops that God does not will.... Be of good cheer and don't worry about me. I am in the hands of God and I am happy. My guardian angel is watching over me![12]

On August 20, 1900, a local official took Crescitelli into his home under the guise of protecting him. When a pre-arranged signal was given, dozens of violent men surrounded the house and demanded the missionary be handed over to them. The official told Crescitelli to flee out the back door into the mountains, but the Italian knew it was a ruse, so he knelt down and prayed.

When his attackers surrounded him breathing threats of violence, Albericus Crescitelli asked them, "What have I done to you? If you have something against me, some accusation to make, speak; take me to the authorities." In response the Boxers

> inflicted a fierce blow to his left arm, almost severing it, and then another directly to his face, breaking open his nose and his lips. Dazed by the blows of the clubs and by his wounds, he was at first dragged, and then ... after tying his hands and feet to a pole, they carried him like an animal on the way to the butcher.[13]

Crescitelli was taken to the market town of Yanzibian where he was beaten throughout the night, causing him to pass out. When he regained consciousness, the brave Italian prayed for his attackers who had spent the night playing cards and drinking. At about noon the following day, Crescitelli was "humiliated and tortured very cruelly. The Boxers bayoneted him to death and dismembered his body, throwing his arms, legs and head into the river. He became a martyr at the age of 37."[14] The example left by Albericus Crescitelli's martyrdom resonated for over a century. The Chinese Communist Party considering him such a threat that they issued vile slanders against the missionary in 2000, a century after his death. All records indicate that he was a much loved man of God who lived a humble and sacrificial life for the people of Shaanxi.

Consolidation and growth

Although Shaanxi emerged relatively unscathed from the Boxer Rebellion, the effects of the slaughter in other parts of the country deeply affected all believers, and a time of consolidation and reflection was needed. During that time, many believers who had been lukewarm in their commitment to Christ crossed the line and became wholehearted disciples. The news that thousands of their brothers and sisters had laid down their lives for Jesus Christ inspired the Shaanxi believers to take a similar stand for the gospel.

A gathering of believers at Fengxiang on New Year's Day, 1909

In the following years, reports flooded in showing that despite continual struggles and setbacks, a new openness to Jesus Christ was seen throughout the province. Many churches at least doubled their membership. The body of Christ in Shaanxi continued to grow, and the salt and light of Jesus was given out in many places where previously there had been little or no gospel witness. For example in early 1906, the *China's Millions* magazine printed this snippet: "Mr. C. J. Anderson, in announcing 32 baptisms in the stations on the Xi'an Plain, Shaanxi, informs us that in almost all the centers worked by the members of the Scandinavian China Alliance, God is giving conversion blessing."[15]

The first decade of the twentieth century turned out to be one of both tragedy and triumph for Christians in Shaanxi. Although no further surveys were done, it was clear that the Evangelical churches had experienced steady growth. They had broadened their base, and fellowships had been established in most cities and counties throughout the province.

The Xi'an Bloodbath of 1911

The period leading up to the 1911 Revolution—which marked the fall of the Qing Dynasty after 268 years of rule—was a time of great danger for missionaries and Chinese believers. Many people blamed foreigners for propping up the corrupt Qing rulers, and when the tide turned against these rulers, many missionaries and their converts were also targeted.

For decades, a growing resentment against the Manchu rulers had simmered among the Han Chinese. Strangely, China had been controlled by two ethnic minority dynasties—the Yuan Dynasty of the Mongols from 1271 to 1368 and the Manchu-led Qing Dynasty from 1368 to 1911—a total period of 640 years. The emperor and empress of China had both died in 1908, leaving their two-year-old son on the throne. The Han Chinese seized the opportunity to launch a revolution which resulted in China becoming a republic. Manchu people throughout China

The new mission school at Xi'an, which was destroyed during the 1911 riots

were slaughtered by angry mobs, and those who were considered to be friends of the Manchus faced grave danger.

An anti-Manchu and anti-foreign sect called the Ancient Society of Elder Brothers had hundreds of members throughout Xi'an. Violence erupted at noon on October 22, 1911, when members of the sect and other rebels captured the arsenal of the government troops. Xi'an had long been a center of Manchu power, and at least 20,000 imperial troops and their families lived in the northeast suburb.

For days soldiers were butchered throughout the city, and at least 10,000 Manchu people were slain in the streets before the carnage spread to other parts of the province and all over China. A missionary shared her memories of those dark days:

> For three days there was a ruthless slaughter of men, women and children. Those who tried to escape were cut down as they passed through the gates. In the darkness a few managed to scale the city wall, descend the other side, wade through the moat and flee to the open country. Many set fire to their houses rather than let their enemies seize their possessions....
>
> At the English Hospital, when the first fury was past, men were brought in a shocking condition. Many had attempted to cut their throats. Asked why they had done so, they answered simply: "The wells were full."[1]

In the mayhem, a Catholic school near Hanzhong was destroyed and forty teachers and students were slaughtered. At first "it was reported that 40 foreigners were murdered. However, it was later made known that these 40 were Chinese Catholics who had cut their hair short, and were therefore termed 'foreigners.'"[2]

The English Baptists

A Catholic priest was murdered in the suburbs of Xi'an, and when the English Baptist Mission came under threat, the leaders decided to separate the students into small groups and send them to safe locations throughout the city. Missionary-teacher Jennie Beckingsale wrote this detailed report of her experiences:

> We sent out to try to hire carts, but found all inns and shops closed and barricaded by the frightened inhabitants. That night, the school in the South suburb was burned, six children and two adults being killed, and this news was brought to us early the next morning. Several of our servants fled and the schoolgirls were panic-stricken and begged to be allowed to leave.
>
> Upon receiving confirmation of the sad tidings, we decided to leave the compound as word was brought to us by trustworthy helpers that a band of ruffians was coming to attack us also. We divided the girls into companies and sent them out to different villages where we had friends....
>
> When all had gone, the remainder of our party, six in number, set out with two horses, and such luggage as they could carry, to meet an evangelist at a village where he would advise us as to further plans. Before we reached the place, we were attacked by a large band of men who took the horses and everything we had and drove us back to the city with horrible threats and insults. We were permitted to enter one of our houses, while the leader rode on for orders, and we waited for about two hours expecting certain death....
>
> About 6 p.m., Mr. and Mrs. Donald Smith were brought in, terribly hurt by the brutality of a band who had attacked them with great violence, beating them cruelly, and breaking both of Mr. Smith's arms. The party of schoolgirls returned unhurt, however. Next morning, another band of girls came back without injury, though much frightened, and on the following day the number was completed by the return of a third party who had a terrible tale of exposure, persecution, and threats; but by the mercy of God not one of them was injured in any way.
>
> During the whole of this time, for four days and nights, the sounds of fighting were continuous. Bullets flew even into our compound, our houses were shaken by explosions, and the sky

was lit up by the lurid flames from the burning houses of the Manchu.[3]

The Scandinavian Alliance

The Scandinavian Alliance Mission had quickly grown from its humble beginnings in 1890 to become one of the largest Evangelical organizations in north China. In 1909, the work in the West suburb of Xi'an was taken over by Richard and Ida Beckman.[4] They soon constructed a school which offered a Christian-based education to missionary children, but the Revolution brought tragic results for this mission.

The Beckman family in 1904

The violence against the Scandinavian missionaries broke on the night of October 23, 1911, when a mob rushed into the school, setting fire to the gate as they attempted to break down the wall. The missionaries and their children were huddled together on the second floor of the building as Richard Beckman and a young teacher named Wilheim Vatne fetched a rope and a wheelbarrow to help the children escape over a back wall.

Vatne went over the wall first, and Beckman had just helped his eldest daughter Selma over when shots rang out. The mob had gained entry to the compound. Beckman, his wife Ida, and six remaining children tried to hide in a small outbuilding. Richard Beckman later wrote,

> I sat down and took our smallest girl in my arms. We began praying, and asked God to prevent the mob discovering where we were, if it was His will to deliver us. At the same time we committed ourselves into His hand, to live or to die. My wife took our youngest girl from me for a moment, pressed her to her bosom, and kissing her tenderly, said, "I must say goodbye to you, my darling."[5]

Moments later their hiding place was discovered. One account said,

> They all dashed out, trying to run through the crowd milling around the yard. Beckman, carrying little Thyra, became separated from his wife and the others. Oblivious to blows from the fanatics who saw him, he rushed through the gate and ran into a grove of trees on the south bank of a large pond. Hearing voices behind him, he jumped in and waded to the middle of the pond where he and his child huddled in the thick vegetation which had grown out of the shallow water.[6]

Beckman and his daughter were surrounded by mobs of bloodthirsty men who crowded around the pond and waited for their prey to emerge from the dark. Beckman recalled, "I sat there for

Ida Beckman (left) and Ruth Beckman with her sister Thyra in front

an hour or more until my arms were numb from exhaustion, and the little girl's legs dropped into the water. Still she did not cry or make a noise."[7]

Just before daybreak, Richard Beckman and his daughter carefully made their way out of the pond and back to the mission station where they were told that the beloved mother of their family, Ida Beckman, and five children had been butchered by the mob. The murdered children were Ruth Beckman, age 8; George Ahlstrand, age 10; Hilda Nelson, age 15; Hulda Bergström, age 12; and Oscar Bergström age 13. Apart from the Beckman girl, the youngsters were the children of missionaries stationed in other parts of the province. Richard Beckman painfully recalled his reaction:

> There lay my wife and little Ruth, as well as the other dear children, slain! How the hearts of the parents of these children would bleed, as well as mine, when they should learn what had

> happened—the thought of this called forth deep pain. With the addition of the uncertainty concerning Mr. Vatne and Selma, I was nearly overcome.[8]

A Chinese seminary student later told how the martyrs had died. Beckman wrote that the student had found Beckham's dead wife

> clasping our girl Ruth with one arm, while on the other side Hulda Bergström had sought refuge. The other children had pressed through the gateway, but had not come far before they were slain. Hilda Nelson had run a short distance towards the south, seeking refuge among some graves. Oscar Bergström had reached halfway to the place where I leaped into the water. George Ahlstrand had fallen in the road a short distance from the gate, and at his side lay his pet, the big dog, keeping watch. One of the boys had been shot. Judging by their appearance they must have had a quick death.[9]

George Ahlstrand with his parents (left) and Hilda Nelson (right)

Ida Beckman was born in Sweden in 1865. She was converted at a Salvation Army meeting and afterward became an active Christian worker on the streets of Stockholm. After emigrating to the United States in 1888, she settled in the city of Brooklyn. Soon after she heard the famous preacher Frederik Fransen speak on the need for missions. Ida attended training classes and soon felt the Holy Spirit calling her to China.

Richard Beckman was in a state of shock at the death of his beloved wife and daughter Ruth. But he wanted to know what had happened to his 13-year-old daughter Selma and the 21-year-old teacher Wilheim Vatne, both of whom had scaled the wall before the mob entered the mission station. Three days later it was discovered that the pair had escaped into the night and taken shelter with a Chinese family. The grieving Richard Beckman was once again called upon to tell what happened

Wilheim Vatne (left) and Selma Beckman (right)

> As the people had heard that all foreigners in the city had been killed, they dared not let these live. They constantly pelted them with broken bricks and hard lumps of earth. Mr. Vatne, taking hold of Selma's hand, was occasionally knocked to the ground, but sprung to his feet again, still holding her fast. About noon they were separated. Mr. Vatne was killed first, and shortly after, darling Selma, my eldest child, breathed her last. They passed through severe suffering. Their pierced bodies were found buried in a field.[10]

Wilheim Vatne was born in America to Norwegian parents. He grew up in North Dakota, where he placed his trust in Jesus Christ at a young age. After graduating from high school early, Vatne became a teacher at the age of just 18. A few years later he heard that the mission school in Xi'an was looking for a consecrated Christian to teach the missionary children. Vatne accepted the call, arriving in China in September 1910. After hearing of his son's martyrdom, Vatne's aged father wrote,

> You can hardly believe how we feel these days. It was a hard stroke when we heard that our beloved Wilheim has already been taken away from us. How strange that his day of work should be so short! Oh, Wilheim was a dear son to us!… I am weak and weary, and this heavy sorrow is weighing me down, but sweeter will be the rest when I reach Home…. I could have written this letter with my tears! Yet, the Lord had the greatest claim to him: He gave him to us, and He took him. Blessed be the Name of the Lord![11]

The mob thoroughly destroyed the new Scandinavian Alliance Mission school and all the adjoining buildings. On the day following the bloodbath, Beckman felt

> crushed to despair. All possible ways of escape now came to my mind, but too late! Why had I not attempted this or that method by which I could probably have rescued them all?… During the forenoon little Thyra cried bitterly. No words could comfort her, save when I prayed. As soon as I ceased praying she wept again.

> This continued until the afternoon. I continually called on the Lord, paying no attention to whoever came or went. I resigned myself wholly to the will of God, to live or to die. Thus I regained peace and calmness of mind.[12]

When Beckman told his little daughter that her mother and sisters had gone to be with Jesus, she asked, "Did they go to our Jesus?" When her father replied "Yes," she said, "Then I am glad, for I can go to them."

Evil did not have free rein in these days, however, and testimonies emerged of God's protective power. Christine Anderson was fleeing to safety after hearing news of the massacre when a Chinese evangelist found her and assured the single missionary that she was safe. The evangelist had risked his life by going to

Richard Beckman and Thyra after arriving back in Sweden

the bandits and preaching the gospel to them. The leader was so touched by the evangelist's courage and message that he assured him they would not lay a hand on Anderson or any of the other Christians. The leader promised, "I know of your Jesus. I won't hurt you."[13]

The mission school in Xi'an was rebuilt in 1915 on the same spot where the martyrs had spilled their blood. The Scandinavian missionaries "returned and went bravely on with their work, teaching and preaching the Word of God, that Christ is the Savior of all men."[14]

Richard Beckman and his daughter Thyra returned to Sweden to recover from their ordeal. While there, Thyra developed "measles, croup, diphtheria and inflammation of both lungs," and was close to death.[15] Doctors held little hope for her recovery. But many Christians prayed fervently, and she experienced a complete recovery. Years later she married a missionary and returned to serve in China, among the people who had taken her mother and sisters from her. This great act of grace and forgiveness amazed all the Chinese who heard about it.

1910s

"The Christian God has come down!"

Powerful revivals in other parts of the world during the first decade of the twentieth century—including the great Welsh Revival and the Azusa Street Revival in Los Angeles—affected multitudes of people and ushered them into the kingdom of God. The flames of revival spread to the Korean Peninsula and then into some parts of China as God brought thousands to faith and repentance in places where there had previously been few Christians.

Despite the faithful labors of many dedicated believers, Shaanxi Province had not experienced a true outpouring of the Holy Spirit at any time in history, except perhaps more than a

A crowded tent revival meeting in Xi'an

thousand years earlier through the first Nestorians. This situation began to change in 1910, however, just before the Boxer Revolution and the subsequent Xi'an massacre detailed above.

Annie Olsen of the Scandinavian Alliance Mission gave a thrilling address at a prayer meeting in January 1910. She shared about a move of God at Sangjiachuang in Shaanxi, and her report is worth repeating in detail:

> The missionaries in Shaanxi, having heard of the great blessing in Manchuria and Shanxi, prayed for a similar blessing to be granted in their province.... Meetings were arranged in four centers, and the churches of the three mission organizations gathered. The first meeting was in Xingping, and from the commencement a spirit of conviction was noticed.
>
> At first the Christians were sad; then they became fearful, so that they hardly knew what the trouble was. There were 400 or 500 people present, and the conviction of sin was so strong on the third day that they broke out into groaning and crying, their sins being too heavy for them to bear. We felt the Spirit's presence very near.
>
> An old woman had a bowl of opium, which was practically all her savings, and she had kept it for five years. This, she felt, was very wrong, and feeling that she could not sell it as it could harm others, she decided to burn it. The opium was brought to a meeting in a basket, and the young men joyfully took it outside where it was burnt. The outsiders could not understand why the Christians were burning so much valuable opium.
>
> Fear came upon the heathen population, and they said, "The Christian God has come down in their midst!"
>
> Many of the Christians confessed to various kinds of sins, and to unfriendly feelings among themselves, each one taking the blame. Quarrels were made up, and money that had been obtained dishonestly was restored.
>
> Similar manifestations of the Spirit's power were witnessed at each of the centers, and a deep work of grace was evident, for

> which we praise God.... The women took off their silver ornaments and laid them on the table as an offering to the Lord. The deepening of the spiritual life of the Church since has been very manifest, for which we are thankful to God.[1]

Further meetings in the western suburb of Xi'an were conducted by three conservative mission agencies—the Baptist Missionary Society, the Scandinavian Alliance, and the China Inland Mission. Many missionaries had expressed skepticism about reports of revival elsewhere. But the Holy Spirit fell on the people with great power, and spontaneous public confessions of sin occurred in each meeting. News of the revival told how

> Sins were confessed by leaders; a backslider, who had been put out of the church years before, and was threatening to kill a missionary, confessed sins and was reconciled to his father. But the outstanding evidence of the Spirit's power was in the theological college. Most of the students, though moved by one's confession of great sin one morning, so resisted the Spirit that at night some became unconscious in consequence....
>
> Students were stretched out on the ground, having tried to hide from the majesty of the Lord.... At last, peace obtained, voices rose in praise and in prayer for the students in the East suburb.... Since then, there has been further blessing among them.
>
> The women and girls were also moved at the meetings. The prayer for the meetings in the East suburb, where James Watson had a tent for 700 erected, were in no small measure answered.... One came up and took half an hour to confess. Students and others followed in a stream, so that the meeting lasted four hours, and confession continued at the evening meeting, and at the following Sunday meetings.
>
> On the Saturday at 11 a.m., the teacher called us to the girls' school, and before we got there, we heard a great sound of weeping, for all 39 girls were weeping.[2]

The revival continued to spread throughout Shaanxi. Three months after the initial outpouring, veteran New Zealand missionary Annie Harrison wrote of the effect the revival was having on her Sunday school students at Xixiang:

> In one class the response on the part of every boy but one was immediate. Several said: "I have already accepted Jesus Christ," and the others were all ready to do so. They did not wait for the after-meeting, but there and then got down on their knees and prayed.
>
> A touching incident occurred in a class of small boys. A dear lad stood up before his teacher had even begun to speak to them and said with much agitation: "I want to accept the Lord Jesus."
>
> "Yes," she said, "wait a little while, for we are going to ask all who wish to do so to stay after the meeting."
>
> "I can't wait," he replied. "I want to accept Him now."
>
> About 120 boys responded to the invitation, and I shall never forget the sight of that room full of earnest young faces, all eager to own Jesus Christ as Lord and Savior. They have been well-grounded in gospel truth, so that they knew perfectly well what they were doing. After they had been spoken to, they were asked to kneel and, one by one to offer up a short prayer, but they were in such a hurry that they all prayed together. Then one of the teachers asked all who had really accepted the Lord to stand up and say so. Nearly all responded....
>
> May the Lord keep us faithful to the great trust He has given us and enable us, through His grace, to lead these dear lads on to fulness of life in Christ Jesus. Many of them are well-educated and just verging on manhood. What a blessing they may become to the whole province![3]

Today, over a century later, many people in Xixiang continue to stand for Jesus Christ. An estimated 14,000 Evangelicals and 6,700 Catholics live in the county, making up over six percent of the total population there.[4]

The chaos subsides

In time, the chaos in Shaanxi caused by the collapse of the Qing Dynasty in 1911 subsided. As the leaders of the new Republic of China gained control of the nation, law and order was slowly restored in most places. At this time, Chinese Christians increasingly took the lead in church life and evangelism throughout the province. This 1914 report from Lantian County, east of Xi'an, details seven days of special meetings in which the Holy Spirit deeply touched those in attendance:

> The Lord gave us and the church a mighty blessing. There was weeping, praying, confession and forgiving of old grudges. The church was stirred as it has not been for several years. There are now 24 members, and they volunteered no less than 500 days for the preaching of the gospel.... Many families have put away their idols; but many of them have not yet become real followers of Christ. Our prayer is that the Spirit may gain victory in their hearts....
>
> An old sturdy vegetarian, who had for some time been under the influence of the gospel, came forward one evening and asked for prayer. The next morning, he cleared his ancestral shrine of all idolatry and enjoyed a breakfast with his family for the first time in many years. They all rejoiced that his "mouth was opened again," as they call it, and the pleasure at his being able to partake of such food was as great on his part as theirs. He is a good man with a splendid reputation among his neighbors.[5]

The work in Lantian, which had been under the leadership of missionary William Englund, was set alight by the Spirit of God. In the year after the 1914 meetings—when they had just twenty-four church members—the mission reported startling growth with "seven outstations beside the head station; ten evangelists, four Biblewomen, two colporteurs [traveling Bible salesmen], four unpaid helpers, and up to this time 241 who have been baptized and added to the church."[6]

Later, in 1936 when Mao led his Communist forces through Lantian during their famous Long March, the Christians there suffered awful persecution. Church buildings and homes were burned to the ground, and many believers fled into the mountains until the danger passed. God had the last say, however, and the Christian community experienced strong growth in the aftermath of the onslaught.

Jessie Gregg

The second half of the 1910s saw an increase in the number of Christians in Shaanxi as the presence of the Lord Jesus continued to grace His children in meetings that brought deep conviction of sin and deliverance from bondage. God used various servants to achieve His purposes at this time, but prominent among them was a single female evangelist named Jessie Gregg (1871–1942), who ministered to women across north and central China with great effect. Although much of her work was done in other provinces, Gregg, who was affiliated with the CIM, held many meetings in Shaanxi that left a trail of new converts, and thousands of believers were strengthened in their commitment to Christ.

In 1917, Gregg and her team visited Xi'an. A missionary joyfully reported,

> You will rejoice to hear that God is blessing the ministry of Miss Jessie Gregg in Shaanxi. During her recent meetings for women at two centers in Xi'an, 47 women professed

Jessie Gregg after forty years of service in China

Jessie Gregg and her team of Chinese workers

Lunch break during one of Jessie Gregg's 1917 meetings in Shaanxi

> conversion.... The Lord again in His mercy manifested the power of His Spirit. Wrongs were righted, sins confessed, and crooked things straightened. Many hearts were deeply stirred. To God be the glory.[7]

Gregg also visited the strategic city of Fengxiang where the CIM's Charles Stevens and his wife had served for many years. They were deeply encouraged by the visit. Mrs. Stevens wrote,

> We have been more than 20 years in Fengxiang, and this is the first time we have ever had any special help such as Miss Gregg is now giving.... Surely, He who has given gifts to His Church has greatly enriched us in China through this ministry. The women are won by Miss Gregg's personality and manner, and the message of the Cross, grand in the simplicity and clearness in which it is delivered, seems mighty through the Holy Spirit's working.
>
> She left us yesterday for Qianyang, and I have never seen in China anything like the loving manifestation the women showed as they watched, in the distance, the very last glimpse of the sedan bearing the Lord's messenger on her way to needy Gansu. Here we have sown in tears, and she has helped us to reap in joy. On the Xi'an Plain many have found forgiveness, life and hope in Christ.[8]

Mayhem returns

The government had struggled to gain full control of Shaanxi since the 1911 Revolution, and with the economy in tatters, gangs of bandits formed in many parts of the province, terrorizing the population. With each passing year, lawlessness gained ascendency in Shaanxi so that by the end of the 1910s, the province seemed worse off than even during the aftermath of the 1911 Revolution.

Foreign missionaries, both Evangelicals and Catholics, were called to lay down their lives during this time. A Franciscan priest named Francis Bernot was assassinated in June 1913, while at the end of the decade, in August 1919, the American Franciscan Capistran Goette finally succumbed to injuries he had received from beatings over a quarter of a century before.

On the morning of January 4, 1918, the Swedish Missionary Alliance's Christine Villadsen was murdered by bandits while trying to protect Chinese believers at Sanshui in western Shaanxi. A report said, "It appears brigands entered the city, robbing and killing the people. Miss Villadsen and one of the Chinese Christians lost their lives."[9]

Christine's last letter home had excitedly broken the news that seventy-three Chinese women had made commitments to Christ. Just weeks before her martyrdom, Villadsen was with Jessie Gregg when the pair of single women were accosted by

Christine Villadsen—murdered by bandits in 1918

bandits while riding their horses near Sanshui. The bloodthirsty men raised their guns and were about to shoot the two ladies when Gregg removed her hat. Seeing her grey hair, the bandits allowed them to pass.[10] Upon hearing of Christine Villadsen's death, Gregg wrote,

> News of the tragic death of Miss Villadsen has almost overwhelmed me.... She wept and cried when she saw the beginning of the harvest in Sanshui. That city is a very lonely place, but she loved it and was so very happy there. She was a keen missionary, and nothing was too much trouble where the Chinese were concerned. Certainly, the mission has lost a capable and consecrated worker by her death.[11]

The 1910s drew to a close, and Christians in Shaanxi looked back on a decade through which they had endured intense persecution after the overthrow of a dynasty. On the other hand, the Lord Jesus Christ had breathed life into many parts of His church, and strong growth had been experienced throughout the province.

Stress was ever present in Shaanxi, however. This China Inland Mission report from 1919 offers a glimpse into the difficult challenges faced by Christians at the end of the decade as much of the province risked being plunged back into a state of chaos:

> In Shaanxi the conditions are still very disturbed, and our workers at Hanzhong, Fengxiang, Xixiang, Ankang and elsewhere have been passing through a time of considerable strain and anxiety.
>
> The city of Ankang was attacked by brigands on November 4, and within 24 hours 1,000 women and children came to the mission premises for refuge. Strong men with tears rolling down their cheeks came begging for protection....
>
> Bullets fell all around us. One man lying in bed just opposite our door was shot dead, but not one stray bullet hit our walls. Oh! We shall never forget that Wednesday: screams of people being murdered rendered the air that day, and the noise of houses burning and being torn down... was too awful for description.

Hell itself seemed let loose all around us.... Never again do we want to go through such an experience....

The chapel has been well filled each Sunday since, and many are apparently truly enquiring. If souls are going to be saved here as a result of all that has happened, what a privilege is ours to have suffered for Him who gave His life for these very people.[12]

1920s

A decade of discontent

After the intense decade of the 1910s, the church in Shaanxi prayed for relief in the 1920s so that they could freely worship God and continue to share the gospel with the millions of people throughout the province who had yet to hear the Name of Jesus. At the start of the 1920s, the Catholic Church in Shaanxi continued to be much larger than their Evangelical counterparts, although the ratio was shrinking quickly. In 1891 there were eighty Catholics for every Evangelical believer in the province, but by 1904, this ratio had been cut in half to 40:1. An extensive survey in 1922 found that Catholics were only seven times more

Missionary Charles Stevens and two Chinese evangelists at Fengxiang

numerous, with 48,948 Catholics in 313 churches throughout Shaanxi at the time,[1] compared to 7,081 Evangelicals.[2]

An uprising in China known as the White Wolf Rebellion began in 1913 and grew until it numbered 12,000 bandits. The leader Bai Lang, whose name sounds like "white wolf" in Chinese, was a man with little conscience. His army conducted mass rape, looting, and murder across several Chinese provinces, and Christians were often in their crosshairs. Even after the rebellion officially ended, thousands of men joined armed gangs, and violence continued to plague Shaanxi throughout the 1920s and 1930s. In many places—especially rural areas where government troops were less prominent—bandits wreaked havoc on the church.

A joyful Shaanxi Christian in 1925

Lantian was a favorite target because nearby rugged mountains gave the bandits an easy escape route. A deacon in the Lantian church was shot dead by a bandit. Later an evangelist named Yang was instrumental in leading many people to faith in the town before one Sunday, "a robber gang entered the church and shot him dead while in the pulpit preaching to a large gathering of refugees."[3]

Elsewhere, death came to God's servants in other ways. Andrew Young, a brilliant and much loved doctor from the Scottish lowlands, died after contracting typhus in April 1922. The 53-year-old had served in the African Congo before transitioning to China, and his loss was deeply felt by everyone involved in the work.[4]

Andrew Young

Young initially served at Yan'an in northern Shaanxi, and from there he traveled around ministering to people's physical and spiritual needs. He was one of a very small number of doctors in the region at the time. But after the 1911 Revolution, he felt compelled to relocate to the provincial capital where he served until disease claimed his life.

Feng Yuxiang, the Christian governor

Feng as vice premier of China in 1928

Shaanxi became so wracked by lawlessness in the 1920s that the people cried out for deliverance. The economy had collapsed, and inflation reduced even wealthy families to beggars. Hundreds of bandit gangs brought terror to the entire society. Even nature seemed to conspire against the people of Shaanxi. Severe earthquakes in 1920 and 1921 caused widespread panic and loss of life.

In the midst of this mayhem a Chinese Christian and general in the Chinese army named Feng Yuxiang emerged. His remarkable story divided Christians at the time. Some believed his faith was a front, assumed for convenience, and that he was really a renegade warlord. Others, including the veteran missionary Jonathan Goforth, befriended him and held him in high regard.

Feng had an imposing physical appearance, standing 6 feet 2 inches (1.88 meters) tall, and weighing more than 200 pounds (91 kg), which enabled him to tower over other Chinese of his generation. He was stationed in Beijing when John Mott—the American preacher and founder of the Student Christian

Movement—conducted a series of meetings. Feng signed up for one of the classes, and the gospel gradually convicted his heart. He became a true disciple of Jesus Christ in 1914.

Because of his integrity and God-given wisdom, Feng rose through the ranks from brigade commander to general. While the rank and file troops in most army divisions were known for their unruly behavior and for pillaging and raping wherever they went, Feng's division was markedly different.

After a series of battles between government forces and bandits had killed or wounded thousands of people in and around the provincial capital, Florence Broomhall shared her joy at the general's visit, to the hospital and their home in Xi'an:

> To our great delight the famous General Feng sent word on the fourth day after his entry into the city that he wished to come and see his wounded men and the hospital, and within a few hours he, accompanied by his bodyguard, rode up to the hospital gate, where my husband met him and ushered him in. He is a most striking-looking man, very tall and well built, with a kind, genial face.
>
> As he entered the wards his men, recognizing him, struggled to salute but he forbade them all even to try, and went graciously from one bed to another, gently patting them or stroking their hands in a lovely fatherly manner which was most touching. He seemed to be brimful of love for them and so genuine in his sorrow that they had been wounded.
>
> After seeing the hospital my husband brought him home for tea in our drawing room, and he greeted me with a sweet courtesy, and on hearing children's voices upstairs immediately asked to see them….
>
> We were deeply impressed by his charming humility…. He was so utterly different from the usual type of pompous bragging Chinese soldiers, and so suggestive of the gentleness of Christ. We felt it a mighty honor to have him in our home, and when, as he left the house … my husband put up his umbrella over him

> to escort him to the gate, General Feng simply took his arm and walked arm-in-arm with him to the gate to mount and ride away, my cup of joy was full.[5]

Throughout Shaanxi, the impact of General Feng's leadership was great. Numerous Christians were encouraged and emboldened by Feng's witness, and Christianity was held in much higher regard than previously. In a surprising move, Feng was appointed governor of Shaanxi, which caused a missionary to remark,

> No province has needed a Christian governor more than Shaanxi, for since the Revolution it has taken the lead in all that pertains to misgovernment, treachery, robbery, public stealing, and injustice on the part of officials, and all the evils of the opium traffic, with the overburdening of the people having to support countless hordes of robbers and soldiers. We have all prayed much for General Feng. Let us now pray even more for Governor Feng.[6]

Alas, Feng Yuxiang's time as governor of Shaanxi was short lived, for he was needed elsewhere. In 1924, he led a coup that

General Feng preaching to thousands of his troops

seized control of Beijing, and he personally handed the order to the last emperor, Henry Puyi, notifying him that he had been removed from the throne of China and had three hours to leave the Forbidden City. This incident brought approximately five thousand years of imperial rule in China to an end. Henry Puyi was the last in a long line of emperors dating back to the legendary Emperor Youchao, who is reputed to have begun his rule in 3162 BC, or to the Yellow Emperor Huangdi who began his reign in 2698 BC. By some counts, Puyi was the last of 559 kings and emperors spanning Chinese history.[7]

Feng Yuxiang, meanwhile, continued to rise in rank and became the vice premier of the Republic of China from 1928 to 1930.[8]

Salvation for the rebels

Despite almost all of Shaanxi Province being riddled with banditry, the good news of Jesus Christ was still proclaimed among the people, and even some bandits were humbled and received Him as Lord. From Sanyuan County in central Shaanxi came this report from James and Evelyn Watson of the English Baptist Mission:

> There has not been much peace in Sanyuan for three years. It is a storm center. On one occasion 10,000 robbers paid a visit, taking away all that was valuable. Yet the missionaries and the Christians are respected by these different robber bands, of which there are four or five. None of them trust each other, but all respect the Christians. To possess a Bible is as good as having a passport.... Colporteurs are about the only people who can travel in Shaanxi without being molested.
>
> There is a spiritual work going on among these rebels. One of them came one day, saying they were thinking of starting a Bible class, and wanted the preaching hall and an evangelist put at their

disposal.... This work has gone on for one-and-a-half years. It began with 10 men, but has now branched out into two classes, and about 50 now meet every day to study the Word of God.

In the spring three young officers were baptized, after being kept a long time waiting. They came last July but were put off until October. Then again, they were put off till January, and asked why they could not be received. Was it because they were in the rebel movement? They were quite willing to be delayed, but, they said, "We cannot trust God more than a year hence than we do today." In April they were baptized, with the commander-in-chief and several officers being present at the service.[9]

Solomon Bergström

Meanwhile, Solomon Bergström of the Scandinavian Alliance Mission continued to faithfully serve in the town of Xingping, a short distance west of Xi'an. By 1906, the work at Xingping had already gathered 193 converts,[10] but a huge blow struck the Bergströms when two of their children, Oscar and Hulda, were killed by an enraged mob in 1911. The surviving family members returned to the United States to recover from the ordeal, then returned to China two years later.

By 1927, God's blessing was so strongly on the work that 1,580 people were baptized since the beginning of the mission at Xingping, and over 2,000 inquirers had enrolled in Bible study classes. There were 11 churches and 13 outstations in the district. Bergström commented, "The work is now fully budded and ready to burst forth into beautiful blossom. God gave the increase, and despite difficult circumstances the bud did blossom forth."[11]

In 1927, Bergström wrote about some of the many transformed lives in Xingping:

Nine of our out-stations have been affected by the civil war, and some of these have suffered severely. This city was nearly surrounded by the opposing camp, which at one time was only seven miles away. By the grace of God, this was averted in time....

Tent work was maintained throughout the year, with the three tents having all been in use. The aggregate number of days spent in this special ministry were 330, and as a result 332 persons expressed a willingness to believe in the Lord. In addition, 418 persons confessed Christ at the central station and out-stations....

School work has been carried on in three schools with 97 students. About 2,000 patients have been treated at the dispensary. A helpful Bible school, attended by 50 or 60 men from the out-stations, was held in the month of August.

One of the out-stations suffered severely at the hands of 2,000 brigands in the early part of the year. Some of the houses of the Christians were burned down, others were looted, and nearly all were driven from their homes and compelled to wander for days among the mountains, uncertain of what might happen to them.

One poor fellow was brutally put to death by those evil men. His body lay exposed by the wayside for days, as no one dared to remove him for burial.

The suffering has been very severe, but God has been glorified through it all. The fiery trial has cleansed the Church, and the members have been drawn nearer to the Lord. No one has lost faith, they have stood firm. We thank God for this![12]

After a visit home to Minnesota in 1928, the Bergströms returned to Shaanxi with renewed vigor. The following year Solomon held eighteen evangelistic campaigns that resulted in an additional 484 converts and inquirers, most of whom became baptized church members.

The prospects for the work in Xingping had never looked brighter, but in December 1929, Solomon Bergström was unexpectedly called to his eternal reward after thirty-five years of faithful service. The level of respect the people of Xingping felt for the missionary was so great that his casket lay in state over the Christmas period, and "hundreds of Christians and unconverted

Chinese leaders associated with the Scandinavian Alliance Mission

people came to see that blessed smile on the face of this saint of God.... At that time, the churches he had gathered and organized, prayed for and safely and wisely guided numbered over 2,000 souls."[13]

More than a decade after Bergström's death, despite years of lawlessness, war, plagues, and pestilence, the church in Xingping continued to be a tower of strength having 18 churches, 25 Chinese preachers, and 2,465 church members reported in 1940.[14]

Nearly a century after the Christians in Xingping endured many years of persecution and fiery trials, the body of Christ in the county remains one of the brightest lights in Shaanxi. Today an estimated 56,000 Evangelical believers reside in Xingping City, worshipping in both house churches and more than thirty registered Three-Self congregations.[15] Christians in the city comprise 11.4 percent of the population, meaning that Xingping has the third highest concentration of Christians among the 107 cities and counties in the entire province of Shaanxi.

Civil war

The years rolled on, and many courageous Christians continued to spread the light and salt of the gospel among the people of Shaanxi, despite overwhelming difficulties. By the late 1920s, lawlessness evolved into open civil war between Mao's Red Army and the Guomindang (Nationalists). In the spring of 1928, mobs marched through the streets of Xi'an, shouting, "'Down with Christianity!' They broke up church meetings, carried off church members and threw them into prison…. They killed two evangelists in a midnight raid and seriously injured several others. One of them, Min, lost his right arm. But he still carried on bravely with his work."[16]

God's people continued to boldly and lovingly serve Him despite waves of hardship. Against all odds they succeeded in reaching multitudes with the message of eternal life. The arrival of the Communists, however, cast a dark shadow over Christianity in Shaanxi. The Communists' highly disciplined structure and promises to restore order to the distraught society soon made them extremely popular, but discerning church leaders knew that even darker times awaited if the Communists managed to seize power.

1930s and 1940s

The horsemen of the Apocalypse

The church at Mei Xian (Mei County) in western Shaanxi was a favorite target of bandits due to its close proximity to their mountain hideouts. In 1933, the church was holding a series of special meetings when a large group of bandits raided the town and carried off ten Chinese Christian as hostages. They were taken into the mountains, and ransom demands were issued. One night the guards wandered away from the camp, and some of these captives tried to escape. Unfortunately,

> Two of the older men, already weakened by hunger and cold, had not gone far when they stumbled on the side of a hill and

A group of evangelists from Mei Xian in Shaanxi. The man on the right was killed by bandits in 1933

> fell to the bottom. They were discovered and beaten to death. A third Christian was recaptured and badly beaten, but not long afterwards he got another opportunity to escape when the bandits moved away owing to the approach of soldiers.... He was more like a dying man than a living one when he finally reached home. Two of the younger men managed to evade being recaptured.[1]

In the 1930s the people of Shaanxi saw no respite from the natural disasters that had afflicted them for generations. In addition to the rampant banditry and violence and the never-ending cycle of floods and famines, a plague of locusts devastated crops in 1930, and a cholera epidemic two years later resulted in the deaths of many key Chinese Christian leaders. It was as if all the judgments symbolized by the four horsemen of the Apocalypse was visited on them: conquest, famine, war, death. One source remarked on the extraordinary sequence of disasters that blighted the province:

> Unusually destructive natural disasters struck northern China: drought, locusts, blizzards, hail, floods, and epidemics, one after another, hit eight provinces in all, but especially Shaanxi and Gansu, with Shaanxi being hit the hardest. Out of a total population in one region of 750,000, only 40 percent remained. In many places the entire population perished.
>
> Three years of disaster and famine left piles of bodies everywhere, with more than three million dying of diseases and starvation. Profound grief prevailed. Multitudes took to banditry as the only way to survive. Robbery and looting were widespread; there was no social stability.[2]

Despite these huge challenges, the gospel continued to advance among unevangelized areas of Shaanxi. Believers even emerged among the Hui Muslim community. Missionary Alma Artibey wrote from Fengxiang in western Shaanxi,

> There are quite a number of Muslims in Fengxian. We have one lad about 18 years old, a converted Muslim, who loves the Lord with his whole heart. We also have a Muslim girl, about 13 years old, who recently accepted the Lord as her Savior. I am praying the Lord will give me many opportunities to present the Word of Life to the Muslims of this community.[3]

In the ancient city of Xi'an, however, the large Hui population remained almost completely untouched by the claims of Christ. Missionary George Young lamented,

> Truly this field is white unto harvest but the laborers are lacking. Here in one of the oldest and most historic cities of the world, among its quarter of a million souls, lives a big Muslim community of 20,000 people. They occupy the northwest quarter of the city and are an exclusive people racially and socially....
>
> There is a spirit of friendliness towards foreigners. We get a warm welcome from the ahungs when we visit their mosques, and they are happy to show us round and to have a talk about religion. Muslims who come as patients to our hospital listen intently to the gospel story and often buy Gospels and Bibles when they leave.
>
> Despite these sporadic efforts, it is a sad fact that there is no serious attempt being made by any mission to evangelize this big Muslim community of Xi'an. They are sadly neglected spiritually, and our conscience is not easy about this.... Who will answer this call?[4]

Mary Anderson

A single Swedish-American missionary named Mary Anderson came to China in 1891 with the first group of recruits sent by her mission. She proceeded to live the rest of her life as the only foreign Christian in the small, unfashionable town of Yingjiahui, about 18 miles (29 km) south of Xi'an.

In early 1900, Anderson was knocked unconscious by a mob, and her possessions were ransacked when agitators were angry at her for using an umbrella to shade herself from the blazing sun. The mob accused her of offending the rain god by using an umbrella on a cloudless day, and they punished her to placate the spirits. Though small in stature, Anderson had the heart of a lion, and she refused to be cowed by the attacks. She remained in Shaanxi for decades and led dozens of school children to faith in the Living God. On several more occasions she was attacked and robbed, but she gained strength by regularly quoting her favorite Bible verse: "If we suffer, we shall also reign with him" (2 Tim. 2:12 KJV).

When in 1928 the US embassy ordered Anderson and the other missionaries to evacuate and return home, many local Christians thought they had seen the last of the aging woman. They were both shocked and delighted when she returned in October the following year and promised to remain and serve them for as long as the Lord gave her strength. Although bloodthirsty mobs had failed to stop her, the dreaded typhus fever

The memorial service held to honor the life of Mary Anderson

struck, and she was finally laid to rest in June 1930. At the time the church at Yingjiahui numbered about 300 members, most of whom had been led to faith in Jesus Christ by Anderson and her Chinese co-workers.

To honor their fallen friend, the local believers held a special memorial service at which they unveiled a tablet that contained a beautiful tribute to Mary Anderson's life and service for God. It says, She loved her Chinese people and would rather be among them than in any other place in the world. They loved her and looked upon her as their teacher, preacher, doctor, counselor, and faithful friend. Practical and sensible in all her ways, for 34 years she labored faithfully in this field, most of the time alone. She traveled on foot through this mountainous region, preaching the gospel, ministering to the needy, and scattering Christian literature. She was beloved by all.[5]

Gustaf Tornvall

The Swedish missionary David Tornvall served Christ in neighboring Gansu Province for thirty years until his health broke down and he died in 1925. The work of the Tornvall family carried on, however, as they had been blessed with seven children—six girls and a boy named Gustaf who was born in China. Despite his youth, Gustaf Tornvall took over his father's ministry. He "preached, taught, and managed the work with skill and conscientious fidelity. The people loved and trusted him and listened to his helpful messages."[6]

During a terrible famine in 1929–1930, Tornvall did all he could to alleviate the people's suffering. He took a job as manager of a road construction crew with the International Famine Commission and helped provide thousands of men with an income to keep their families alive. However Tornvall never lost

Gustaf Tornvall preaching to a group of laborers

sight of his spiritual responsibilities, and he frequently preached the gospel to the workers.

Tornvall paid his workers in cash, so he frequently traveled by horseback to Xi'an to collect their wages. During one of those trips, on July 23, 1932, Tornvall and three other men were "robbed and murdered by bandit soldiers and their bodies so disposed of that they could not be found. The seed of another beautiful life, having given a full measure of devotion to Christ, was planted in China's soil—an honor to the Scandinavian Alliance Mission and to the glory of Christ."[7]

The Bethel Band in Shaanxi

John Sung, whose Chinese name was Song Shangjie, emerged in the late 1920s and 1930s as the greatest evangelist China had ever produced. Wherever he went, both within China and throughout Southeast Asia, thousands of people repented of their sins and placed their faith in Jesus Christ. A remarkable trait of his ministry is that even decades after his death, lasting fruit remains, and many churches still functioning today can trace their origins back to a visit by this spiritual dynamo.

John Sung

Sung was in great demand all over China; so unfortunately he only visited Shaanxi once, in 1937. The demands on his time made it impossible for him to linger long in any one location. However, to extend his ministry, evangelistic teams or bands were established in each location. Dozens and sometimes hundreds of local Christians committed to sharing the gospel in villages and towns in their area, and a far greater harvest was reaped from that outreach than from Sung's meetings alone. The evangelist's diary recorded the highlights of his brief visit:

> I went to Xi'an, whose churches had for years wanted me to come. Ever since July, Xi'an had been deluged by daily rain, but the day before the meeting the rain stopped, and the clouds receded. More than 20 Western missionaries were there to cooperate with me. 400 to 500 people came from out of town, added to the more than 1,000 orphans and local people. The meeting place was really congested....
>
> Among the 574 people who received salvation were the former mayor, school principals, and wealthy merchants. Over 100 evangelistic teams were set up, and two days after the meeting the rain resumed. The interval of clear weather allowed the people to safely reach their homes.[8]

As a result of the evangelistic outreach, revival broke out in Shaanxi in 1934 and 1935. Revival historian J. Edwin Orr details the impact the preaching bands had in Shaanxi:

> In one locality 700 people were baptized within 12 months, with 600 eager inquirers receiving counsel. It was noted that all 700 converts faithfully attended worship. In early 1935, a Bethel Band composed of two minor prophets—John Shi and James Chang—were ministering in Shaanxi. Neither evangelist had a reputation like John Sung or Andrew Gih, yet men and women were falling under deep conviction of sin.... Shi and Chang were faithful in preaching, Christ-like in demeanor, and earnest in spiritual life. They left behind a spirit of unity among believers.[9]

As they traveled on foot over the mountains of Shaanxi, the two Bethel preachers met a Daoist priest who had spent his life seeking to make merit and earn his way into heaven. Shi and Chang shared the gospel with the man, and he admitted that the teachings of Jesus were true and just. But he had spent so many years pursuing self-righteousness through penance that he could not cross the line and leave his old life behind.

After praying with the priest for several days, John Shi felt led to make an offer to him that was a great personal sacrifice, for the evangelists had little money on which to survive. He told him, "If you will lay aside your priestly robe, I will give you a whole new change of clothing." The very next day,

> The Daoist priest came to see Pastor Shi and said he was now willing to cut off his long hair, which was his badge of religion, and surrender his Daoist gown and cap for the suggested one from Shi's own scant wardrobe. And this he did, afterwards joyfully testifying, "My burden of sin fell off with the cutting of my hair! I have exchanged my Daoist cap for the crown of life, and my priest's garments for the Lord's robe of righteousness!"[10]

As they continued their wonderful ministry in Shaanxi,

> The Bethel Band found that, in one city, membership of the church was only 15, but the evangelists took to the alleys and streets, with Chang playing his trumpet. Eighteen people professed faith in the first chapel service. On occasion, there were so many inquirers that no message could be given.
>
> They were interrupted in the arduous work. The Red Army units traversed Shaanxi on their Long March, and both evangelists and missionaries were forced to flee. In 1935, 1,000 conversions were reported in Shaanxi, as the work of God went further in that province. Missionaries and national leaders alike rejoiced in the good health of the churches.[11]

Other encouraging accounts tell of the impact that the Bethel workers had in diverse parts of the province. At Yangxian in southern Shaanxi, missionary Miss R. J. Begbie was thrilled by the visit of the Bethel workers. She filed this report:

> Our fellowship with the Bethel brethren was for a brief eight days, and the gracious working of God's Spirit in all our hearts, with the inevitable blessing of outflow to the heathen, may be truly described as "days of heaven upon earth." It is hard to express in words the full joy of seeing prayer answered for our Chinese helpers, or to tell how our own hearts have been blessed and uplifted by these dear servants of God. The power of the adversary was terrible, but God prevailed over his many devices. Some 87 names were given in as having confessed the Lord.[12]

Another report of the Bethel duo's visit to the south of the province says,

> In Chenggu some 300 souls have been to the altar confessing their sins to God and seeking forgiveness, and we believe many really found peace through the blood of Christ. In Yangxian some 180 heathen men and women gave their hearts to God besides a number of unbelieving wives or husbands of church members, who have withstood the truth and tried to hinder the other member of the family from following the Lord.[13]

The Red Army

In the 1940s, the hardships and deprivation throughout Shaanxi continued, and the ongoing civil war brought devastation to millions. As the decade progressed, it became apparent that the Communists had gained the upper hand, and it was only a matter of time before they would seize control of the whole nation. Shaanxi had effectively been under Mao's control since the conclusion of the Long March in 1936. Their base at Yan'an remained the control center for all Communist activity in China until 1947.

The town of Lantian had experienced renewal from the Holy Spirit in the 1910s, and the number of church members there increased from a handful to 241. When Mao led his forces through the Lantian area during their famous Long March, the Christians there suffered terribly. Church buildings and homes were burned to the ground, and many believers fled into the

In 1935, the Communists seized the St. Mary's Cathedral at Yan'an and used it as a training base and granary until 1947

mountains until the danger passed. In the aftermath of the Communist onslaught, the gospel flourished in Lantian. A 1940 summary of the work in the town says

> There have been onslaughts of the enemy and evil devices of many kinds, but the Lord used even weak earthen vessels to overcome and be more than conquerors, so the church continued and kept true to the mission of saving the lost and winning many to the faith, for the believers were fellow workers with God. From the beginning, nearly 1,000 have been baptized in Lantian and in 1939 the total membership of the church was over 800.[14]

The good seed that was faithfully sown generations ago in Lantian has continued to produce a mighty harvest. There are an estimated 11,000 Evangelical Christians in Lantian today, comprising nearly 10 percent of the entire population of the county.[15]

As the 1940s progressed, missionaries found that their presence in the province was increasingly unwelcome. Their numbers dwindled as many moved back to their home countries or to

Back to Jerusalem workers at their farewell meeting in Shaanxi, alongside a table of gifts which included a wash basin for each missionary

other parts of China that were not yet under Communist control. As a result, few reports emerged from Shaanxi during the 1940s as the church prepared for a long period of persecution.

Catholics were harshly treated by Mao Zedong's militant atheists as they passed through Shaanxi. Aloysius Liang, a Chinese priest, was allowed to minister under the watchful eye of the Communists in the Red stronghold of Yan'an. However, they seized the main cathedral and used it as a training base and then a granary. In 1947, the Red Army abandoned Yan'an, taking hundreds of Catholic hostages with them. Showing all the characteristics of a loving shepherd, Liang volunteered to go with them to serve the flock that had been entrusted to his care. During the journey he was tortured to death.

The 1940s was a decade of suffering and trouble for Christians in Shaanxi, but outreach continued as brave men and women risked their lives to exalt Jesus Christ. In May 1943, the province saw the launch of the Back to Jerusalem Evangelistic Band which was established at the Northwest Bible Institute in Xi'an under the leadership of Mark Ma Peixuan. A constitution was adopted and officers elected, and the Back to Jerusalem Evangelistic Band was formally established. The constitution defined the target area of the Band as

> The seven border provinces of China; and to the seven countries on the borders of Asia: Afghanistan, Iran, Arabia, Iraq, Syria, Turkey, and Palestine.... In pioneer districts we plan to establish churches according to the example of Scripture. In places where churches already exist, we plan to serve such churches. We look to the Lord alone for all financial supplies.[16]

The actual Chinese name adopted by the group was the "Preach the Gospel Everywhere Band." Their vision was to plant churches among all the Muslim, Buddhist, and other unreached people groups in northwest China, and ultimately to establish the kingdom of God all the way from China's borders "back to Jerusalem."

In 1944, the first team consisting of three women and two men were sent to Gansu Province for a short term of service. The following year another two workers were sent to preach Christ among the Hui Muslims in Ningxia, and in 1946, the Lord called two men, Mecca Zhao and Timothy Dai, to long-term service in Xinjiang. Several pioneer Chinese missionaries reached Kashgar near China's borders with the nations of Central Asia. When the Communists took control of the area, however, most of the missionaries were arrested and sent to prison for many years. None of the original workers ever managed to step foot outside China.

Although on the surface the Back to Jerusalem initiative appeared to fail, the vision God had given His church in China survived. Decades later in the 1990s it burst back into life among the millions of house church believers that had come to faith in China's great revival.[17]

Annie Skau

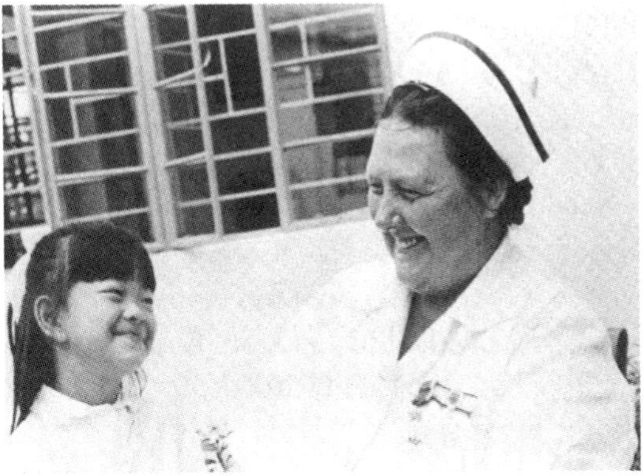

Annie Skau selflessly served the people of Shaanxi for thirteen years

Annie Skau Berntsen was born in Oslo, Norway, in 1911. Her early years offered no hints that she would one day be a powerful witness for Christ in China and a scourge to the Communists. In her teens she was a leader of a Karl Marx youth club, and she later decided to become a nurse. It was at nursing school that Annie first heard the gospel and discovered that she could have a personal, life-changing relationship with the Living God. The would-be Marxist changed course and became a dedicated Christian.

In 1937, the China Inland Mission offered a course on tropical diseases, and Annie signed up. While there, she contracted the "mission bug" from the staff and students. A year later she was sent to China where she began a thirteen-year association with Shaanxi Province which only ended when she and the other missionaries were forced to leave China in 1951. For most of her time in Shaanxi, Skau was based at Shangxian (now Shanzhou District) in the province's southeast. She was loved and accepted from the moment she arrived, which caused her to say of the local Christians, "They were bound together by hardships and persecution, and they took me in as one of their own."[1]

For the next decade Annie Skau and her co-workers offered sterling service to the people of Shangxian. She helped treat thousands of sick and injured people and was eager to share the gospel with everyone she encountered. The locals nicknamed Annie "the Giant Woman" as she was much larger in stature than Chinese women. She did not take offense at the name, and over time it became clear that she was also a spiritual giant who was never flustered by trials. She was forced to flee the area when the Japanese army invaded in 1943, but throughout the ordeal, she remained a calm, consistent witness for Christ with a loving smile adorning her face.

Confronting the rain god

Annie liked to spend time walking through the mountains surrounding the city, often accompanied by her Chinese friend Yu Chen. One afternoon they encountered a procession of villagers carrying idols, as firecrackers were let off and drummers banged out a deafening beat. Drought was afflicting the area, and the procession was to honor and placate the rain god. As Annie watched from under the brim of her straw hat, two idol bearers came straight to her, angrily shouting at her to take off her hat because the superstitious villagers believed the deities were infuriated if someone's head was covered during a drought.

Annie refused to submit to their idols by taking off her hat. So a group of men pulled the poles from their idols and marched toward her, threatening to beat her to death. "I can't take my hat off to your gods. My God is Jesus," Annie courageously told them.

When they replied, "We don't know anything about your God," the Norwegian firebrand declared, "If you want to be worthy of His love, stop this procession … and turn your attention to the true God, and you will have rain tonight."[2]

Stunned by her boldness, the procession dispersed, and Annie continued on her way. When she told a church elder what had happened, he was deeply concerned and said that if a person predicts rain and it remains dry, that person will be judged to be evil and put to death. At eleven o'clock that night the sky was still cloudless, and the local Christians were anxious that their beloved missionary-doctor had overstepped the mark and would pay with her life. Annie remained calm, however, and her face was covered with a broad smile as though she knew something of which the others were not aware. As the clock counted down to midnight, the elder entered the mission house and excitedly declared, "The rain has started to fall! God is good."[3]

Abundant supplies

During the latter part of the Second World War, Annie asked God to provide much needed equipment and medicine to the mission. The Lord answered with an unexpected windfall. When Hitler positioned 350,000 troops in Annie's homeland of Norway, neighboring Denmark assumed the Nazis would never leave without a fierce battle. So they donated a huge amount of medicine to Norway in expectation of mass casualties. When Germany lost the war, however, their forces withdrew from Norway leaving tons of spare supplies. Much of these were donated to foreign missionaries to aid their work, and the medical clinic in Shaanxi was one grateful recipient.

God also used this provision to extend Annie Skau's work. At a time when many missionaries were leaving China, Annie's services were much sought after, and it was said she was the last remaining doctor among two million Chinese people in south-central Shaanxi Province. Not everyone was appreciative of her work, however. When a young civil servant named John Ma heard that Annie was still in Shaanxi and that her ministry was thriving, he flew into a rage and went to a meeting she was conducting with a large rock in his hand, intending to smash it into her head when he had a chance. As Ma pondered his violent plan, the Holy Spirit came upon him. He walked to the front of the church and told Annie that he wanted to give his life to Christ and become His disciple. When his workmates discovered that John Ma had become a Christian, they beat him severely. But even as they were pummeling him with their fists, the new believer prayed for their salvation. This prayer caused the men to feel ashamed, and they too asked to become Christians.

Old Grandmother's prayers

During these years of fruitful service, when most other missionaries had been evacuated from Shaanxi, Annie Skau owed much of her success to the friendship and intercession of "Old Grandmother"—a precious Christian woman in her late seventies who had been the first convert to Jesus Christ in the town decades earlier. She loved Annie deeply and called her "Little Girl," in contrast to the common nickname "the Giant Woman" that others called her.

Old Grandmother had a special gift of intercessory prayer, and she rose at four o'clock each morning to lead a group of women who cried out to God in a little chapel near the medical clinic. Each patient was fervently prayed for, and as a result Annie and the Chinese evangelists often encountered little resistance when they shared the gospel. Hundreds of people subsequently found new life in Christ during those years of reaping.

They also saw numerous miracles in response to fervent prayer. One sick woman with a malignant tumor on her tongue was told by Annie that there was nothing she could do to save her life. But Old Grandmother took the matter to the Lord in prayer. A few months later, Annie was perplexed why a woman in a church meeting was sticking her tongue out at her. She then recognized the woman as the "hopeless case" she had sent home to die. The woman had been completely healed, and her tongue looked perfectly healthy.

On another occasion a wounded soldier was carried into the clinic. He was in terrible condition, having been shot and then thrown off a cliff. Compassionate locals rescued the unconscious man and carried him ten miles to the city. As Annie knelt beside the man and exhorted him, "Put your faith in the Lord Jesus and He will save you," Old Grandmother was storming God's throne in prayer for him. Annie needed to perform surgery quickly on the dying soldier, but no operating table was available. So she had the door of the clinic removed from its hinges and used it to perform the surgery. It took four intense hours to remove the bullet from his chest. But a faint pulse was detected, and the man opened his eyes and declared, "The Lord Jesus has saved me!"

Days later after he had recovered his strength, the soldier explained what happened when he was on the cusp between life and death: "Three times I heard voices coming to me from a great distance, telling me that the Lord would save me." After receiving a thorough grounding in the Bible, the man returned to his home village as a zealous evangelist, eager to share the good news about Jesus with his friends and relatives.

Because of the chaos in society and a lack of food, packs of wolves began entering the towns of Shaanxi where they attacked and killed many children and frail adults. On one occasion the wolves entered a house and bit a baby's face. When the baby was brought to Annie,

> The wounds were already crawling with maggots, and the prognosis was wholly negative. She picked up the baby and carried it to Old Grandmother's bed. While Annie bathed and treated the terrible wounds, Old Grandmother prayed and fed the baby. In two weeks the wounds were healed. The healing of the beautiful baby was the work of God.[4]

A worthy servant of God

In December 1948, a dozen missionaries from Annie's area were ordered to evacuate to Chengdu in Sichuan Province because violence and instability had engulfed Shaanxi. Annie went on the six-day journey and enjoyed a wonderful Christmas with fellow missionaries, most of whom decided it was time to wind up their careers in China and return home. It was assumed that Annie would return to Norway, but as she prayed about it, she had a sense that the Lord wanted her to remain in Shaanxi and continue her work. She wrote, "More and more it seemed to me that God was guiding me to stay, but then I wondered if this was just my own choice, rather than what He wanted. One thing I knew for certain: I would obey His will, whatever it was."[5]

The final decision to stay was confirmed when Annie met with the Chinese church leaders in Shangxian. Throughout China the general view was that the presence of foreign missionaries had brought persecution to local Christians. Annie mentioned these concerns, but the church leaders replied, "If you leave us now, when we have so much need of you, then you aren't worthy to be called a servant of God."[6] The matter was settled. Annie and the church leaders formed a prayer circle right there in the mission compound, and together they promised to remain faithful to the Lord Jesus unto death. Annie Skau recalled the powerful moment:

> We thought we were going to receive a martyr's glorious crown quite soon, and we rejoiced in the thought. We started to

> memorize portions of the Scriptures, with each of us choosing different parts. My heart was overflowing with joy, for at last I knew that I was acting in accordance with God's will. In knowing that, I experienced a perfect peace I had never felt so fully before.[7]

In June 1949, the Nationalist government abandoned the area. On the final Sunday before the Communist army marched in to fill the void, the little church was filled to overflowing. Many believers wept openly for Annie, convinced she would be killed by the soldiers. The courageous Norwegian missionary felt no fear, however, and she enthusiastically led the singing.

Life had been difficult enough for Christians in Shangxian, but the danger escalated exponentially when the Communists took control. Annie was an eyewitness of the depravity and brutality exhibited by Mao's forces. Almost twenty years after being forced to leave China, her voice still quivered as she recalled the horrific scenes:

> The Communists … tacked up a public notice, listing the names of all the people they had shot. Do you know that all those poor victims had to dig their own graves and kneel beside them? The Communists killed everyone at once—and hurled their bodies into the graves.
>
> So many died! So many times we heard the iron tires on the cobblestones and saw the death roll posted in the villages and towns. I knelt and prayed for all those poor, helpless human beings—and every time, I had to face the awful fact that I could do nothing to save their lives. No one in China knew what would happen from one second to the next. I knew I could be killed at any minute, yet I was happy in my faith; it was like an island of peace in a maelstrom of hatred and destruction.[8]

Nothing but good

Despite the violence, Annie felt no bitterness toward the Communist soldiers who were mostly exhausted and hungry young men. She refused to take sides in the conflict and treated all who needed help. Her selfless actions caused a quandary for the Communist leaders. Some wanted to kill Annie. But others felt ashamed because her service for the people was greater than their own, and the community held her in the highest regard.

Finally, the day came when "the giant woman" was ordered to go to the town's market where a stage had been erected. The Communists' patience had run out, and she was to be "struggled against" in a public trial. The leaders of the meeting called on the large crowd to make accusations against the beloved missionary. After a long period of silence,

> Not one person came forward with the anticipated denunciations. The whole carefully rehearsed performance appeared to have bogged down, leaving the members of the court embarrassed, frustrated, and angry. Finally, the chairman of the court spoke out in great irritation: "Is there not one word about the evil this missionary has done?"
>
> Absolute silence followed. The lack of response was acutely painful to the court, and there was not another voice heard until some young people at the rear of the crowd ventured to speak out. Their words were not those the court had been waiting for: "She has never done anything but good!"[9]

Prison

The 1950s dawned with China fully under Communist control, yet Annie Skau remained in Shaanxi, still faithfully fulfilling the call God had given her. The persecution of Christians greatly intensified, and many Chinese believers were arrested or simply vanished from their homes. Annie was told that two Christian brothers were being held hostage in prison at Shangnan, about 40 miles (65 km) away. Without hesitation, she rode her bicycle to Shangnan and appealed for their release. When the prison guards refused to let them go, she offered to take their place in the cell.

After some discussion they agreed to her proposal, and Annie was locked in a tiny cell just long enough for her to lay down in.

Thinking the middle-aged Westerner would beg for her release, the guards were surprised when they heard her singing joyous songs all night. When asked what she was doing, Annie replied, "I must praise God. It is the happiest night of my life." Not knowing what charges to bring against the woman of God, the Communists invented a ludicrous accusation—blaming her for polluting the river when she had conducted baptisms!

Upon reflection, the charge didn't seem serious enough to the accusers, so they charged her with going around the countryside and setting fire to eleven villages. When Annie was told the new charge, "It struck her as so funny that she doubled over with laughter, and the young official made no real effort to conceal his own amusement."[10] Realizing the foolishness of their actions, they released Annie, and she returned home.

The final stretch

As almost all missionaries had been expelled from Shaanxi, many mission stations were abandoned throughout the province. Annie was asked to take over the empty properties. Remarkably the simple woman from Norway, who once wanted to be a Marxist, found herself with forty mission stations under her control in the Marxist heartland of China. She carried on serving the people, but increasingly distressing reports reached her of Chinese pastors and church members being arrested and tortured in prison. After much prayer, Annie felt the time for her departure from China was near. She had done all she could for God there by the power of the Holy Spirit, but the nighttime was about to come when no one could work.

Before leaving, she attended one memorable prayer meeting in the town of Danfeng that was attended by more than 400

Christians. She was asked to speak, and she shared on Daniel in the lion's den which was an apt message for the gathered believers who were about to face their own dangerous trials. On July 15, 1950, Annie Skau was rearrested and charged with being a spy. She was sent to a lice-infested prison where despite the miserable conditions and frequent interrogation sessions, she was allowed to keep her Bible. She read it every day, gaining strength from the Spirit of God.

For months she endured persecution, but with Christmas approaching, she completely ran out of money. Not only was she unable to buy food, but Annie was worried that if they expelled her from the country, she would have no ability to pay for her travel. Then a letter arrived from missionaries in Shanghai saying they had sold some of the medical supplies Annie had left in storage, and funds were available for her needs. Instead

Annie Skau ministering to Chinese refugee children in Hong Kong

of spending the money on herself, however, she bought toys to give to the children as Christmas presents.

Finally, in early 1951, Annie Skau knew her service in China was complete. She left her beloved Shaanxi with her head held high after thirteen years of witnessing to God's grace and power. After a time back in her homeland, Annie again felt the call of God to go to East Asia. In 1953, she began ministering in a refugee camp in Hong Kong where she had daily contact with hundreds of desperate people who had fled across the border from Communist China. Two years later she founded the Hope of Heaven rehabilitation center in the British colony, and thousands of needy Chinese were blessed by her work.

During her years in China, Annie Skau was not well-known to most Western Christians, but after more people learned of her story and uncompromising faith, accolades were made in her honor. The greatest of these was given in 1979 when Annie was 68 years old. She was awarded an MBE, Member of the British Empire, in recognition of her decades of service to the Chinese people. Her home nation also awarded her the prestigious King of Norway's St. Olaf's Orden, and she received the Florence Nightingale Medal.

Before she passed to her eternal reward in 1992, Annie reflected on her full and exciting life for Jesus Christ:

> To be allowed to wear oneself out serving God, that is the greatest happiness. That is why I would have chosen the same path if I were to be young again. What I would have changed are all the stupid and clumsy things I have done....
>
> Nobody knows what death contains, we can only believe. My belief is so strong that I have no fear. Now I just look forward to meeting Jesus.
>
> The most magnificent thing that can happen to me is to be allowed to serve Him day and night in His temple. Nothing in the world is as glorious as serving the Lord Jesus Christ![11]

1950s and 1960s

Mao Zedong surrounded by smiling teachers and students in 1959

What the Communists failed to understand

Annie Skau was one of the last Evangelical missionaries to be expelled from Shaanxi Province. Almost all Catholic priests and other foreigners had already been deported, many after suffering persecution and imprisonment. In what would be the final survey of Christians in China for decades, in Shaanxi in 1949 there were an estimated 30,000 Evangelical believers.[1] Although the gap had narrowed, Catholics still held a sizable advantage over Evangelicals at the onset of Communist rule with 103,199 Catholics scattered throughout the province in 1950.[2]

The new government had accomplished their goal of removing the "foreign crutch" of the Chinese church, and they believed that Christianity would soon collapse without the leadership and money provided by overseas Christians. Just before China came fully under Communist control, a senior officer of the People's Liberation Army made this revealing statement to a missionary:

> You missionaries have been in China for more than 100 years, but you have not won China to your cause. You lament the fact there are uncounted millions who have never heard the Name of your God. Nor do they know anything of your Christianity.
>
> But we Communists have been in China a far shorter time, and there is not a Chinese who does not know or has not heard the name of Stalin or something about Communism.... We have filled China with our doctrine. Now let me tell you why you have failed, and we have succeeded.
>
> You have tried to win the attention of masses by building churches, missions, hospitals, schools and what not. But we Communists have printed our message and spread our literature all over China. Someday we will drive you missionaries out of the country, and we will do it by means of the printed page.[3]

What the Communists failed to understand, however, was that for decades a process had been underway to transfer the leadership of churches into local hands. By the time Mao swept to power in 1949, there were few fellowships still relying on foreigners for their sustainability. Rather, the church in Shaanxi was filled with thousands of redeemed Chinese men and women who had not become Christians for material reasons but because their lives had been transformed through a relationship with the Living God who promised eternal life to all who keep the

A women's Bible class in Shaanxi. It was in small groups like these that the faith survived and later flourished

faith and endure until the end. Because the kingdom of God is spiritual in nature, the Communists found themselves incapable of completely crushing the body of Christ, even though they did their best to try to eliminate it over the next three decades of harsh persecution.

As Shaanxi had been under Communist control for longer than almost any other part of China, the Christians in the province were aware of the brutality of the Communists' atheistic philosophies. There was no middle ground with the Communists. Their goal was complete domination, and any person or entity that refused to submit to the Revolution was suppressed. If they still refused to align with the will of the Party, they were eliminated.

Chinese mission leader Andrew Gih, whose Chinese name is Ji Zhiwen, was a clear-thinking servant of God who saw how Communism was directly opposed to the kingdom of God on every level. He wrote the following comparison to help Christians understand the differences between the two:[4]

Communism vs Following Christ	
Communism is materialistic	Following Christ is spiritual
Communism is godless	Following Christ is God-centered
Communism is God-hating	Following Christ is God-loving
Communism is God-defying and blasphemous	Following Christ is God-honoring
Communism divides people into classes	Following Christ unites people in Christ
Communism pulls the higher classes down	Following Christ raises the lower classes up
Communism spreads hatred and strife	Following Christ spreads love and peace
Communism says, "Blood must be shed for revolution."	Following Christ says, "Blood has been shed for salvation."
Communism aims for a class-less society	Following Christ says, "Thy kingdom come."
Communism advances by propaganda	Following Christ advances by the preaching of God's Word
Communism is maintained by the sword	Following Christ is maintained by love

The curtain closes

By 1952, every foreign Christian had been removed from Shaanxi, and all communication overseas was strictly forbidden by the government. A curtain of silence fell on the church, and for nearly thirty years, very little information squeezed through the cracks to the outside world. The hundreds of expelled missionaries and concerned intercessors scattered around the world hungered for an occasional crumb of information about the state of God's people in Shaanxi. But their hunger went unfulfilled.

When information came from other provinces about widespread arrests, imprisonment, and killing of Christian leaders, it was like a dagger in the heart for all who loved the church in China.

Many observers thought it was impossible for the Chinese church to survive the onslaught, especially when the persecution reached its zenith during the Cultural Revolution which began in 1966. It was generally believed that if the doors to China ever opened again, no trace of Christianity would be found, and the missionary enterprise would have to start again from scratch.

The total silence from the church in Shaanxi continued until well into the 1970s when the first glimmer of light began to emerge after Mao's death in 1976. Although Mao and the leaders of the People's Republic of China ruled from Beijing, the province of Shaanxi was still considered to be a Communist stronghold, and the persecution of Christians there was particularly severe. Pastors and evangelists faced the harshest judgments, and many were killed or sent to prison labor camps for periods of twenty years or longer. Most died in captivity.

One of millions of executions performed by Red Guards in 1966

1970s

A famine of the word

Initially when the first news from the church in Shaanxi in decades began to trickle to the outside world, many Christians were unable to believe the reports. Many assumed the writers had exaggerated the situation from a sense of hope rather than reality. A pastor from Shaanxi, Zhu Chengxin, shared how a

These 25,000 Gospel booklets were smuggled into China in 1973
VOM Canada

visit to neighboring Henan Province in 1975 invigorated his faith, even though China was still in the grip of the Cultural Revolution. Many foreign observers feared that Christianity had been completely wiped out by Mao, and that no believers could have survived the two decades of brutal persecution. Zhu spent twenty-eight days traveling across the Henan Province conducting many services each day and then returned to Shaanxi to share what he had learned. The following account of Zhu's travels provides a sense of how the Holy Spirit was moving at the time:

> Every evening we hurried out after eating to reach the place of worship in time for the midnight service. Seeing the hunger and thirst of the Christians moved me to tears.
>
> When I felt it was finally time to leave, local Christians were reluctant to let me part. One Christian brother stood up and said: "You cannot leave; I have prayed to the Lord not to let you go." He then abruptly rode off on his bicycle. I was puzzled by the man's statement and action. Not until two days later did I understand what he meant. Knowing exactly what route I would take in leaving the village, the brother had rushed to inform the woman in charge of the home gathering along the road that the servant of God was coming her way. She immediately sent several sisters to wait at the crossroad.
>
> When I passed that way, I was easily identified because of my Shaanxi accent. I pleaded with the women to let me proceed. Instead, they fell on their knees and cried out for God's mercy. They had been longing for someone to preach to them and had waited two days on the road for my arrival. Seeing no way out, my companion and I agreed to return to the village with them.... Over 100 people came to hear us preach that evening.[1]

The greatest need in the Chinese Church in the 1970s was for the Word of God. On the rare occasions when Bibles, or even Scripture portions, were smuggled into the country, they quickly disappeared like a cup of water poured out in a sandy desert. The

An outdoor church meeting in 1974, during the Cultural Revolution
VOM Canada

authorities had destroyed every Bible they could find, and those caught in possession of one faced years in prison, or worse, for their "crime." By 1978, a few courageous ministries decided to do whatever they could to smuggle Bibles into China, but the quantity they were able to get through the border was minuscule compared to the size of the need.

Remarkably, a few letters were received from believers in Shaanxi telling of the great impact that resulted when Bibles made it through. One letter in 1978 said,

> We have received the 1,000 Bibles you mailed to us. Our happiness, love, and warm tears have mixed together. The love of the Lord flowed toward us like a river from His throne and made us leap with joy! The deepest part of my heart is filled with living water, and the Holy Spirit has made me braver. Whether I live or die means nothing to me. God is enlarging His territory inside of me.
>
> The Lord blessed our work over New Year and we have seen far greater progress than in recent years. Those who know Jesus

> are spread everywhere like water in the ocean. These are the wonderful works of the Lord and the answer to our prayers.[2]

Another letter was received at the end of 1978 which told of a rapid increase in the number of Christians, despite the many years of intense hardship. By that time, Christians around the world had been made aware that God had done something remarkable in China. Not only had His children survived the long season of darkness, but the church was also alive and well! The letter said,

> My heart is melted because of the Lord's abounding love.... Our Father's house is prospering day by day. The old and young alike in the family are full of life, peace, and the joy of the Lord. The sons of Abraham have risen up and cannot be counted. They are like the stars in heaven.
>
> God's Spirit is working, rebuilding, and filling His whole family with glorious light, new experiences, and unending grace. The number of saved people is increasing all the time. When we are working with the Holy Spirit, we feel peaceful, joyous, and safe. This is the result of all your prayers for us. Thanks to the Lord![3]

Zhang Guanru—the gentle pastor

Apart from Bibles, the greatest need of Christians in Shaanxi during the 1970s was for solid Bible teaching. All church buildings had been demolished or confiscated, and a generation of church leaders had been imprisoned or killed. Despite these obstacles, the Spirit of God was moving in the hearts of many people, and new believers were springing up across the province. Without the Scriptures or Bible teachers, however, many were at risk of being deceived by cults.

At this time, God revived the ministry of a man nicknamed "the gentle pastor" who went on to become a key figure in the rise of Christianity in Shaanxi. Zhang Guanru was born in 1924 across the border in Henan. His father died when he was just 6 years old, and he first heard the gospel after his grandfather and uncle met some Christians. Two pivotal events occurred in 1936 when Zhang was 12. As was the custom in China at the time, his arranged marriage to Jia Qingyun was formalized; and he was converted to Christ after attending an evangelistic meeting led by the famous preacher John Sung.

The Holy Spirit touched Zhang's life so deeply that he began to preach immediately after his conversion, purposely copying the style and mannerisms of the great evangelist. Consequently, some Christians nicknamed him "the little Dr. Sung." In 1940, Zhang desired to know more of God's Word, so he enrolled in a Bible school run by American Mennonite missionaries. Two years later the invading Japanese army took over the school, and he was forced to end his studies. By 1946, the Second World War had concluded, and Zhang moved to Sanyuan at the heart of the civil war that was raging in Shaanxi at the time.

Zhang Guanru and his wife, Jia Qingyun, in 2004

For the next decade Zhang served God fervently, reaching thousands of people for Christ. He led the church at Sanyuan until 1966 when the Cultural Revolution erupted. Zhang recalled the atmosphere of fear that filled China:

> In those days everyone was guarded against not just their neighbor, but even their own family members. Even father and son did not talk to each other at the dinner table; one might belong to one camp while the other belonged to another. Tension was high in families. Even husbands and wives could be from rival camps. It was an abnormal society.[4]

In Sanyuan, the authorities became aware of the existence of local Christians. Suddenly, in a single day, twenty-two Evangelical and Catholic believers, including Zhang, were arrested and labeled "counter-revolutionaries." Zhang was sentenced to fifteen years in a prison labor camp. Looking back on those years, he remarked,

> All I wanted was that 15 years would pass by quickly so I would be able to return home.... Every human being has weaknesses, but I had never given up my faith. When I gather with other old people these days, we often say that our generation went through the worst time and suffered the most, yet we had the richest experience.
>
> We could not have imagined how great God was had we not lived through the period of the Cultural Revolution. Faith was what mattered most. God knew what was happening and was watching over us.... We could not read the Bible because everything was confiscated from us. But we could pray within ourselves without appearing to be praying. Religious behavior was banned in prison. But we could remember His Word.[5]

Feeling bewildered and not knowing what had become of his wife and children, Zhang Guanru suffered terribly in the labor camp. He nearly lost his life when a wolf attacked him as he slept in a cave while working in a remote area. He said, "I could have died easily if not for God's protection. It was a real danger."[6]

In 1980, after Zhang had been in prison for fourteen years, the atmosphere in China began to improve, and Zhang was released a year early and "rehabilitated" by the government. He was sent back to Sanyuan to work in a milk factory, and two years later he led a campaign to have his former church building returned so the believers could recommence their meetings.

During his years of incarceration, Zhang had only seen his wife a few times because of the prison's remote location and her extreme poverty. Jia had struggled each day to keep the family afloat and feed the children. As the wife of a prisoner, she couldn't find work. For years she had been cut off from all Christians because just having contact with the family members of a counter-revolutionary caused a person to become a suspect. Zhang realized his wife had suffered much more than he had during the years he was in prison.

A fresh beginning

Although he had been badly abused by the authorities, Zhang felt he could serve God most effectively in the second half of his life by joining the government-sanctioned Three-Self Church. He was ordained as the pastor in Sanyuan and immediately began to train a new generation of shepherds because God's people were like a wandering flock of sheep at the time, knowing little of God's Word and susceptible to being ravaged by spiritual wolves. In 1983, he started the "Shaanxi Pastoral Staff Training Class" at his church which quickly grew to train workers from across the country. Over the years more than one thousand people were equipped to be church leaders in Xinjiang, Ningxia, Qinghai, Gansu, and other remote parts of China.

Zhang always told his students that he was available to receive their call if they encountered any special problems or needed prayer. His daughter Zhang Fengquan said of her father's compassionate heart, "He always said that you must not grumble in doing church work, though it is not easy. Sometimes people remain dissatisfied no matter what you do, but my father said a preacher should be like a rubbish bin, open to the views and criticisms of brothers and sisters."[7]

In 1988, the pastoral training class was replaced when Zhang founded the Shaanxi Bible School on the premises of the Sanyuan church. The need was so great that the school was relocated to Xi'an, where it has continued to train church leaders to the present day. "The Gentle Pastor," meanwhile, continued to serve God's people in Sanyuan, and by 2006 there were 6,000 registered believers in 24 churches in the county.[8]

Zhang Guanru continued to encourage God's children into his nineties, when he finally left his earthly tent to be with the King of Kings forever. The gospel has continued to thrive in Sanyuan, and today there are an estimated 35,000 Evangelical believers in the county: 11,000 Three-Self Church members and a further 24,000 unregistered house church Christians.[9] Many thank God for the influence Zhang Guanru had on the kingdom of God in their location.

Communists come to Jesus

Several precious reports on the state of Christianity in Shaanxi were received by mission organizations in the late 1970s. One of them said,

> In a village in Shaanxi the believers were gathered in a home meeting when suddenly the Production Brigade leader with several others forced their way through the door and stood

among the believers. He shouted, "You are forbidden to believe in Christ and are forbidden to pray!"

No sooner had he finished speaking when his neck and mouth began to swell to an enormous proportion, and he was unable to breathe. Seeing this, the Christians said, "You must repent and believe in Jesus." He accepted their advice and began to pray. Right away the swelling went down, and the man praised God out loud. His whole life was changed. Not only did he stop persecuting Christians, but he witnessed everywhere and led many people to the Lord. All glory to the Lamb that was slain![10]

At a university in Xi'an, a professor who was also a Communist Party cadre approached a foreign Christian who was teaching at the university and said, "My wife and I would like to become Christians. Please help us." The foreigner was suspicious, as the man had threatened all the students against becoming Christians just months earlier. When asked for the reason behind his sudden change of mind, the professor said,

> My wife is working in the villages of our province, and I am only able to see her a few times a year. She told me amazing things that I have never heard before. She said one 70-year-old woman was going from village to village preaching good news to the people and praying for the sick. My wife went to investigate and saw many outstanding miracles of healing. Even the dead are being raised! Entire villages are turning to God and becoming Christians. We know this is real and we want to believe in Jesus. Will you please help us?[11]

1980s

The stages of the cross

After the death of Mao Zedong in 1976, the long dark winter experienced by the church in Shaanxi—and by the entire Chinese population—began to thaw, and shoots of growth appeared. At first, just a few reports indicated God's Spirit was moving. It soon became apparent that not only had the Christian faith survived, but in many places the number of believers had markedly increased. The late Chinese church expert Jonathan Chao details the painful stages that the churches went through before they experienced revival:

Revival brought tens of thousands of new believers into Shaanxi churches in the 1980s
RCMI

> The Church in China has been transformed from a timid, "foreign-colored" institutional church into a bold, indigenous, institution-less church, and it has been changed from a dependent "mission church" into an independent missionary church. It is a Church that has gone through the "steps of the Cross," following in the footsteps of her Lord: betrayal, trial, humiliation, abandonment, suffering, death, burial, resurrection, and the gift of the Spirit of Pentecost.[1]

In the years prior to Communism, the provincial capital Xi'an tended to have the lowest response to the gospel of all the cities and towns in Shaanxi, but by the early 1980s, God was at work in the strategic city. Veteran China missionary Leslie Lyall, writing from his home in Britain, says, "There are 70 house churches in Xi'an alone, attended by several thousand Christians. One church not far from Xi'an has baptized 7,000 people in two years."[2]

Not all were quick to rejoice in the rise of the house churches, however. The state-sanctioned China Christian Council in Shaanxi condemned house church activities and complained that the growth of one church in Xi'an was due to an evangelist converting 800 people from his work unit of 12,000. As a result, "All itinerant evangelists became targets for arrest, and one was suspended by his thumbs and beaten."[3]

Jesus from Henan

The main factor behind the growth of Christianity in Shaanxi in the 1980s was not churches within the province itself, but the overflow of a tremendous revival that swept neighboring Henan Province. This revival empowered simple farmers and factory workers and transformed them into bold evangelists. Many crossed the border and preached the good news of Jesus to the people of Shaanxi, and thousands were saved.

Peter Xu in the 1980s

In an extensive interview, Peter Xu Yongze—the founder of the large Born-Again house church movement that grew to contain millions of believers throughout China—told the author about his network's foray into Shaanxi:

> God used a severe persecution in 1983 to give many of our leaders a vision for the salvation of all of China. During the summer of that year, many Christians took refuge in the mountains of Shaanxi, and in so doing spread the flame of the gospel to those areas. Within two years our movement had expanded from a church based predominantly in Henan to one that was sending teams of workers all over the country.
>
> I was arrested and sentenced to prison, but after my release in 1984 I was invited to Ankang City in Shaanxi to preach the gospel. I was taken to a house where I found that three of the six family members were extremely sick and unable to get out of bed.
>
> When I looked around their house and saw many idols, I told the family, "You must destroy all these idols. You have trusted in them, and they have made you sick and miserable." The family was afraid of demonic retribution if they destroyed their idols, so I told them, "If you agree, I will destroy them for you, but I will only do it in front of you as witnesses."
>
> They agreed to my proposition. After the idols were smashed, the three sick people were able to get out of bed for the first time in many days and they gradually regained their strength.
>
> On the second day I was invited to another home. The simple people there had heard a rumor that "Jesus from Henan" had come to their area, and a crowd of about 70 unbelievers gathered to watch me. That family also owned many idols, which they agreed to destroy.

As I began to share the gospel with them, however, the Holy Spirit gave me a word of knowledge, and I prayed aloud, "Lord, thank you for bringing me here. May every idol in this home, both those displayed openly and those hidden in a box, be destroyed."

The family members were shocked and repented when they realized that God knew their secret. They brought the hidden idol out. But it was made of hard wood and I couldn't smash it, so we burned it instead.

A few minutes later a crying mother came to the house, carrying her young daughter. She asked, "Where is Jesus from Henan?" The people pointed at me and said, "He's the one." These people were so innocent-minded. A rumor had spread that I could do the works of Jesus, heal any sickness, and that I could even raise the dead back to life!

I tried to explain that I had no power to do any of these apart from the Name of Jesus Christ, but they couldn't grasp that simple truth. I grew frightened when I realized that the girl had already been dead for at least several hours, and the blood had drained from her face. Not knowing what to do, I shouted, "Everyone kneel!" All the people knelt with their eyes wide open, looking to see what I would do next.

I knelt next to the mother of the dead girl and prayed with tears in my eyes, "O Lord, please confirm your Word and have mercy on this girl."

About three minutes later, the mother felt her daughter move. Then she helped her stand on her feet. The whole room full of people saw the girl raised from the dead by the power of God.

I preached the gospel of repentance and faith in Jesus, and all 70 people bowed and surrendered their lives to the Lord. The new believers formed a house church and met regularly as they grew in grace and the knowledge of God.

Within two years we had established Bible training seminaries in Shaanxi Province. Many workers graduated from the schools, and Xi'an became one of the headquarters for our work to Tibet, northwest China, and southwest China. Over the years, many miracles took place in Shaanxi. Our schools often lacked basic food, but God constantly provided through miracles. Although many of our workers and students have been arrested in Shaanxi, some were able to escape through sovereign interventions by the Lord.[4]

Martha's quest for Bibles

In the 1980s, Bibles were extremely scarce in Shaanxi and throughout China. Believers did all they could to obtain God's Word when it was smuggled into the country from Hong Kong. The precious Scriptures were distributed first to the neediest Christians, especially those who taught other believers. In 1983, a mission leader traveled to Xi'an to meet a house church Christian known only by her English name, Martha. She was 27 years old at the time and had committed her life to Christ during the Cultural Revolution. From that moment on, all she wanted to do was preach the gospel and see her fellow citizens know Jesus like she did.

Martha had been engaged, but decided to postpone her marriage for two years to concentrate on delivering Bibles to wherever the need was the greatest. The meeting with the mission leader was scheduled for 9:00 p.m., but Martha did not turn up until about 1:00 a.m. the next morning. She apologized, "and explained that she had been delayed because the local commune leaders discovered she was delivering Bibles to a nearby village. They beat her up, robbed her, and threw her onto a deserted road."[5]

The mission leader noticed something was wrong with Martha. Even though her body was thin, her face appeared bloated and distorted. He asked what the matter was, assuming her condition was a consequence of the beating she had received. "Oh, no," she said. "I've had this problem for some time now." She rolled up her trousers to show her legs covered with stings and mosquito bites. As she traveled around the remote countryside, she often had to sleep in abandoned shacks or in the open fields. She was literally being eaten up by bugs and mosquitoes. When she was urged to see a doctor, Martha replied, "No. I have to catch an early train to Inner Mongolia. Where are the Bibles?"[6] Her only concern was to get God's Word to the hungry believers in Inner Mongolia.

In August 1983, Martha disappeared while she was traveling with another load of precious Bibles. It was in the midst of a nationwide crackdown against crime and religion, and when she failed to appear, many friends were concerned for her life. Later, a scribbled note was received from Martha. She had been arrested and charged with "distributing superstitious materials," and she didn't know what the penalty would be. The little note quoted the apostle Paul's words from Ephesians 6:19–20 (AV): "Pray also for me, that whenever I speak, words may be given me so that I will fearlessly make known the mystery of the gospel, for which I am an ambassador in chains."[7]

A few weeks later news emerged that Martha had been executed. She had paid the ultimate price for her energetic and unabashed love for Jesus Christ. God had counted her worthy to receive a martyr's crown.

The Heavenly Man in Shaanxi

Another Henan Christian who ministered in Shaanxi during the 1980s was Brother Yun whose life story later became well-known through his best-selling autobiography, *The Heavenly Man*. In his book, Yun detailed a dramatic visit he made to the province:

> Our church leaders told me they had received a letter from Shaanxi, begging us to send workers into their midst to train them how to plant new churches.... Three of us—two young sisters and I—arrived in Shangnan County in southeast Shaanxi. Most of the

Brother Yun in the 1980s

impoverished people there had never seen outsiders before….

On the first day of the meetings, I shared the history of the cross throughout church history and mission. At about 1 p.m. on the second day I lost my voice, and I was taken to a room to rest.

Suddenly, several Public Security officers kicked down the door to my room. They grabbed me and held me down on the bed. One officer lay on me, pinning me down with his weight. With one hand he held me by the throat, and with his other hand he reached into his pocket and pulled out his ID card, shouting, "I come from the Public Security Bureau. Where do you come from?"

The officers took a rope and bound my arms tightly behind my back. One of them noticed a red wooden cross attached to the wall, with the words "For God so loved the world" inscribed on the horizontal section, while on the left and right were written: "He hung on the cross" and "He took our sins upon Himself." The officers read those words and laughed aloud, before tearing the cross from the wall and tying it to my back with the ropes. Then they started to kick me furiously. Blows rained down on my legs, arms, chest, and ribs.

The owner of the house came and knelt before the officers, begging them to release me. He said: "This is a good man. He's done nothing wrong. Please arrest me in his place." The officers kicked and pushed him out of the room, shouting, "You can never pay this man's debt!"

For the first time I had the honor of literally bearing the cross of Christ on my body! They triumphantly marched me off, bloodied and bruised, to Shangnan township. When people saw me bound with rope and that I was carrying a big red cross, a crowd gathered to witness the remarkable sight.

As I was paraded through the streets, a police car drove slowly in front, with a loudspeaker proclaiming: "This man came from Henan to preach Jesus. He has seriously disturbed the peace and has confused the people. Today the Public Security Bureau has captured him, and we will punish him severely."

I was forced to kneel in the dirt while officers punched me in the chest and face and repeatedly kicked me from behind with their heavy boots. My face was covered with blood and due to the unbearable pain, I nearly lost consciousness as I lay on the ground. They lifted me up and made me stagger down another street, determined to make an example of me to as many people as possible....

I was paraded through the streets for half a day, and when night fell they took me to a big courtyard inside the police station. They didn't loosen my ropes, but they did take the wooden cross off my back. They then locked me inside a large interrogation room with an iron door and bars on the windows....

I felt that God wanted me to pretend I was crazy, like David had done in the Bible, so I lay down on the ground and acted insane. I rolled my eyes back in their sockets and spat like a madman. The officers were frightened and were convinced I was crazy....

At that moment, the Holy Spirit spoke to my heart: "The God of Peter is your God." I remembered how angels had opened the prison gates for Peter to escape. The rope that bound my arms behind my back suddenly snapped by itself! I didn't tear the ropes off but kept them loosely in place. I decided to try to escape, and if caught I would claim I was trying to go to the toilet. With my arms still positioned behind my back, I used my mouth to turn the door handle and I walked out of the room!

God gave me faith and courage. I reminded myself that the blood of Jesus Christ protected me, and I walked through the middle of the onlookers in the courtyard. Nobody stopped me or said anything to me! It was as though God had blinded their eyes and they didn't recognize who I was. I walked to the toilet

> block in the northern part of the compound, about 30 feet away from the interrogation room....
>
> Because the front gate had been locked, the only way out of the compound was over an eight-foot-high cement wall, which had sharp glass embedded in the top. I stood there for a moment, stared at the wall, and prayed, asking the Lord to heal my numb hands and body.
>
> Then I decided to try to leap over the wall. I saw no other choice. I was trapped, and at any moment the officers would grab me. What happened next is not possible from a human perspective....
>
> I pulled myself up onto the wall as high as I could manage. Looking over the top, I saw that on the other side was a ten-feet-wide open septic tank. As I hung grimly onto the side of the wall, suddenly it felt as if somebody hoisted me up and threw me over! I jumped so far that I even cleared the septic tank! The God of Peter helped me leap over the wall and escape![8]

Remote Shangnan continued to be a place where Christians were intensely persecuted for their faith. In 1988, 80 house church evangelists were captured and imprisoned there.[9] But the believers in the area persevered and have faithfully continued to share the gospel. Today, Shangnan County has a population of about 220,000 people. Of that number, an estimated 16,000 are followers of Jesus Christ, with 10,000 being members of illegal house churches.[10] The example set by Brother Yun and others has resulted in many people coming to faith.

Signs and wonders in Shaanxi

Because of the bold and uncompromising witness of house church evangelists, the gospel began to fan out across Shaanxi. Tens of thousands of people who had never heard of Jesus discovered His life-changing teaching, and they enthusiastically embraced God's free offer of eternal life. In 1986, a Sister Liu moved from Henan and began working in a factory in Shaanxi. When she asked if there were any Christians in the area, she was met with blank stares until someone told her they knew of Christians in a village 40 miles (65 km) away.

Determined to be connected to her brothers and sisters, Liu started out early the next morning. When she finally reached the village, she was dismayed to find that only three old ladies there were believers. But Liu was excited and started a house fellowship with them. Soon, they had more than ten believers. Feeling she needed help, Sister Liu wrote to her church in Henan, and another sister was dispatched to Shaanxi to assist in the promising work.

The believers poured out their hearts before God in prayer, and miracles occurred each time they went into surrounding villages to share the gospel as God confirmed His Word with signs and wonders. A report of those wonderful days says,

> A man who had been blind for years received his sight. Many people came from near and far because of this miracle. Some walked up to 12 miles (19 km) through the night over mountain trails with their lanterns. Many were sick, but the Lord healed them. Thus, the church grew daily.
>
> There was a beautiful middle-aged woman who had been confined to bed for seven-and-a-half years after a medical procedure went wrong. One day, her mother heard that a woman in the next village who had been ill with tuberculosis for many years had been healed because of her faith in Jesus.
>
> When her daughter heard the story, she began to call on the Name of the Lord. She immediately felt better and the next day she was able to get out of bed and walk. That Sunday, she attended Sister Liu's meeting, where the believers prayed for her and she was completely healed. She then asked Sister Liu to preach in her village. As a result, many turned to the Lord and a woman who had been blind for eight years received her sight.[11]

When the authorities learned about this move of God, they tried to arrest Sister Liu and the other leaders. They fled to other districts, however, and everywhere they went they preached the gospel with great results. In one town,

> A fortune-teller accepted the Lord after listening to Sister Liu's sermon. He returned home and burned all his books on fortune-telling. He experienced a powerful conversion and God gave him a great burden for souls. Within a year, he had led more than 300 people to the Lord. He suffered much persecution, but God helped him overcome....
>
> The flame of the gospel spread quickly to other counties, and many were added to the church daily. In one village where there had been no believers two years earlier, 60 percent of the villagers became Christians. This infuriated the village head, who interrupted their meetings and reprimanded them. This made the believers pray even more fervently for him.
>
> A few months later, the village chief's only son fell ill, and the doctor gave no hope of recovery. Desperate and helpless, he went to the church and sought help. The believers prayed for him, and he accepted the Lord. They also prayed for his son, and he was healed! The village chief became a zealous Christian and eventually opened his home for the believers to meet in.[12]

Another of the indigenous house church networks that grew quickly in Shaanxi during the 1980s was the controversial True Jesus Church which had been founded by Paul Wei Enbo in Beijing in 1917. Pentecostals and Charismatics around the world claim the True Jesus Church as part of their movement because members believe in the baptism of the Holy Spirit and practice healing and speaking in tongues. However, their theological beliefs are a complicated mix of several denominational strands. One of many testimonies to emerge from the True Jesus Church in Shaanxi occurred at the end of 1988, in Qindu District. There a 53-year-old woman named Zhao Guifang was suffering from hepatitis, appendicitis, and cancer of the womb. She was reduced to skin and bones, and the doctors had given up trying to cure her.

One day, a strange woman came to Zhao's village, and a crowd gathered around her as she sung and prayed. Zhao was confined to bed but heard the commotion outside and wanted to find out what was happening. Her husband didn't want to trouble her and told her it was nothing. Undeterred,

> She tried very hard to walk with her hands on the wall. The gathering was only just around the corner from her home, and when she arrived, the evangelist asked her to pray. She didn't know what praying was, however, so the evangelist laid hands on her head and prayed for her. After a while, Zhao felt the pain in her head had gone. She joyfully told the crowd what had happened, but they jeered at her, for they did not believe in miracles. Zhao, however, knew it was true....
>
> Two hours passed, and Zhao felt greatly relieved. Her stomach was no longer swollen, and she was completely healed. The whole village stared at her in great astonishment.
>
> Before Zhao was healed, her husband had been unhappy about her going to church meetings. Afterwards, however, he changed his attitude and agreed to be baptized. Since then, they have turned their home into a meeting point, and their door is open every day from early morning to late evening. The sick are welcomed and allowed to eat and stay there for free until they have recovered. On average, about 30 people come to her daily.[13]

A dead woman is raised to life

In the 1980s, the power of the Holy Spirit continued to sweep across the province, quenching the thirst of desperate believers. Pentecostal teaching influenced the house churches and brought a new dynamic to the body of Christ in Shaanxi. A Sister Yu in Xi'an shared this testimony:

Although both my parents and my husband's parents were believers, we rejected Christ for years. Due to many problems, we returned to Christ, and with our three daughters, we became active in the ministry. After we first returned to the Lord, due to lack of teaching, we attended the Three-Self Church, where the pastor never preached the gospel, but just made political speeches.

One day, an elderly engineer in his 70s preached on the baptism of the Holy Spirit. He was warned by the church officials not to preach on the subject, but he replied: "I will preach whatever the Lord gives me."

After that we traveled to Henan Province and received the baptism of the Holy Spirit. We learned about worship and praise and brought this teaching back to the churches in our area. The Lord told us to come out of the false Three-Self Church, so we began to meet in our home. Then the Lord led us to construct our own church building. It seemed impossible given the situation in China, but everyone gave sacrificially, and now we have our own church building, and up to 1,000 people meet there regularly.

Now is a time of revival, and all the brothers and sisters are baptized in the Holy Spirit. We have seen many miracles, and people have even been raised from the dead. Of course, there are those who fight us and say this is all of the devil. We don't believe we are of the devil, however, for if we were how would we be able to raise the dead?

One sister passed away and had been dead for almost a whole day. An elderly sister in her 70s knelt beside her body and prayed, "Lord, you brought me here to serve her, so how can I possibly leave her as a dead woman?" Thus, she knelt at the side of the body and prayed for almost a day from the time she died.

After her death was confirmed by a doctor, the government workers prepared a grave to bury her, and the next day they came to collect the body. But upon entering the room, they found her healthy and alive! This burial team had been working for years and nearly fainted when they saw this.[14]

By the end of the remarkable decade of the 1980s, the church in Shaanxi had experienced unprecedented growth. A 1981 estimate determined there were just 30,000 Evangelical Christians in the entire province,[15] but by the end of the decade the number had swelled six-fold to 180,000.[16]

The government-approved Three-Self churches had stagnated in Shaanxi, however, and the white-hot revival experienced by the house churches had produced almost all the growth in the province. One report noted, "Internal Public Security statistics on the number of Christian converts in Xi'an (Shaanxi Province) showed that only two percent had been baptized and received as members in the 'open church'. The other 98 percent had all been converted through the witness of independent house church evangelists."[17]

For the first time in history, Evangelicals in Shaanxi had caught up to their Catholic counterparts, who were also estimated to number 180,000 church members in 1989.[18] Soon, however, further revival in Shaanxi caused the Evangelicals to numerically shoot far ahead of the Catholics as multitudes of people were transformed by the power of Jesus Christ.

Letters from Shaanxi

We conclude this chapter by reprinting several letters that were received from Christians in Shaanxi during the 1980s. Letters were few and far between at the time, and these precious communications reveal both the strengths and weaknesses of Christianity in the province while offering a snapshot of the ever-changing conditions experienced by the body of Christ.

1988

Persecution is normal for us, but what is most painful is when the leaders of the Three-Self churches accuse us to the authorities, even when the police have not been bothered with us. Those Three-Self people claim to believe in the same God, but they betray the Lord and His brethren. This makes us suspect that they are not really born-again or saved. May our Savior forgive them....

At the beginning of this year, whole villages in the mountains of Shaanxi turned to Christ, as they were drawn by the great love of the Lord on the cross. There are not enough Bibles. Some teenagers want to dedicate themselves to God for full-time Christian service. Turned out of their homes, they are willing to spend their entire lives as evangelists.[19]

1989

Please help me and pray for me. I am going to die soon because I am suffering from unrequited love. I pour out my sorrows wherever I go, and even though I believe God is all-knowing and all-present, I feel lonely and don't belong anywhere. No one loves me and they all look down on me because I only finished Middle School. I know I am not pretty, but I have a kind heart and am gentle and soft. My boyfriend left me, and I don't know what to do now. Several times I prayed earnestly to the Lord, but He has not given me an answer. Please help me.[20]

I heard a rumor that overseas people are saying there is no longer any persecution in China. We find this hard to believe. There are more than 100 brethren in prison here, and many young Christians under 18 are under strong pressure from the police. Some were thrown into manure pits, others were beaten with electric stun-batons, and some were beaten so severely that they could not stand and could only crawl to the toilet.

A few could not endure and revealed the names and addresses of their fellow workers to the police. The betrayers were sentenced, however, whereas those who said nothing were eventually released because of insufficient evidence... Our 500 to 600 full-time Christian workers and 50,000 to 60,000 believers will have to stand on their own feet now.[21]

1990s

A house church meeting in Shaanxi in the 1990s
RCMI

Bold believers advance the kingdom of God

The revival that swept through many parts of Shaanxi in the 1980s continued into the new decade, and multitudes of people were introduced to Jesus for the first time. The Communist authorities in the province had a big problem on their hands. They spent the decade trying to dampen the revival flames wherever they broke out, only to find that the more they tried to extinguish the fire of the Holy Spirit, the more it spread.

Many bold Christians became vessels of blessing to the people of Shaanxi. One of them was a 54-year-old woman named Ma Songcao whose husband regularly beat her because of her faith in Christ. In 1991, she contracted various diseases, but after being prayed for she was completely healed. In response, Ma dedicated the rest of her life to spreading the gospel, which further infuriated her husband. To shame her, he stripped her naked and tied her to a wooden cart, then paraded her around the village. Instead of humiliation, Ma Songcao felt joy that she had been counted worthy to suffer shame for Jesus Christ, and neighbors scolded her husband for his evil actions. From that time on, people listened to Ma's preaching more intently, and by 1997, "she had led 150 villagers to God, although her husband was not among them."[1]

As the authorities in Shaanxi began to feel more helpless in their losing battle to destroy the church, pressure was brought to bear from the central government in Beijing because they viewed Shaanxi as the heart of Communism in China. In yet another bid to crush Christianity, the provincial authorities were ordered to crack down mercilessly on Christians. Across the province, God's children experienced especially brutal treatment in 1992 and 1993. According to one report,

> There were cases in which victims were bound and hung up, had boiling water poured on them, were hit with glass bottles, burned with cigarettes, or whipped with leather belts. Handcuffs and shackles were often used not simply to restrain prisoners, but also to inflict pain. Suspension by the arms or legs, being made to adopt physically painful or exhausting postures for long periods of time, deprivation of sleep or food, exposure to cold or heat, and prolonged solitary confinement were other frequently cited practices.[2]

In January 1993, even a government-approved Three-Self Church was destroyed by the Public Security Bureau as part of their campaign to suppress Christianity. After approximately 300 officers surrounded the building while a service was in progress, the Christians were ordered to leave, and those who refused to stop worshipping were brutally dragged outside. Then bulldozers moved in and razed the building to the ground.[3] But as Christians came under more severe attack, God mocked the atheistic persecutors by pouring out His Spirit, and the number of Christians continued to grow throughout Shaanxi Province.

In one village an evangelist proclaimed, "Jesus Christ is a great God. He is the one who created the universe. He can cause the blind to see, the deaf to hear, and even the dead to rise." A man who heard those words ran to the hospital where a boy had just died. He told the boy's parents what he had heard, and they carried their lifeless son to the meeting and laid him before the preacher. The evangelist was scared because he had not expected to have to prove his claims in such a dramatic fashion. He grew anxious realizing that if the boy did not come back to life, the people would consider him to be a liar and would never believe in Jesus. He prayed for the boy with dozens of onlookers watching intently, but nothing happened. Then he prayed again saying,

> "Lord, I don't mind losing face, but I really do not want this to cause people to mock your Name and not believe in you. Please show your glory in this place." As he was praying, the mother of the child said, "Look, my son is alive again!" The child stood up and ran around the house. Due to this miracle, many people in that area burnt all their idols and believed in Jesus.[4]

Lai Manping

Persecution continued to rain down on many Shaanxi Christians during the 1990s. Countless arrests, tortures, and imprisonments continued, but a particularly brutal incident in 1993 brought Shaanxi into the news.

Lai Manping was a 22-year-old farmer and house church Christian from Ankang in southern Shaanxi. He was part of a team of five preachers who traveled to Taoyuan village in nearby Xunyang County to hold a gospel meeting on March 27, 1993. The village leaders reported the meeting to the local Public

Security Bureau (PSB) who dispatched eight or nine officers to investigate. They arrived and without saying a word began to wildly beat the gathered Christians with their batons. The preachers from Ankang, including Lai, were arrested and taken away. The first report of the incident stated,

> Three brethren were stripped naked from the waist down and beaten by the PSB. When they finished, they also forced each of the 26 others in the meeting to beat these brethren 100 times with bamboo rods. If they failed to comply, they too were beaten by the PSB. These brothers were totally covered with blood, gaping wounds, and injuries all over their bodies. They were then hung up and beaten with rods until they were unconscious and barely

The body of Lai Manping, who was beaten to death by the Public Security Bureau. This picture was published around the world, sparking outrage from the authorities in China

> breathing. The PSB also cursed them loudly with the most vile and filthy language.[5]

Female believers were also treated contemptuously. Two were thrown over a stove, and millstones weighing 130 pounds (59 kg) were placed on their backs while they were beaten and bashed. Their trousers were ripped open in front of the men to humiliate them. One of the sisters, 21-year-old Xu Fang, later reported,

> They ripped open the pants of us sisters with rods and showed our nakedness, abusing us terribly and using the most cruel methods to beat our private parts. It was absolutely repulsive, disgusting, and base beyond description! Then they suspended us from the ground with the brothers and took turns beating us with constant swearing until the next morning.
>
> A sister from Ankang had brought her 12-year-old nephew to the meeting. Not only did they beat this innocent boy on the head until blood flowed out, but they then lifted him like a stone and threw him, smashing into the people.[6]

At daybreak, the three men and two women who had been beaten the most were forced to walk from the remote village to the PSB headquarters in Lijia, about 18 miles (30 km) away. They painfully crawled along the paths, taking a day and a half to reach their destination. The district officials then tried to send them to the county authorities in Xunyang, but the officials there refused to accept them after seeing the terrible injuries they had received. They were sent back to Lijia where they were held for another eight days. The five Christians lay in agony on the floor of a cell, more dead than alive.

The worst affected was the young man Lai Manping. One of the other detainees testified that "Lai's face was totally black and clots of blood came out when he relieved himself. His breath smelled terrible and everyone in the room could smell it. He had sustained severe internal injuries as a result of the beatings."[7]

The guards were concerned that a prisoner might die in their custody, so they called a doctor to examine Lai. She was horrified at his condition but offered only some external medicine before leaving. The guards thought it would be better if Lai died outside the prison, so they forced him to leave. Mustering all the energy he could, Lai attempted to crawl back home. He "struggled, walking and crawling six miles (ten km).... He just collapsed. The local people found him and carried him to a small house, but after one day and night he died."[8]

Lai's parents heard of their son's release and rushed to Lijia to collect him. After an exhaustive search they discovered their beloved son was dead. Lai's uncle was outraged and demanded that the PSB take full responsibility for the murder. Instead, they claimed he had died because of a heart condition. An autopsy revealed the young Christian's heart had turned completely black. In the debased minds of the local officials, this finding only confirmed their narrative.

A local believer who owned a camera photographed Lai's brutalized body. The pictures were then carried to Hong Kong and published in newspapers around the world. The British Parliament took up the case with the Chinese government who denied any wrongdoing and repeated their claim that Lai had died of heart disease.[9] Amnesty International was told by Chinese officials that there was "no such case as the persecution of Christians."[10] More details later emerged about the brutal treatment Lai Manping had endured before his death. One reported noted,

> It is very rare that PSB officers require a detainee to be whipped 100 times by as many as 26 persons, meaning a total of 2,600 stripes. Under traditional Chinese law, 80 stripes with a wooden board was considered the maximum. It is also highly unusual for law enforcement officers to partially strip men and women in front of each other, force them to make contact, and even beat

> the private parts of the women.... All these practices are entirely illegal, even when judged by the laws of the People's Republic of China.[11]

Furious that their dark deeds had become worldwide news, the authorities determined to hunt down those who had reported the story and taken the pictures. Ninety house church Christians were arrested in retaliation. They were released more than two months later after being forced to pay fines of between 500 to 700 Yuan (US $90 to $125)—a virtual fortune for a farmer at the time in this impoverished part of China.

In September 1993, the police rearrested twenty-five of the Christians who had suffered during the original incident in March. They were again beaten mercilessly. By November six still remained in custody, including the brave Xu Fang who had documented the murder of Lai Manping. She was tortured in an attempt to make her retract her statement, but Xu refused saying, "I am prepared to spend several months in prison or even be killed by them, but I will stand by the facts of this persecution, including the fact that the PSB killed Lai Manping."[12]

If not for Xu's persistence and the local believer who owned a camera, this incident would have never been known outside the local area where it occurred, like dozens of similar cases that go unreported each year. The courageous witness of thousands of Christians like Lai Manping, who willingly laid down his life for Jesus Christ, resulted in explosive growth among the churches of Shaanxi during the 1990s.

The murder of Lai did not deter the Shaanxi authorities, and arrests and savage beatings intensified. However, the gospel continued to transform entire communities so that in 1994, a total of 318 house church Christians were arrested in the single village of Shechiang.[13] The power of the Holy Spirit had blazed throughout the village, setting thousands of people free, and the local authorities were ordered to stop the movement before it spread to surrounding areas.

The cave seminary

For centuries, caves carved out of the soft clay terrain in Shaanxi have been used as homes by the population. Mao's soldiers stayed in many such caves, and the current Chinese President Xi Jinping famously grew up in a cave during his formative years in the province.

In 1999, the author interviewed a young single Christian woman named Sister Ling who was one of the first of two workers to establish house church Bible schools in Shaanxi. She said,

> In early 1987, God called me to launch a Bible training program along with another sister who became my dear co-worker in the

Christian women witnessing through song and dance outside their "cave church" in Shaanxi
RCMI

gospel. We found a cave in the Shaanxi countryside, outside the city of Xi'an. With our own hands we dug the dirt out until the cave was large enough to contain more than 20 people.

We were able to occupy the cave without objection from the locals because they believed it was inhabited by demons that they called "spirits of the Yellow Caves." The locals didn't dare to go anywhere near the cave, so we had it all to ourselves!

Shaanxi is very cold in the winter, with temperatures plummeting to minus 10 degrees for much of the time. Inside our cave we were surprisingly warm, however, because of the insulation provided by the walls. Although to human eyes our Bible school was wretched and pitiful, to us it was the most special place in the world because God was with us!

Because we had no money or financial support we faced great difficulties, but God faithfully provided our needs in unexpected ways. By His grace, after a while we obtained some chickens which produced much needed eggs, and we were given a dog for protection against bad people and wild animals.

When it came time to open our little Bible school, we had 16 brothers in the first class! For security reasons, we decided it was best to sleep during the daytime and study God's Word at night, when the prying eyes of police and villagers were fast asleep.

This was the humble beginnings of how the Lord started our cave seminary. By 1995 the work had spread, and Bible schools sprung up across north China, including in Shanxi, Gansu, Ningxia, and Qinghai provinces. Within seven years the ministry grew to include more than 200 co-workers, and many people entered the Lord's service after being strengthened by His Word and empowered by the Holy Spirit.[14]

Sister Lan

The government-approved Three-Self churches in Shaanxi also reported strong growth throughout the 1990s as revival continued to spread and impact the lives of many who attended registered churches. Some of this growth was intentional after a number of house church Christians, grieved by the state of the Three-Self Movement, studied hard and gained the credentials needed to become official pastors. After being appointed to lead churches across the province, they boldly preached the true gospel to their spiritually thirsty congregations.

Some Three-Self leaders were infuriated by the success of one new preacher, Sister Lan. They told her not to hold any more meetings, but Lan refused saying she would obey God and not men. One night she preached with such a strong anointing of the Holy Spirit that according to a report, "Among those who came to listen to Lan's preaching were three sisters from the Three-Self church. Their eyes were opened and they began to see the light. The three later led other believers out of the Three-Self. At least a few hundred people left the government church!"[15]

Sister Lan was invited to hold meetings in other parts of the province, and God continued to use her mightily. In one desolate and impoverished city in northern Shaanxi, she was led to the hut of a man who had been paralyzed for eight years. There she found a dilapidated hovel with the man lying on a small bed in the middle of the room. Around him sat four emaciated children. Lan began to weep when she saw the condition of the family, and she encouraged them to repent of their sins and place their trust in Jesus Christ. After initially refusing to soften his heart,

> The man wept and repented. Lan laid hands on him and prayed, and he was healed instantly. He got out of bed, leaping and crying and praising God. He jumped all over the house and then went to tell his neighbors.... They all repented and accepted the Lord. The meeting went on until four o'clock in the morning and everybody went home rejoicing![16]

Lan's meetings continued to attract the attention of the authorities. At one gathering a sister whispered in her ear telling her that men from the Public Security Bureau, the United Front, and two pastors from the Three-Self Church had come to the meeting and were planning to arrest her. The United Front representative stood up and spoke first, warning people that all meetings without the approval of the government were illegal, and anyone who preaches would be dealt with severely.

The Three-Self pastors, Chan and Wang, then spoke for twenty minutes, sarcastically telling the crowd that a woman who had the power to make paralyzed people walk would speak at the end. When it was finally time for Sister Lan to speak, the power of God's Spirit surged through her fragile body, and everyone's heart was touched. Many wept and repented of their sins. God had turned the government's intentions on their head, and

> The two Three-Self pastors wept even more bitterly. They said to the officers from the PSB and the United Front: "This sister is a nice woman; she only came here to visit her relatives. We assure you that she did not cause any trouble at all." So the officials left.
>
> Then the two pastors said to Lan, "We thank the Lord for sending you to us. He opened our eyes to see the truth and has granted us repentance. It was we who reported you to the authorities. They have left now but they may come back tomorrow. We suggest that you leave early tomorrow morning."[17]

Heeding their advice, Sister Lan left that city. But she continued to faithfully and boldly proclaim the gospel all over Shaanxi Province, and thousands of people came to faith in the Living God.

The spread of the revival from the house churches to the registered churches is reflected in official statistics from Shaanxi. In 1989, at the end of the previous decade, the Three-Self leaders in the province reported 180,000 members.[18] Despite only counting baptized church members over the age of 18, by 1997 they had reportedly doubled in size to 360,000 believers in their churches.[19]

The Catholics also continued to grow in Shaanxi, albeit at a slower rate than the Evangelicals. Catholics increased from an estimated 180,000 in 1989[20] to 200,000 in 1994,[21] and 220,000 in 1997.[22]

Letters from Shaanxi

1990

Although the government claims to be open-minded in religious affairs, the number of believers is restricted. More than 2,000 Yuan (US $350) from one church's building fund was seized by the PSB. Some churches must pay bribes to have their meetings approved.[23]

At first, I requested a Bible from you only for its literature value. After careful consideration, however, I came to faith in God, and now I believe that He is with me always. Faith in Christ has given me new strength and courage. I used to be overwhelmed by a sense of void and loss. Now I am convinced that God exists, and my feelings are markedly different than before. The Lord has given me courage to overcome all obstacles.[24]

1992

My husband, who was an atheist, became a Christian after listening to gospel radio broadcasts from overseas. He took notes habitually while listening to your programs. Recently he suffered a stroke and is paralyzed from the waist down, but he still preaches the gospel to the other patients in the hospital.[25]

1993

I have good news! God has heard my prayers, and He has prepared a brother in Christ to be my husband, even though we are part of a church where there are few available men. Although we have different personalities and interests, our common faith binds us together, and I believe that if God brought us together then He will continue to guide our way.[26]

1995

We organized a huge evangelistic outreach to more than 60 mountainous villages, and we preached the gospel on every street corner. In the mountains alone, 500 to 600 people accepted the Lord. Hallelujah! In response to this revival and the need to nurture the new believers, we are organizing a mass discipleship training program to establish the new converts in the faith.[27]

1996

There are many people in my neighborhood who have repented of their sins and converted to God after listening to your broadcasts. I believed in Christ long ago, but during the Cultural Revolution the church was closed, and I lost my faith. One summer day in 1991, I turned on my radio and heard Jesus Christ being proclaimed. I listened attentively, attended a church, and returned to the Lord.[28]

I am a rural woman from Liuba County. We have no church buildings here, so we meet in believers' homes. There are many such meetings, and we suffer continual persecution. In March, three brothers were taken away to prison, and we have not seen them since. It is exceedingly difficult to share the gospel here. When preachers come, they are often arrested, beaten, and fined.[29]

1997

Two years ago my younger sister visited, and we rode our bicycles to a church meeting. On the way I fell and badly injured my head. I was bleeding profusely and only semi-conscious, but when I cried to God for help, I was immediately revived. Christian sisters took me to a clinic, and one of them changed her clean clothes for mine and paid my medical bill. I really saw God's love shining through them. As I lay on the bed I thought about how Jesus died on the cross, and I realized His suffering was far greater than what I was experiencing. After the accident, my work supervisor told me to abandon my beliefs or I would be expelled from the Communist Party. My mother and I prayed for God's help, and since that time they have not come to bother me any more about my faith.[30]

We are an elderly retired couple who accepted the gospel in June 1994 when we asked God to forgive our sins. We knelt down and pledged to serve Him with all our hearts, minds, and strength. With Jesus as head, we formed a small fellowship that meets twice a week. Usually, a sister reads a Bible passage and then we discuss its meaning. Then she leads us in prayer. Because of God's grace, the congregation has been steadily increasing, and we are too numerous to meet in a home. Thankfully, a brother offered his office to God, and now all of us worship there on Sunday mornings. The Lord fills us with joy whenever we worship and pray, and He strengthens us to endure hardship.[31]

1998

Your various courses have helped me greatly. I am leading two meeting points with a total of 200 members. It is difficult shepherding God's flock, so I am studying the Bible diligently. I thank God that His words are powerful, and He protects me from heresies and cults. I'm praying for all of you, and I have committed my whole life to Jesus Christ.[32]

The factory where I am employed is not doing well, and workers are continually being laid off. We have dropped from 1,500 workers to only 500 at present, and we are not paid on time. Everyone knows the factory will likely close. Unemployment and anxiety cause many family problems, with disputes, fighting, and divorces. Some believers have left God, and the number of people attending our meetings is falling. For ten years God's grace has been sufficient for me, but I am weary and distressed. I don't know what to do apart from crying out to God for help.[33]

I am the only believer in my workplace, and I listen to your radio broadcasts regularly. I have learned a lot from God's Word, and I share the gospel with my unbelieving colleagues. When I work the nightshift, I bring my radio with me. They enjoy the messages but are afraid to believe in God as they worry their supervisors will harass them if they become Christians.[34]

1999

When I was in high school my father got cancer, and my family was plunged into despair. At that time, a Christian sister visited us and shared the good news about Jesus. She prayed for my father with tears flowing down her cheeks, and as she wept I was struck by her sincerity. Although my atheistic upbringing meant I shouldn't believe what she said, I accepted Christ nonetheless as I was moved by her kindness and gentleness.[35]

There is a 70-year-old lady in our church who walks three miles to our meetings. Several years ago, she heard the gospel for the first time and was touched by the life of Christ. She has never missed a meeting since, and she strives to learn all she can from God's Word and to glorify Him. She offered her living room for us to meet in, and the ministry has prospered, with new believers being continually added to our church.[36]

I am a new believer and conditions here are quite basic. Bibles and study material are scarce, or maybe I should say that we have none. Although we live in the suburbs, we still face persecution from the authorities. We cannot meet openly, but the brothers and sisters still come to worship every Sunday.[37]

Within 40 miles (65 km) of my home are several churches, but all of them are lacking workers, and the Bible teachers have limited knowledge. Although a few pastors in our area graduated from seminary, they are engaged in church administration and don't concentrate on preaching and pastoring. As such, our spiritual growth is lacking, and our faith is very weak. When the pastor asked the believers to give their tithes, most immediately said, "No!" When he requested that we observe the Sabbath, most ignored him. We love the world more than we love God. However, when I shared what I learned from your broadcast, one said it was the best message he had heard for years. The brothers and sisters began to change, and now they attend services faithfully and have even given almost 1,000 Yuan to help construct a new church building.[38]

Here in Shaanxi the government has been cracking down on the Falungong sect, and many Christian meetings have also had to stop. We cannot gather, and many believers are frightened and tossed about in their faith. Now we can only meet in an elderly sister's home. Please pray for us.[39]

We were a flock of sheep lost in the swamp of the world, waiting for the gospel to rescue us. We yearned to be baptized by God's love and to know His sweetness. We often discussed the meaning of life, and it eventually led to us believing in Christ. In the future we plan to resume our meetings and learn more from God's Word; however we do not have enough Bibles.[40]

2000s

A packed house church Bible school in Shaanxi
RCMI

Attacked by a satanic cult

In November 2000, the author of this book visited Shaanxi and met many house church leaders from one of the largest networks in the province. The main leader of the network had about 400 house churches under his care, but he was deeply discouraged at the time. For years, this group had been under intense pressure from the authorities, and many of their workers had been tortured and imprisoned.

The group had also lost many believers to the Eastern Lightning cult over the previous few years, including some church leaders who had been enticed by the attractive monthly salaries that were offered to workers who would join the cult. Whereas most house churches were extremely poor, the cult received funding from overseas and benefited from the profits of several large corporations inside China.

After the Eastern Lightning lures some church leaders into joining the cult—which believes Jesus has already returned as a woman living in central China—the mask comes off, and they realize they are trapped in a wicked group that refuses to let them go. One sister had been deceived into joining the Eastern Lightning earlier in the year. She saw the danger and tried to escape, but the cult leaders would not let her. They beat her legs so severely that she had trouble walking and was in constant pain.

In June 2001, a female house church preacher named Dong Xiulan was deceived by the cult in Xi'an who forced her to travel to Gansu Province to study their doctrines. Dong and other recruits were controlled by drugs and brainwashing, and she reported that those who did not submit to the Eastern Lightning leaders were bound, put into sacks, and thrown into the river. She finally gained her release after her desperate husband took an Eastern Lightning member hostage and demanded the cult set his wife free. It took a long time for Dong Xiulan to recover spiritually, mentally, and emotionally from her ordeal.

Zhou Dianyu, a widow in her 40s, lived in the eastern suburb of Xi'an. She and her daughter were known for their zealous evangelism for Christ. In their eagerness to understand the Bible better, they attended a training course, only to discover they had been tricked. It was actually a meeting led by the Eastern Lightning. However the cult believed the pair had accepted their teachings and allowed them to return home to recruit other Christians. Zhou's house church leaders immediately discerned that she had been indoctrinated by the satanic group, and they earnestly prayed that she and her daughter would be set free by the power of Jesus. Zhou Dianyu saw the error of her ways and decided to visit the cult headquarters and return the books she had been given. She didn't come home that night, and the next morning her dead body was found in a house. The official reason for her death was given as asphyxiation by inhaling coal fumes, but the Christians knew she had been murdered by the cult.

The Eastern Lightning continues to operate throughout China today, wreaking havoc among Christians in many areas. Western believers have also been targeted by the cult, and attractive young women have been sent to sexually entice and blackmail some missionaries.

Fire and blood in Shaanxi

Despite the ongoing tribulations experienced by God's people in Shaanxi, the kingdom of God continued to advance in the new millennium. Being a mountainous and widespread province, there were still hundreds of isolated communities where Jesus Christ had never been named. House church evangelists from other parts of China were often surprised by the extreme poverty of believers they met in Shaanxi. The great economic boom that much of China experienced in the previous decades had not reached the remote corners of Shaanxi. It was common practice among Chinese churches for local believers to cover the travel expenses and food of those who came to minister to them, but many preachers brought their own food to Shaanxi so they would not be a burden to the extremely poor local Christians.

As house church networks flourished in many parts of the province, the growth was met with strong persecution from the authorities. Each year hundreds of pastors and evangelists were arrested, beaten, and fined. If the government captured someone whom they believed to be a key leader, they would be formally charged and imprisoned. Most arrests were never reported, but one incident that did emerge into the public realm was that of twelve church leaders who had distributed Bibles at a marketplace in Jiaocheng County on June 9, 2007.[1] Four were released the same day, but eight other leaders were sent to prison.

In June 2009, the authorities illegally seized and demolished the Taochuan Christian Church in Luonan County, in the southeastern part of the province. They first confiscated Bibles and teaching books and then arrested and imposed stiff fines on the church leaders. To send a warning that people should avoid Christianity, the three handcuffed pastors—Liu Caili, Huang Shumin, and Xi Fenying—were shown on the television news being taken to prison.[2] The land and church building had been legally purchased by approximately one hundred church members the previous year. It appears that the number of Christians in Luonan County had increased so rapidly that it caught the government off-guard. This crackdown was one of many in Luonan which today boasts an estimated 28,000 Evangelical Christians.[3]

Despite the constant pressure and harassment, many courageous preachers continued to proclaim the gospel in Shaanxi. Brother Luo Ying, who was nicknamed "the healing evangelist" by fellow Christians, concentrated his ministry on the Ankang region in southern Shaanxi. Luo once lamented, "In one place there has been a sudden increase of 500 new believers, but we could only supply them with 50 Bibles. Growing demand for Bibles is found all over China."[4]

Defenseless nuns beaten

Catholics also suffered for their faith in Shaanxi. On November 23, 2005, a mob of forty armed men descended on the South Cathedral in downtown Xi'an where a group of nuns was protesting the demolition of a school that the government had promised to sell to the registered Catholic Church. The thugs attacked the defenseless nuns and bulldozed the school. Sixteen nuns suffered serious injuries, and five needed to be hospitalized. It later emerged that the mob had been hired by the Chinese Bureau of Education, and the authorities charged eleven men who led the attack.

Zhang Yinan – a man feared by China

Born in Henan Province in 1958, Zhang Yinan was trained in technology but also took a strong interest in history and religion. After surrendering his life to Jesus Christ and being baptized in 1990, he was awakened in the middle of one night and heard a loud voice saying, "You must be filled with the Holy Spirit." This voice was followed by

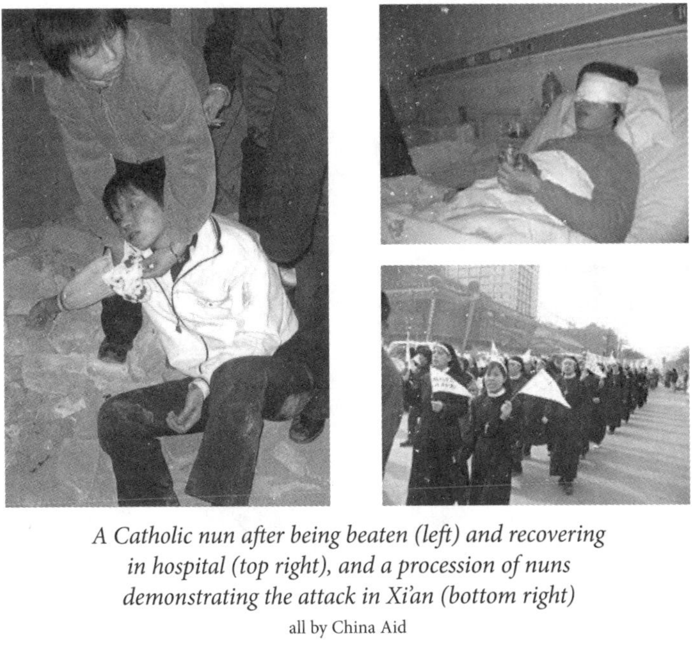

A Catholic nun after being beaten (left) and recovering in hospital (top right), and a procession of nuns demonstrating the attack in Xi'an (bottom right)

all by China Aid

> a sensational feeling of electric current passing down through his hands and legs. Sometime later Zhang received a prophecy through the laying on of hands that God was calling him to embark on the writing of church history. This he obeyed and he spent many rewarding hours … making friends with spiritual doyens and interviewing various house church leaders.[5]

By 1998, Zhang had come into the crosshairs of the Chinese authorities who did not want their dark deeds exposed by an historian who was determined to document the growth of the kingdom of God in China. When the police raided his home in April 1998, Zhang fled to Shaanxi. There he remained for several years until he was finally arrested in September 2003 and sentenced to two years in a prison labor camp for "subverting the government and disturbing the social order."

The judge at Zhang's brief trial used his personal prayer journals against him, citing entries such as "We ask the Lord to destroy all strongholds in China" as evidence of a sinister plot

Zhang Yinan
Paul Hattaway

to overthrow the government. Being a deep thinker, Zhang had also composed a "Christian constitution" for China, expressing his desire that one day believers would be free to openly practice their faith. The court prosecutor claimed these statements proved that Zhang held "anti-Party and anti-socialist feelings."

Zhang Yinan wrote a touching letter to his son from behind prison bars. In part, he said,

> My son, you have been blessed by God, and although you are young you have great vision. I hope that you will continue to pursue the truth of Christ and grow into a deeper knowledge of God, so that a strong foundation is laid in your life.... I hope you will love the brothers and sisters in the Lord, respect your teachers, and follow the regulations of the school. I hope you will be courageous and wise, careful and strategic, passionate and persistent. Give my greetings to all who have cared for you. Do not be distracted. I am doing fine here.
>
> Emmanuel, and God's mercy be with you forever. May the Almighty God bless you and may signs and wonders follow you.
>
> Your father on earth, written from the labor camp, November 11, 2003.[6]

Zhang Yinan after his release from prison

Compass Direct

Zhang Yinan was well-known to many foreign Christians and ministries, and prayer support from around the world was mobilized for him and his family. He was released from prison on September 25, 2005, but his journals and writings were not returned to him.

Zhang was driven by an acute sense of justice and passion for the gospel to reach every part of his country. After his release he could not remain silent, and he boldly went before the Religious Affairs Bureau in Beijing to argue the cause of the house churches. His stand caused the authorities to act, and their intentions were made clear in 2018 when Zhang applied for a passport to travel overseas. The same day that the application was received, dozens of Public Security officers surrounded his home and followed his wife to the hospital where she worked, even entering the operating theater while she was assisting doctors with a surgery.[7] A squad of armed officers swarmed his church, broke down the doors, and carried off every possession they could get their hands on. Zhang was paraded down the middle of the street in a bid to humiliate him and to dissuade anyone who might want to follow his example.

The Chinese authorities remain terrified of this simple Christian scholar and the explosive information they fear he possesses. When Zhang was invited to attend the National Prayer Breakfast in Washington DC—even though he had no passport allowing him to travel—fifty to sixty officers were assigned to 24-hour surveillance of his home to ensure that he did not leave his apartment until the American meeting concluded.

For decades, estimates of the number of Christians in Shaanxi had varied greatly, mostly because official figures failed to include the unregistered house church believers who make up most Evangelicals in the province. An official figure of 250,000 Three-Self Church members in Shaanxi was published in 2001,[8] which rose to 458,500 four years later.[9] The respected mission book *Operation World*, however, published a much more realistic figure of 1,362,600 Evangelicals in 2001, consisting of both registered and unregistered believers.[10] The authors of *Operation World* also estimated 294,600 Catholics in Shaanxi,[11] meaning that Evangelicals outnumbered Catholics by a ratio of nearly five-to-one in the province. This number also represents a significant increase of Catholics, up from 220,000 just four years earlier in 1997.[12]

Letters from Shaanxi

2000

Churches from several counties joined together for evangelism last winter, preaching the gospel in many villages. Thanks to God, many people were added to our family. We did a good job following up, and teams of brothers and sisters were dispatched to visit new converts and invite them to meetings. We are thankful that not only have adults been saved, but many young children as well. They are so innocent and pure.[13]

God moved me to set up a meeting point this March with several believers who converted to the Lord up to six months earlier. However, because there had been no fellowship or nurturing, they didn't know God deeply, and their spiritual lives were poor. However, the Lord blessed us, and several brothers and sisters from my previous church came to help me. The believers did their utmost to learn God's Word, and now our church is flourishing, and we have grown to more than 20 believers.[14]

While we were holding a Bible study last September, our meeting was raided by the Religious Affairs Bureau, and several brothers were thrown into prison on the pretext that they refused to join the Three-Self Patriotic Movement. They are still in prison suffering physical and mental torture. Pray the house churches in Shaanxi will be strong under persecution and the gospel may spread even in the prison, although we hope they will be released soon.[15]

I have been a Christian for six years, and we belong to a rural fellowship in Shaanxi which two years ago constructed a new church building with six main halls and five smaller rooms. Now every seat is taken, and we are wondering what to do next! We have two deacons in charge—one is over 80 years old and serves as the janitor. The other one is 50 years old, but neither are well-educated. Nonetheless, we now number 400 believers, 200 of whom have been baptized. Praise the Lord, for we have now set up two other meeting points. We are very weak and have many newborn babes who need spiritual milk. In our mountainous district there is a nearby village without a single believer, and in other villages there are just one or two Christians. For years we have wanted a reference Bible and a Bible in modern Chinese, but we can't buy these here.[16]

2001

The gospel first arrived here a long time ago and many believed in Christ. However, no one came to nurture us in the faith, so we do not know how to properly seek or please God. Our churches are lukewarm—neither hot nor cold. Please also pray for me. I left home and began to serve God, but my family's economic condition deteriorated, and they can no longer afford to support me. I am deeply burdened and pray the Lord will make a way for me.[17]

Is there any hope for my miserable soul? Many years ago I chose to follow Christ. However, the path was full of difficulties and dangers, and I was weak, foolish, and ignorant. My body has been weak since childhood, and I am an introverted, self-contemptuous person. In my final year at school, overwhelming pressure stretched my nerves to the limit, and I became mentally disordered.

When I was at the darkest point in my life, my boyfriend left me and my best friend betrayed me. I was like a bird with its wings broken, and I was admitted to a mental hospital for five months. It was a miserable time. There were other patients who had been there most of their lives. They never spoke, laughed, or cried. They just sat there quietly, as though they didn't exist. Is there any hope for a miserable soul like me?[18]

2002

For the past three years I have been part of a group of several sisters who meet to study the Scriptures under the Holy Spirit's guidance. It has helped us to grow in the truth of Christ and to be more willing to offer ourselves as living sacrifices. We now have a lively and powerful church that is filled with hope and living testimonies.[19]

I am the most unfortunate person in the world. In May 1998, I was careless at work and fractured my spine, resulting in paraplegia. I borrowed 20,000 Yuan to buy medication, but it didn't help. I have not yet repaid the debt, and now I live in dire poverty. My wife, seeing all my struggles, left without a word, leaving behind our three-year-old child. I thought of committing suicide, but I listened to your Bible program and my faith was strengthened.[20]

I became a Christian in 1991, and two years later I adopted an abandoned handicapped child. God gave me a heart to look after those whom society has rejected. I established a home for old people, and they were well taken care of. Later, the Lord led me to help juvenile delinquents, and He helped me see that each soul is priceless in His eyes. I spent all my money to establish a school, and hundreds of children applied to come. As we live in a remote area, no churches have supported us, but God Himself has taken care of our needs. I make every effort to visit prisons and hospitals, and I share the gospel with everyone I meet.[21]

I became a Christian when my husband fell seriously ill. All our money was spent on his treatment, and we went deep into debt. Many friends and relatives turned their backs on us, but God comforted us and healed my husband. We are thankful for the new life He granted us, and we put our trust in Him. A Communist Party leader interrogated my husband and did all he could to make us renounce our faith, saying my husband's illness had been cured naturally and not by Jesus. We have made up our minds to serve the Lord, and we will never turn back. Only in Jesus is our soul satisfied![22]

I have believed in Jesus for two years but have yet to be baptized. The deacons in my church told me that the foundation of my faith is strong, and they want me to preach publicly. However, I am afraid to serve because I don't know enough of the Word of God. My church lacks ministers and no one is willing to serve, so the fellowship is desolate. Some members have been Christians for years or even decades, but they still don't understand the gospel, and their lives are no different from unbelievers. They have befriended the world, and they have no regrets. Some attend church on Sundays just to gossip and have a sleep. My heart is heavy. What shall I do?[23]

2003

Many people here first believed in the Lord after receiving healing, but my path was different. Whenever I felt depressed, I listened to a sister singing hymns and my spirit was lifted. She frequently shared the gospel with me, but I never took it seriously. Then one night I picked up a Bible, and I knew it was time to trust Jesus. I confessed my sins to God and promised to follow Him for the rest of my life. I am thankful that the Lord chose me and has given me the wonderful gift of eternal life.[24]

I realize that the human heart is deceitful, and life is chaotic. The world is full of unfairness and injustice. To fit into society, I became a selfish and deceitful man and took on many vices. Over time I quit my job and joined a gang. During the day we gambled and got drunk, and at night we committed crimes such as kidnapping and blackmail. Twice I was caught by the police and charged with assault and burglary.

After my friends abandoned me I returned home where my mother invited me to attend her church. I reluctantly went along, and the pastor gently answered all my questions about the Bible. I finally prayed to God with all my heart, and my eyes were instantly opened. I entered another world where He is immeasurably great and wonderful. I was baptized last August and have become a new creation. My mother weeps and says that my conversion is better than all the riches in the world. I know my salvation occurred because of the many sleepless nights my mother spent interceding for me. Now I use my life to serve God, and I praise His great love.[25]

2006

At the age of five I was sent to a Buddhist temple to become a monk. Later, I traveled to India to study the Buddhist scriptures, and while there I came to know the Lord Jesus Christ. My family disowned me when they discovered I had converted to Christianity. Now I have been a Christian for 17 years, and I preach the gospel in my hometown.[26]

I have visited many house churches in our area. Small meetings were previously allowed here. But recently the Three-Self leaders have reported house church meetings to the authorities, and many of us have been arrested. They also slander us in the media, saying house churches are evil cults. Although many of us may be weak in the faith, we are not cult members! We strive to teach orthodox Christian doctrine as revealed in the Bible! We have engaged a lawyer to defend us against the local officials, as we have done nothing wrong. Many house church believers in Shaanxi continue to suffer intense persecution.[27]

2010s and 2020s

Intense intercession at a prayer meeting in Shaanxi
RCMI

At the start of the new decade, hopes were high that the body of Christ in Shaanxi would continue to grow both numerically and in the grace and knowledge of God. Hopes were also high that the freedoms they had sporadically enjoyed during the first decade of the new millennium would expand so that no part of the province would remain without a strong gospel witness. Alas as the decade progressed, those hopes were dashed by the rise of an anti-Christian strongman who, helped by invasive facial recognition and other cutting-edge technology, brought a massive dark cloud over God's people in Shaanxi and throughout the nation.

In 2010, a new edition of the mission book *Operation World* was published. The statistics given for Shaanxi showed a significant advance in Christianity from the previous edition of the book in 2001. Whereas there had been an estimated 1,362,600 Evangelical believers in Shaanxi in 2001,[1] the number had more than doubled to 2,769,800 Evangelicals in 2010, consisting of more than 900,000 members of Three-Self churches, and 1.8 million unregistered house church believers.[2] Similarly, *Operation World* estimated that Catholics in Shaanxi Province had grown markedly from 294,600 in 2001 to 846,400 in 2010.[3]

With a similar explosion of faith in many other parts of China, the Communist authorities realized they had an emergency on their hands, and the scene was set for another major confrontation between the powers of darkness and the children of light.

Living martyrs in Shaanxi

Waves of persecution against house church Christians in Shaanxi continued in this decade. On April 7, 2011, Pastor Wang Zhanhu and members of his Cross Church in Huaxian were worshipping God when three police officers interrupted the meeting and seized the microphone. When Wang demanded to know what laws had been broken, all three officers began to beat him in front of his congregation. They then shocked him with an electric baton, causing him to fall into a coma from the intense pain. Wang had been arrested several times in the years preceding this incident, but he steadfastly refused to compromise by registering with the Three-Self Church.

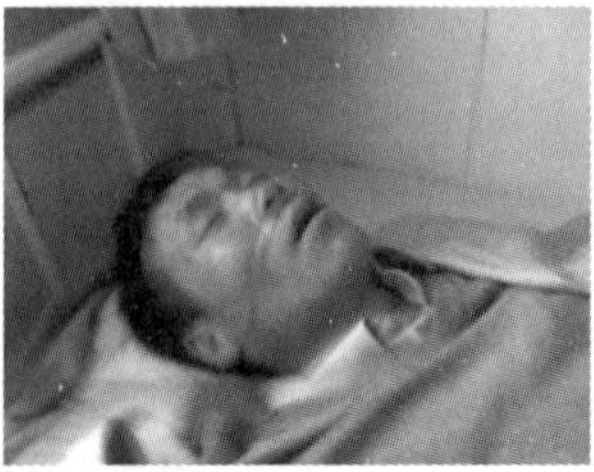

Pastor Wang Zhunhu in a coma after being beaten by the police in front of his congregation
China Aid

As persecution in China became more vicious and targeted in the 2010s, the house churches were filled with a growing number of believers who had suffered physical or mental injuries because of torture and deprivation at the hands of the Communist authorities. Many were unable to work because of their condition. So the mission organization Asia Harvest created a project called the Living Martyrs' Fund to provide financial support for Christian leaders and their families whose lives were in turmoil because of persecution.[4]

Here is a selection of applicants from Shaanxi which provide a glimpse into the brutal treatment many had been forced to endure for their testimony about Jesus Christ:

> Brother Ang is a single man who has faithfully served as a house church leader for years. He has stood the test of government persecution, but because of the filthy conditions in prison, he now suffers from a serious liver disease and requires long-term medication, which he is unable to afford.

> Brother Gen and his wife have one child. He came to the Lord in 1988 and has faithfully led the body of Christ since that time. Despite several arrests and severe beatings, he continues to serve God. Now he is unable to work and has no income because of heart disease. Please help this precious man of God.

> Brother Zong has been a Christian since childhood. He became a full-time preacher at the age of 22, during the dark persecution of the Cultural Revolution. Although he has always tried to lead a quiet life and maintain a low profile, the government severely

persecuted him for years, leaving him with many physical injuries and even more mental scars. He kept the faith and continued to serve as a church elder at his advanced age, but he needs help to survive.

Although Brother Jian was only born in 1980, this young brother has led a full and difficult life. He is married with one child and has served the Lord Jesus full-time in Xi'an since 1999. He has been arrested and tortured on several occasions and spent one year in prison for the sake of the gospel. Now that he has a criminal record, he is unable to obtain work, so Jian and his family are financially destitute.

Brother Xiao came to the Lord in 1997, and his wife died soon after, leaving him to raise his daughter alone. He was caught up in a round of persecution, and a savage beating left him paralyzed. His 80-year-old mother and 90-year-old father are dependent on him too, but with no income, this brother is in distress and would greatly appreciate any help.

After coming to faith in the Lord in 1993, Brother Miao became a full-time evangelist. Since then he has been arrested and beaten by the local police on numerous occasions, but he continues, compelled by the love of God in his heart. His health is now broken due to the terrible treatment he suffered, and his medical expenses have plunged him into dire poverty.

Brother Baixu and his wife are a young couple who serve the Lord wholeheartedly, and local believers meet in their home. Because they refuse to register their church with the atheist Religious Affairs Bureau, they have been strongly persecuted, and twice Baixu has been hauled away to jail. The authorities stole everything of value from their home, reducing them to poverty. They have suffered in numerous ways, and now they are being pursued again. Please help this family, as any assistance would be like a cup of cold water in Jesus' Name.

For many years, Brother Cheng and his wife have shared the gospel with migrant workers from the countryside. He was first arrested five years ago for hosting an unregistered Bible study and was sentenced to two years in prison with hard labor. During that time, he was tortured mercilessly and has been in constant pain since his release. He is now serving again as a teaching elder and is greatly respected by the brothers and sisters. Because of the torture he endured, Brother Cheng is taking long-term medication for bone disease in his back and waist. Please consider helping this man of God.

Brother Long became a Christian in 1994 and has been arrested several times for his faith, enduring beatings and shameful treatment at the hands of wicked men. Now he suffers from bone disease and kidney stones but is unable to afford the medication. Because of his prison sentence he has lost his "political rights," meaning he cannot find employment or provide an income for his desperate family.

The worst persecution in forty years

Xi Jinping rose to the top of the Chinese Communist Party and was elected president of China in March 2013, with 2,952 votes for his appointment and just one against.[5] After a few years of relative calm—during which he silenced all dissent from within the Communist ranks—Xi began to implement severe crackdowns against religion in general but with a special emphasis on the eradication of Christianity.

By 2016, the cry from Christians throughout China was that they were experiencing the worst persecution since the Cultural Revolution forty years earlier. In response, churches in Shaanxi quickly adjusted. They broke their congregations into small groups of four or five believers, and they rotated the location of their meetings to avoid detection, just as believers had done when Mao implemented his harsh policies half a century earlier.

News from the church in Shaanxi quickly dried up, especially after Xi was appointed "President for life" in 2018. Hundreds of foreign Christians—who were serving in Shaanxi as teachers, students, businessmen, and in other roles—were investigated. Often all their communications by email, text, and other means were reviewed. If any contained Christian words, they were used as evidence against them, and they were expelled from China.

One new feature of the crackdown on the church which started in 2016 was that many Three-Self churches were also closed by the government. For more than three decades, the Three-Self Patriotic Movement (TSPM) had enjoyed a relatively peaceful existence because of their cooperation with the authorities. But suddenly the winds of change meant that many TSPM leaders were arrested, and pressure was brought to bear on registered church members. The lines of distinction between registered and unregistered churches in Shaanxi began to blur, and Christian labels became of little importance. All that mattered was whether a person belonged to Jesus Christ or not.

Knowing they were in for a long struggle for their faith, many Christians decided to turn off all electronic devices to prevent the government from tracking their movements. This practice made it difficult for mission organizations to provide Bibles or other assistance to the church in Shaanxi. But by the end of the decade, almost all missionary groups had already ceased working in China.

New challenges in the 2020s

The 2020s began with new challenges both for the church in Shaanxi and society as a whole as the Covid virus spread after its breakout at Wuhan in Hubei Province, which borders Shaanxi to the south. A succession of lengthy lockdowns and Xi Jinping's "zero Covid" eradication policy meant that the lives of the entire population were affected and the economy was severely constrained.

The body of Christ in Shaanxi also had to find new ways to meet and communicate the gospel. Many churches took to social media to hold virtual meetings. But that idea was soon discarded after the government launched a series of raids and arrested church leaders, some even being dragged away while in the middle of their live broadcast. The Chinese church quickly learned that claims by companies like Zoom that their product was safe from Chinese Communist Party surveillance were nonsense. In 2022 a new law was passed that essentially stripped Christians in China from the right to communicate on the internet.

Meanwhile, the Chinese Communist Party seized the opportunity provided by the societal dislocation caused by Covid to crack down even harder against Christians. Each month seemed to bring new laws aimed at controlling—and ultimately destroying—the church. More traditional forms of persecution also continued unabated throughout Shaanxi.

A Christian couple, Chang Yuchun, aged 53, and his wife, Liu Chenhui, aged 44, had run a bookstore that sold Bibles and Christian books for years in Xi'an City. However the Communist authorities felt threatened by this unassuming couple and their literature and charged them with "subversion of state power." Additional charges followed, and on November 16, 2021, Chang and Liu were each sentenced to seven years in prison. They were also fined 500,000 Yuan (about US $75,000) for printing unauthorized books. The court ordered the sale of their house and car to pay the fine, and their four children were sent to live with Li's impoverished and elderly parents.[6]

In June 2022, Long Kehai, a member of the Early Rain Covenant Church, was sent to prison for his faith. His last Facebook posts to friends said, "Goodbye, friends. I will be taken away by national security officers from my new house. What awaits me? Everyone knows!"[7] Long had worked for the China Railway Xi'an Group before an earlier arrest by the Shaanxi authorities in March 2019. He was charged with the generic "crime" of "picking quarrels and provoking trouble." His church requested prayer after his arrest, saying of Long Kehai, "Long is passionate about justice and testifies to the gospel with joy. He has suffered a lot for the sake of justice, and it is not unusual for him to be persecuted, expelled, and detained. May the Lord keep him steadfast, protect him from illegal treatment, and strengthen his faith."[8]

Just a mere handful of arrests of Christians in Shaanxi were ever reported. In addition to Chang, Liu, and Long, who are languishing in prison for their faith as you read this book, hundreds of other unnamed Christians across Shaanxi have been similarly arrested and detained. Some have been incarcerated in formal prisons, while others simply vanished into "black jails"—secret facilities where the authorities mercilessly torture and often kill their victims.

After more than a millennium of Christians being barbarically treated in the "cradle of Chinese civilization," the body of Christ in Shaanxi Province long for the day when a trumpet shall sound and the Lord Jesus Christ shall return in glory to receive His children and to wreak vengeance on the enemies of the gospel.

The Future of the Church in Shaanxi

As we reach the end of our look at the great things God has done in the cradle of Chinese civilization, there is much for which to thank the Lord Jesus Christ. We have learned how the first Chinese people had knowledge of God's creation and the universal flood, and that the very structure of some Chinese characters appears to reflect biblical teachings.

Shaanxi gave the world great inventions including the compass, paper, printing, and gunpowder. Being the southern terminus of the famous Silk Road, the province was also the first place in China to receive the gospel, and the first known church building still stands today near Xi'an, almost 1,400 years after it was erected. Despite these auspicious beginnings, the history of Christianity in Shaanxi has been something of a paradox. Although Nestorian Christians spread the faith in Shaanxi from the seventh century—and signs of Christian influence can be traced back to the dawn of the faith—many centuries passed before Catholics arrived in the province in the 1320s, and many believers suffered martyrdom as they sought to establish churches.

After hundreds of years of spiritual decay, saving faith in Jesus Christ had largely withered in Shaanxi, and only a modest number of Catholics were found in the province by the time the first Evangelicals arrived in the 1870s. Eight decades of missionary endeavor followed, and the kingdom of God was planted in many parts of the province. However, the faith never quite took hold as it did in other regions of China. The conservative, skeptical nature of the Shaanxi natives made it difficult for people to freely embrace the good news of Jesus.

As the tables in the following pages show, Shaanxi Province is currently home to approximately 3.4 million professing Christians, or 8.6 percent of the population. Of those who identify as followers of Jesus, 2.7 million are Evangelical Christians—1.9 million who attend unregistered house churches and 800,000 members of state-controlled Three-Self churches—and the province contains an additional 650,000 Catholics. These numbers may be impressive compared to many countries in Europe and other parts of the world, but in China, Shaanxi ranks below most of its neighboring provinces for the numerical size and influence of the body of Christ. Whereas provinces like Henan and Anhui have been renowned as hubs of white-hot revival over the past forty years, Shaanxi has not experienced a similar widespread outpouring of the Holy Spirit.

Despite its comparatively slow growth, the Shaanxi church has recently blossomed, and today the province is filled with multitudes of faithful believers who, by the power of God's Spirit, continue spreading the light of the gospel.

Appendix

Table 1: Evangelical Christians in Shaanxi (1876–2020)

(both Three-Self and house churches)

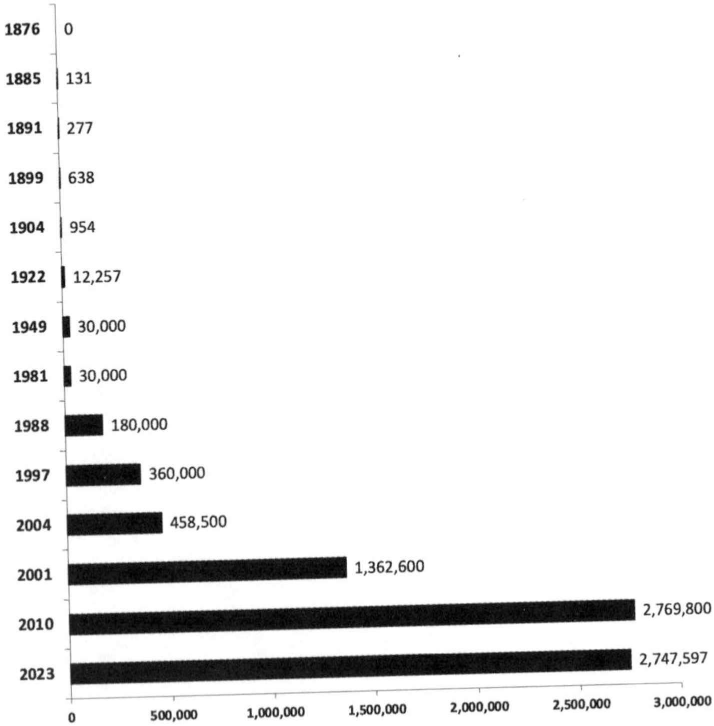

Sources for Table 1:

0	(1876)
131	(1885 – Austin, *China's Millions*)
277	(1891 – Austin, *China's Millions*)
638	(1899 – Austin, *China's Millions*)
954	(1904 – *China's Millions*, November 1905)
12,257	(1922 – Stauffer, *The Christian Occupation of China*)
30,000	(1949 – Lambert, *China's Christian Millions*)
30,000*	(1981 – *Bai Shing*)
180,000*	(1988 – *Tianfeng*, September 1988)
360,000*	(1997 – *Amity News Service*, September 1997)
458,500*	(2004 – *Amity News Service*, November-December 2004)
1,362,600	(2001 – Johnstone & Mandryk, *Operation World*)
2,769,800	(2010 – Mandryk, *Operation World*)
2,747,597	(2023 – Hattaway, *The China Chronicles*)

* These sources may only refer to registered church estimates. TSPM figures typically only count adult baptized members.

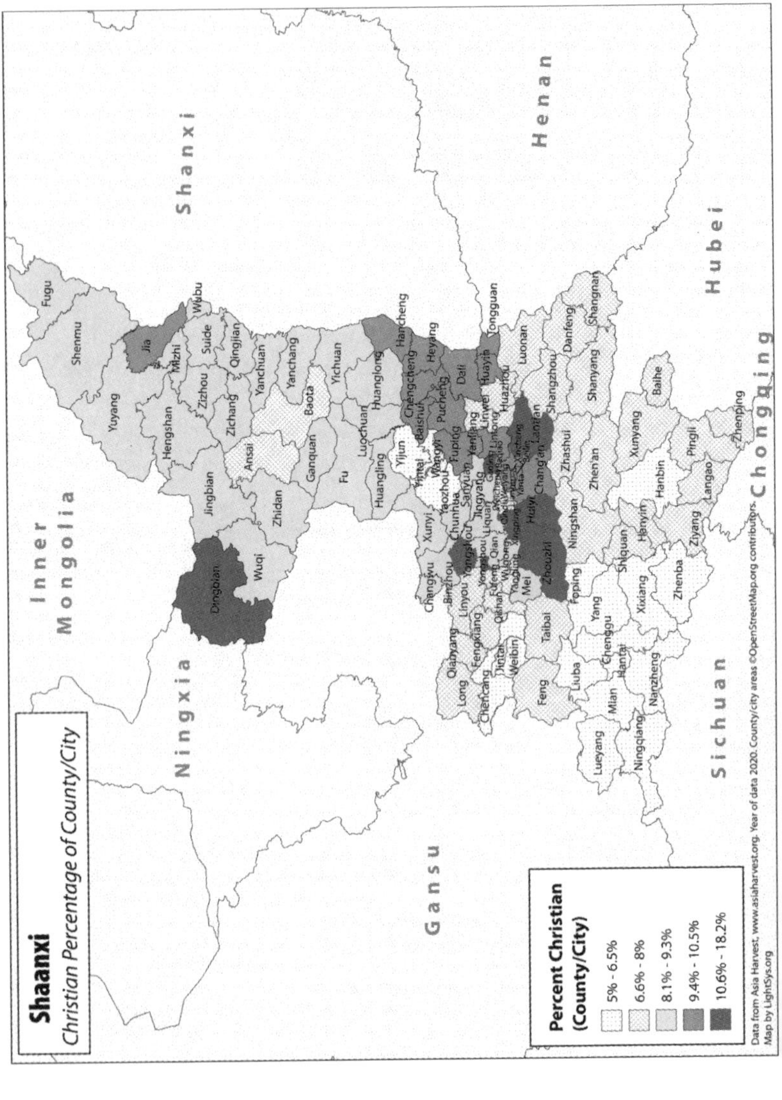
Shaanxi
Christian Percentage of County/City
Inner Mongolia
Shanxi
Henan
Hubei
Chongqing
Sichuan
Gansu
Ningxia
Percent Christian (County/City)
5% - 6.5%
6.6% - 8%
8.1% - 9.3%
9.4% - 10.5%
10.6% - 18.2%
Data from Asia Harvest, www.asiaharvest.org. Year of data 2020. County/city areas ©OpenStreetMap.org contributors.
Map by LightSys.org

Table 2. All Christians in Shaanxi

Shaanxi 陕西		POPULATION					CHRISTIANS							
							Evangelicals			Catholics			Total Christians	
Location		Census 2000	Census 2010	Growth	Growth (percent)	Estimate 2020	TSPM	House church	TOTAL Evangelicals	CPA	House church	TOTAL Catholics	TOTAL	Percent of 2020 population
Ankang Prefecture	安康市													
Baihe County	白河县	180,235	163,395	-16,840	-9.34%	146,555	3,224	7,093	**10,317**	586	703	**1,290**	**11,607**	7.92%
Hanbin District	汉滨区	843,426	870,126	26,700	3.17%	896,826	11,659	25,649	**37,308**	3,587	4,305	**7,892**	**45,200**	5.04%
Hanyin County	汉阴县	240,359	246,147	5,788	2.41%	251,935	5,543	12,194	**17,736**	1,008	1,209	**2,217**	**19,953**	7.92%
Langao County	岚皋县	148,311	154,157	5,846	3.94%	160,003	3,520	7,744	**11,264**	640	768	**1,408**	**12,672**	7.92%
Ningshan County	宁陕县	75,778	70,435	-5,343	-7.05%	65,092	1,432	3,150	**4,582**	260	312	**573**	**5,155**	7.92%
Pingli County	平利县	201,392	192,959	-8,433	-4.19%	184,526	4,060	8,931	**12,991**	738	886	**1,624**	**14,614**	7.92%
Shiquan County	石泉县	159,503	171,097	11,594	7.27%	182,691	4,019	8,842	**12,861**	731	877	**1,608**	**14,469**	7.92%
Xunyang County	旬阳县	426,173	426,677	504	0.12%	427,181	9,398	20,676	**30,074**	1,709	2,050	**3,759**	**33,833**	7.92%
Zhenping County	镇坪县	53,719	50,966	-2,753	-5.12%	48,213	1,061	2,334	**3,394**	193	231	**424**	**3,818**	7.92%
Ziyang County	紫阳县	285,018	283,947	-1,071	-0.38%	282,876	6,223	13,691	**19,914**	1,132	1,358	**2,489**	**22,404**	7.92%
		2,613,914	**2,629,906**	15,992	0.61%	**2,645,898**	50,138	110,304	**160,443**	10,584	12,700	**23,284**	**183,727**	6.94%
Baoji Prefecture	宝鸡市													
Chencang District	陈仓区	729,126	595,075	-134,051	-18.39%	461,024	6,454	14,200	**20,654**	3,227	3,873	**7,100**	**27,754**	6.02%
Feng County	凤县	104,633	105,492	859	0.82%	106,351	2,021	4,445	**6,466**	744	893	**1,638**	**8,104**	7.62%
Fengxiang County	凤翔县	484,464	483,471	-993	-0.20%	482,478	9,167	20,168	**29,335**	3,377	4,053	**7,430**	**36,765**	7.62%
Fufeng County	扶风县	438,324	416,402	-21,922	-5.00%	394,480	7,495	16,489	**23,984**	2,761	3,314	**6,075**	**30,059**	7.62%
Jintai District	金台区	272,193	394,538	122,345	44.95%	516,883	7,236	15,920	**23,156**	3,618	4,342	**7,960**	**31,116**	6.02%
Linyou County	麟游县	85,782	90,728	4,946	5.77%	95,674	1,818	3,999	**5,817**	670	804	**1,473**	**7,290**	7.62%
Long County	陇县	241,751	248,901	7,150	2.96%	256,051	4,865	10,703	**15,568**	1,792	2,151	**3,943**	**19,511**	7.62%
Mei County	眉县	290,315	299,990	9,675	3.33%	309,665	5,884	12,944	**18,828**	4,026	4,831	**8,856**	**27,684**	8.94%
Qianyang County	千阳县	121,532	123,959	2,427	2.00%	126,386	2,401	5,283	**7,684**	885	1,062	**1,946**	**9,631**	7.62%
Qishan County	岐山县	446,579	459,064	12,485	2.80%	471,549	8,959	19,711	**28,670**	3,301	3,961	**7,262**	**35,932**	7.62%
Taibai County	太白县	51,332	50,928	-404	-0.79%	50,524	960	2,112	**3,072**	354	424	**778**	**3,850**	7.62%
Weibin District	渭滨区	328,184	448,189	120,005	36.57%	568,194	7,955	17,500	**25,455**	3,977	4,773	**8,750**	**34,205**	6.02%
		3,594,215	**3,716,737**	122,522	3.41%	**3,839,259**	65,215	143,474	**208,689**	28,733	34,479	**63,212**	**271,901**	7.08%
Hanzhong Prefecture	汉中市													
Chenggu County	城固县	455,408	464,903	9,495	2.08%	474,398	6,167	13,568	**19,735**	4,270	5,123	**9,393**	**29,128**	6.14%
Foping County	佛坪县	33,695	30,075	-3,620	-10.74%	26,455	344	757	**1,101**	238	286	**524**	**1,624**	6.14%
Hantai District	汉台区	503,871	534,923	31,052	6.16%	565,975	6,226	13,697	**19,922**	5,094	6,113	**11,206**	**31,129**	5.50%
Liuba County	留坝县	46,294	43,398	-2,896	-6.26%	40,502	527	1,158	**1,685**	365	437	**802**	**2,487**	6.14%
Lueyang County	略阳县	201,498	201,645	147	0.07%	201,792	2,623	5,771	**8,395**	1,816	2,179	**3,995**	**12,390**	6.14%
Mian County	勉县	397,131	388,123	-9,008	-2.27%	379,115	4,928	10,843	**15,771**	3,412	4,094	**7,506**	**23,278**	6.14%
Nanzheng County	南郑县	478,782	471,634	-7,148	-1.49%	464,486	6,038	13,284	**19,323**	4,180	5,016	**9,197**	**28,519**	6.14%

Table of All Christians in Shaanxi

Shaanxi 陕西		POPULATION					CHRISTIANS							
							Evangelicals			Catholics			Total Christians	
Location		Census 2000	Census 2010	Growth	Growth (percent)	Estimate 2020	TSPM	House church	TOTAL Evangelicals	CPA	House church	TOTAL Catholics	TOTAL	Percent of 2020 population
Ningqiang County	宁强县	313,395	308,885	-4,510	-1.44%	304,375	3,957	8,705	12,662	2,739	3,287	6,027	18,689	6.14%
Xixiang County	西乡县	345,074	341,812	-3,262	-0.95%	338,550	4,401	9,683	14,084	3,047	3,656	6,703	20,787	6.14%
Yang County	洋县	384,374	383,981	-393	-0.10%	383,588	4,987	10,971	15,957	3,452	4,143	7,595	23,552	6.14%
Zhenba County	镇巴县	251,522	246,817	-4,705	-1.87%	242,112	3,147	6,924	10,072	2,179	2,615	4,794	14,866	6.14%
		3,411,044	**3,416,196**	5,152	0.15%	**3,421,348**	43,346	95,360	138,706	30,792	36,951	67,743	206,449	6.03%
Shangluo Prefecture	商洛市													
Danfeng County	丹凤县	295,833	295,349	-484	-0.16%	294,865	6,192	13,623	19,815	1,179	1,415	2,595	22,410	7.60%
Luonan County	洛南县	455,183	441,613	-13,570	-2.98%	428,043	8,989	19,776	28,764	1,712	2,055	3,767	32,531	7.60%
Shangnan County	商南县	227,636	221,569	-6,067	-2.67%	215,502	4,526	9,956	14,482	862	1,034	1,896	16,378	7.60%
Shangzhou District	商州区	530,883	531,696	813	0.15%	532,509	9,585	21,087	30,673	2,130	2,556	4,686	35,359	6.64%
Shanyang County	山阳县	400,993	422,255	21,262	5.30%	443,517	9,314	20,490	29,804	1,774	2,129	3,903	33,707	7.60%
Zhashui County	柞水县	158,421	153,398	-5,023	-3.17%	148,375	3,116	6,855	9,971	594	712	1,306	11,277	7.60%
Zhen'an County	镇安县	276,488	275,862	-626	-0.23%	275,236	5,780	12,716	18,496	1,101	1,321	2,422	20,918	7.60%
		2,345,437	**2,341,742**	-3,695	-0.16%	**2,338,047**	47,501	104,503	152,005	9,352	11,223	20,575	172,579	7.38%
Tongchuan Prefecture	铜川市													
Wangyi District	王益区	190,630	200,231	9,601	5.04%	209,832	2,938	6,463	9,400	839	1,007	1,847	11,247	5.36%
Yaozhou District	耀州区	295,202	325,537	30,335	10.28%	355,872	4,982	10,961	15,943	1,423	1,708	3,132	19,075	5.36%
Yijun County	宜君县	93,141	91,160	-1,981	-2.13%	89,179	1,516	3,335	4,851	357	428	785	5,636	6.32%
Yintai County	印台区	213,627	217,509	3,882	1.82%	221,391	3,764	8,280	12,044	886	1,063	1,948	13,992	6.32%
		792,600	**834,437**	41,837	5.28%	**876,274**	13,200	29,039	42,239	3,505	4,206	7,711	49,950	5.70%
Weinan Prefecture	渭南市													
Baishui County	白水县	277,716	279,679	1,963	0.71%	281,642	7,604	16,730	24,334	1,127	1,352	2,478	26,812	9.52%
Chengcheng County	澄城县	372,150	386,150	14,000	3.76%	400,150	10,804	23,769	34,573	1,601	1,921	3,521	38,094	9.52%
Dali County	大荔县	706,948	693,392	-13,556	-1.92%	679,836	18,356	40,382	58,738	2,719	3,263	5,983	64,720	9.52%
Fuping County	富平县	747,942	743,385	-4,557	-0.61%	738,828	19,948	43,886	63,835	2,955	3,546	6,502	70,336	9.52%
Hancheng City	韩城市	387,041	391,164	4,123	1.07%	395,287	11,068	24,350	35,418	1,581	1,897	3,479	38,896	9.84%
Heyang County	合阳县	432,313	436,441	4,128	0.95%	440,569	11,895	26,170	38,065	1,762	2,115	3,877	41,942	9.52%
Huayin City	华阴市	242,488	258,113	15,625	6.44%	273,738	7,665	16,862	24,527	1,095	1,314	2,409	26,936	9.84%
Huazhou District	华州区	350,228	322,148	-28,080	-8.02%	294,068	5,881	12,939	18,820	1,176	1,412	2,588	21,408	7.28%
Linwei District	临渭区	888,866	877,142	-11,724	-1.32%	865,418	17,308	38,078	55,387	3,462	4,154	7,616	63,002	7.28%
Pucheng County	蒲城县	738,675	743,000	4,325	0.59%	747,325	20,178	44,391	64,569	2,989	3,587	6,576	71,145	9.52%
Tongguan County	潼关县	147,833	155,463	7,630	5.16%	163,093	4,404	9,688	14,091	652	783	1,435	15,526	9.52%
		5,292,200	**5,286,077**	-6,123	-0.12%	**5,279,954**	135,111	297,245	432,356	21,120	25,344	46,464	478,820	9.07%
Xi'an Prefecture	西安市													
Baqiao District	灞桥区	494,084	595,124	101,040	20.45%	696,164	16,012	35,226	51,238	7,658	9,189	16,847	68,085	9.78%
Beilin District	碑林区	698,755	614,710	-84,045	-12.03%	530,665	12,205	26,852	39,057	5,837	7,005	12,842	51,899	9.78%

Table of All Christians in Shaanxi

Shaanxi 陕西		POPULATION					CHRISTIANS							
							Evangelicals			Catholics			Total Christians	
Location		Census 2000	Census 2010	Growth	Growth (percent)	Estimate 2020	TSPM	House church	TOTAL Evangelicals	CPA	House church	TOTAL Catholics	TOTAL	Percent of 2020 population
Chang'an District	长安区	864,269	1,083,285	219,016	25.34%	1,302,301	29,953	65,896	95,849	14,325	17,190	31,516	127,365	9.78%
Gaoling District	高陵区	222,367	333,477	111,110	49.97%	444,587	11,559	25,430	36,990	4,890	5,869	10,759	47,749	10.74%
Huiyi District (Hu County)	鄠邑区	549,252	556,377	7,125	1.30%	563,502	15,215	33,472	48,687	6,199	7,438	13,637	62,323	11.06%
Lantian County	蓝田县	560,283	514,026	-46,257	-8.26%	467,769	12,630	27,785	40,415	5,145	6,175	11,320	51,735	11.06%
Lianhu District	莲湖区	631,224	698,513	67,289	10.66%	765,802	17,613	38,750	56,363	8,424	10,109	18,532	74,895	9.78%
Lintong District	临潼区	639,581	655,875	16,294	2.55%	672,169	15,460	34,012	49,472	7,394	8,873	16,266	65,738	9.78%
Weiyang District	未央区	460,416	806,811	346,395	75.24%	1,153,206	26,524	58,352	84,876	12,685	15,222	27,908	112,784	9.78%
Xincheng District	新城区	526,718	589,739	63,021	11.96%	652,760	15,013	33,030	48,043	7,180	8,616	15,797	63,840	9.78%
Yanliang District	阎良区	235,672	278,604	42,932	18.22%	321,536	7,395	16,270	23,665	3,537	4,244	7,781	31,446	9.78%
Yanta District	雁塔区	795,058	1,178,529	383,471	48.23%	1,562,000	35,926	79,037	114,963	17,182	20,618	37,800	152,764	9.78%
Zhouzhi County	周至县	597,153	562,768	-34,385	-5.76%	528,383	14,266	31,386	45,652	13,738	16,486	30,224	75,876	14.36%
		7,274,832	8,467,838	1,193,006	16.40%	9,660,844	229,772	505,498	735,270	114,195	137,034	251,229	986,499	10.21%
Xianyang Prefecture	咸阳市													
Binzhou City (Bin County)	彬州市	313,216	323,256	10,040	3.21%	333,296	8,666	19,065	27,730	1,333	1,600	2,933	30,663	9.20%
Changwu County	长武县	167,274	167,570	296	0.18%	167,866	4,365	9,602	13,966	671	806	1,477	15,444	9.20%
Chunhua County	淳化县	186,867	193,377	6,510	3.48%	199,887	5,197	11,434	16,631	800	959	1,759	18,390	9.20%
Jingyang County	泾阳县	485,791	487,749	1,958	0.40%	489,707	12,732	28,011	40,744	1,959	2,351	4,309	45,053	9.20%
Liquan County	礼泉县	455,278	447,771	-7,507	-1.65%	440,264	11,447	25,183	36,630	1,761	2,113	3,874	40,504	9.20%
Qian County	乾县	544,846	527,088	-17,758	-3.26%	509,330	13,243	29,134	42,376	2,037	2,445	4,482	46,858	9.20%
Qindu District	秦都区	449,820	507,093	57,273	12.73%	564,366	12,416	27,315	39,731	2,257	2,709	4,966	44,698	7.92%
Sanyuan County	三原县	388,842	403,524	14,682	3.78%	418,206	10,873	23,921	34,795	1,673	2,007	3,680	38,475	9.20%
Weicheng District	渭城区	366,099	438,327	72,228	19.73%	510,555	11,232	24,711	35,943	2,042	2,451	4,493	40,436	7.92%
Wugong County	武功县	389,394	411,312	21,918	5.63%	433,230	11,264	24,781	36,045	1,733	2,080	3,812	39,857	9.20%
Xingping City	兴平市	551,523	541,554	-9,969	-1.81%	531,585	17,542	38,593	56,135	2,126	2,552	4,678	60,813	11.44%
Xunyi County	旬邑县	261,666	261,566	-100	-0.04%	261,466	6,798	14,956	21,754	1,046	1,255	2,301	24,055	9.20%
Yangling District	杨陵区	137,941	201,172	63,231	45.84%	264,403	5,817	12,797	18,614	1,058	1,269	2,327	20,941	7.92%
Yongshou County	永寿县	187,446	184,642	-2,804	-1.50%	181,838	7,819	17,202	25,021	727	873	1,600	26,621	14.64%
		4,886,003	5,096,001	209,998	4.30%	5,305,999	139,411	306,704	446,115	21,224	25,469	46,693	492,808	9.29%
Yan'an Prefecture	延安市													
Ansai District	安塞区	160,771	171,552	10,781	6.71%	182,333	4,011	8,825	12,836	729	875	1,605	14,441	7.92%
Baota District	宝塔区	403,868	475,234	71,366	17.67%	546,600	12,025	26,455	38,481	2,186	2,624	4,810	43,291	7.92%
Fu County	富县	141,760	149,727	7,967	5.62%	157,694	4,100	9,020	13,120	631	757	1,388	14,508	9.20%
Ganquan County	甘泉县	76,705	77,188	483	0.63%	77,671	2,019	4,443	6,462	311	373	684	7,146	9.20%
Huangling County	黄陵县	133,988	129,803	-4,185	-3.12%	125,618	3,266	7,185	10,451	502	603	1,105	11,557	9.20%
Huanglong County	黄龙县	49,039	49,392	353	0.72%	49,745	1,293	2,845	4,139	199	239	438	4,577	9.20%

Shaanxi 陕西		POPULATION					CHRISTIANS							
							Evangelicals			Catholics			Total Christians	
Location		Census 2000	Census 2010	Growth	Growth (percent)	Estimate 2020	TSPM	House church	TOTAL Evangelicals	CPA	House church	TOTAL Catholics	TOTAL	Percent of 2020 population
Luochuan County	洛川县	200,573	220,684	20,111	10.03%	240,795	6,261	13,773	**20,034**	963	1,156	**2,119**	**22,153**	9.20%
Wuqi County	吴起县	112,524	145,061	32,537	28.92%	177,598	4,618	10,159	**14,776**	710	852	**1,563**	**16,339**	9.20%
Yanchang County	延长县	128,551	125,391	-3,160	-2.46%	122,231	3,178	6,992	**10,170**	489	587	**1,076**	**11,245**	9.20%
Yanchuan County	延川县	164,902	168,375	3,473	2.11%	171,848	4,468	9,830	**14,298**	687	825	**1,512**	**15,810**	9.20%
Yichuan County	宜川县	111,685	117,203	5,518	4.94%	122,721	3,191	7,020	**10,210**	491	589	**1,080**	**11,290**	9.20%
Zhidan County	志丹县	124,449	140,489	16,040	12.89%	156,529	4,070	8,953	**13,023**	626	751	**1,377**	**14,401**	9.20%
Zichang County	子长县	207,972	216,910	8,938	4.30%	225,848	5,872	12,919	**18,791**	903	1,084	**1,987**	**20,778**	9.20%
		2,016,787	**2,187,009**	170,222	8.44%	**2,357,231**	58,372	128,419	**186,791**	9,429	11,315	**20,744**	**207,535**	8.80%
Yulin Prefecture	榆林市													
Dingbian County	定边县	285,416	319,370	33,954	11.90%	353,324	7,773	17,101	**24,874**	21,906	17,525	**39,431**	**64,305**	18.20%
Fugu County	府谷县	224,957	260,585	35,628	15.84%	296,213	6,517	14,337	**20,853**	3,555	2,844	**6,398**	**27,252**	9.20%
Hengshan District	横山区	294,674	288,053	-6,621	-2.25%	281,432	5,629	12,383	**18,012**	3,377	2,702	**6,079**	**24,091**	8.56%
Jia County	佳县	238,496	204,666	-33,830	-14.18%	170,836	4,100	9,020	**13,120**	2,050	1,640	**3,690**	**16,810**	9.84%
Jingbian County	靖边县	272,836	355,939	83,103	30.46%	439,042	9,659	21,250	**30,909**	5,269	4,215	**9,483**	**40,392**	9.20%
Mizhi County	米脂县	200,626	154,953	-45,673	-22.77%	109,280	2,404	5,289	**7,693**	1,311	1,049	**2,360**	**10,054**	9.20%
Qingjian County	清涧县	176,644	128,938	-47,706	-27.01%	81,232	1,787	3,932	**5,719**	975	780	**1,755**	**7,473**	9.20%
Shenmu City	神木市	360,774	455,493	94,719	26.25%	550,212	12,105	26,630	**38,735**	6,603	5,282	**11,885**	**50,620**	9.20%
Suide County	绥德县	310,880	296,088	-14,792	-4.76%	281,296	6,189	13,615	**19,803**	3,376	2,700	**6,076**	**25,879**	9.20%
Wubu County	吴堡县	72,781	75,748	2,967	4.08%	78,715	1,732	3,810	**5,542**	945	756	**1,700**	**7,242**	9.20%
Yuyang District	榆阳区	451,337	637,617	186,280	41.27%	823,897	16,478	36,251	**52,729**	9,887	7,909	**17,796**	**70,526**	8.56%
Zizhou County	子洲县	248,619	173,986	-74,633	-30.02%	99,353	2,186	4,809	**6,994**	1,192	954	**2,146**	**9,140**	9.20%
		3,138,040	**3,351,436**	213,396	6.80%	**3,564,832**	76,557	168,426	**244,983**	60,444	48,355	**108,800**	**353,783**	9.92%
Totals		**35,365,072**	**37,327,379**	**1,962,307**	5.55%	**39,289,686**	**858,624**	**1,888,973**	**2,747,597**	**309,378**	**347,076**	**656,453**	**3,404,051**	8.66%

Researching Christians in China

For centuries, people have been curious to know how many Christians live in China. When Marco Polo made his famous journey to "the Orient" 750 years ago, he documented the existence of Nestorian churches and monasteries in various places, to the fascination of people in Europe.

Since I started traveling to China in the 1980s, I have found that believers around the world are eager to know how many Christians there are in China. Many people are aware that God has done a remarkable work in the world's most populous country, but little research has been done to put a figure on this phenomenon. In recent decades, wildly divergent estimates have been published, ranging from 20 million to 230 million.

Methodology

In the following table, I provide estimates of the number of Christians in Shaanxi. Full tables of the other provinces of China can be found at the Asia Harvest website (See the "The Church in China" link under the Resources tab at www.asiaharvest.org). My survey provides figures for Christians of every description. It is arranged in four main categories: the Three-Self Patriotic Movement, the Evangelical house churches, the Catholic Patriotic Association, and the Catholic house churches. I have supplied statistics for all 2,800 cities and counties within every province, municipality, and autonomous region of China.

The information was gathered from a wide variety of sources. More than 2,000 published sources have been noted in the tables published online, including a multitude of books, journals, magazine articles, and reports that I have accumulated meticulously over many years. I have also conducted hundreds of hours of interviews with key house church leaders from many different branches of God's work throughout China.

In compiling the data, I began with this assumption: that in any given place in the country there are no Christians at all, until I have a figure from a documented source or can make an intelligent estimate based on information gathered from Christian leaders in China. I wanted to put aside all personal bias, input all the information I found, and see what the totals came to.

A Note about Security

None of the information provided in these tables is new to the Chinese government. Beijing has clearly already thoroughly researched the spread of Christianity throughout the country, as shown by the Director of the Religious Affairs Bureau Ye Xiaowen's 2006 announcement that there were then 130 million Christians in China.[1] In December 2009, the national newspaper *China Daily* interviewed scholar Liu Peng who had spent years researching religion for the Chinese Academy of Social Sciences. Liu claimed the "house churches have at least 50 million followers nationwide."[2] His figure at the time was consistent with my research.

After consulting various house church leaders in China, all of them were content that this information should be published, as long as the survey focuses on statistics and avoids specific information such as the names and locations of Christian leaders, as it does.

The Chinese Church in Perspective

All discussion of how many Christians there are in China should be tempered by the realization that over 90 percent of its present population face a Christ-less eternity. Hundreds of millions of individuals have yet to hear the gospel. House church leaders in China have told me how ashamed and burdened they feel that so many of their countrymen and women do not yet know Jesus Christ. This burden motivates them to do whatever it takes to preach the gospel among every ethnic group and in every city, town, and village—to every individual—in China, and to do whatever necessary to see Christ exalted throughout the land.

May we humbly give thanks to the Living God for the great things He has done in China. We are privileged to live in a remarkable time in human history, like in the days prophesied by the Prophet Habakkuk:

> *Look at the nations and watch—*
> *and be utterly amazed.*
> *For I am going to do something in your days*
> *that you would not believe,*
> *even if you were told* —Habakkuk 1:5.

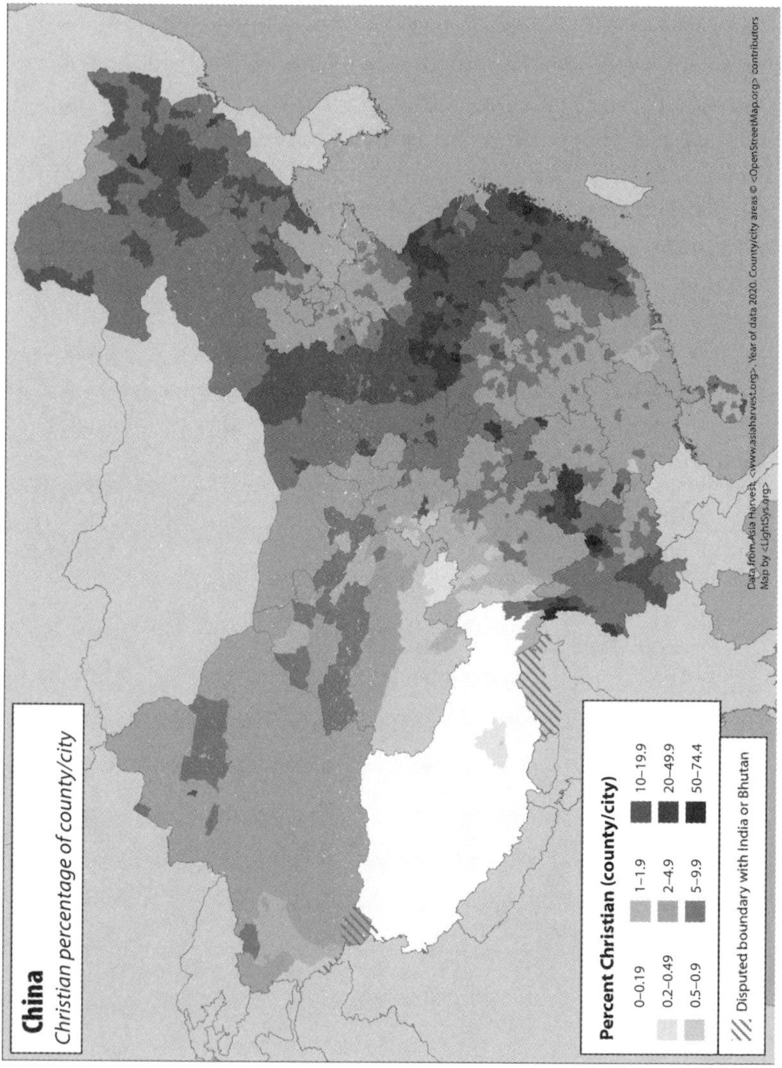
China
Christian percentage of county/city
Percent Christian (county/city)
0–0.19
0.2–0.49
0.5–0.9
1–1.9
2–4.9
5–9.9
10–19.9
20–49.9
50–74.4
Disputed boundary with India or Bhutan
Data from Asia Harvest <www.asiaharvest.org>. Year of data 2020. County/city areas © <OpenStreetMap.org> contributors
Map by <LightSys.org>

Notes

Note: after first mention, short titles are used for the sources.

The China Chronicles overview

1 Quoted in R. Wardlaw Thompson, *Griffith John: The Story of Fifty Years in China* (London: Religious Tract Society, 1908), p. 65.

Introduction

1 Leo J. Moser, *The Chinese Mosaic: The Peoples and Provinces of China* (Boulder, CO: Westview Press, 1985), p. 75.
2 Jonathan Fenby, *The Dragon Throne: Dynasties of Imperial China 1600 BC - AD 1912* (London: Quercus, 2008), p. 165.
3 Marco Polo, *The Travels of Marco Polo: The Complete Yule-Cordier Edition*, Vol. 2 (New York: Dover, 1903), pp. 24–25.
4 Quoted in Manuel Komroff (ed.), *The Travels of Marco Polo, the Venetian* (New York: Horace Liverlight, 1926), p. 183.
5 See "1556 Shaanxi earthquake" at https://en.wikipedia.org.
6 "Dungan Revolt (1862–1877)," Wikipedia (n.d.), www.wikipedia.com.

The Cradle of Chinese Civilization

1 Other sources go back even further to the legendary ruler Youchao who is said to have ruled in China for approximately two centuries from 3162 BC.
2 The Chinese have identified the village of Banpo as probably the first community in China. The Banpo Neolithic Village, located in the East suburb of Xi'an, is the second most visited tourist attraction in the province after the Terracotta Soldiers. The government claims Banpo was first inhabited between about 4500 and 3750 BC.
3 Quoted in Wu Qinglong, et al., "Response to Comments on 'Outburst flood at 1920 BCE supports Historicity of China's Great Flood and the Xia dynasty,'" *Science* 355 (31 March 2017): pp. 579–82, quote p. 579.
4 Lo-pi, author of the *Lu-shi*, quoted in Joseph Marie Amiot, Francois Bourgeois, et al., *Memoris des Chinoise*, Vol. 1 (Paris: Nyon, 1776), p. 157.

5 David Crockett Graham, "Songs and Stories of the Ch'uan Miao," *Smithsonian Miscellaneous Collections* 123, no. 1 (Washington DC: Smithsonian Institute, 1954): p. 59.

6 Chan Kei Thong with Charlene Fu, *Faith of Our Fathers: Discovering God in Ancient China* (Singapore: Campus Crusade for Christ, 2007), pp. 123–26.

7 Chan with Fu, *Faith of Our Fathers*, p. 130.

8 Chan with Fu, *Faith of Our Fathers*, p. 132.

9 Chan with Fu, *Faith of Our Fathers*, p. 134.

10 Spencer M. Harrington, "Vintage Altar of Heaven," *Archaeology Magazine* Archive (March–April 2000).

11 Chan with Fu, *Faith of Our Fathers*, p. 113.

12 Stephen Chen, "Scientists Find What Could Be the Face of a King at an Ancient Pyramid in China," *South China Morning Post* (9 August 2022).

13 Brook Larmer, "Mysterious Carvings and Evidence of Human Sacrifice Uncovered in Ancient City," *National Geographic* (7 August 2020): p. 579.

14 Chen, "Scientists Find What Could Be the Face of a King."

15 Scholars disagree on the approximate timeframe for the Xia Dynasty. The 2205 to 1600 BC estimate is based on traditional chronology. Liu Xin believes the dynasty ended earlier, in 1766 BC, while a project commissioned by the Chinese government in 1996 concluded that the Xia existed between 2070 and 1600 BC.

16 Although most historians agree on the basic fact of Shang rule, estimates of the years when the dynasty came to power and when it was replaced differ greatly. According to the traditional chronology based on calculations made approximately two thousand years ago by Liu Xin, the Shang ruled from 1766 to 1122 BC, but chronology based on the *Bamboo Annals* suggests their rule was later, from 1556 to 1046 BC. A 1996 Chinese government project dated the Shang Dynasty from c. 1600 to 1046 BC, and these dates are the most commonly accepted today.

17 John Ross, *The Original Religion of China* (Edinburgh: Oliphant, Anderson & Ferrier, 1909), p. 37.

18 *Historical Records*, vol. 38 (Genealogy of Song Wei Zi).

19 *The Works of Mencius*, Book 4, Part 1, Chapter 7. See English translation with notes by James Legge at http://nothingistic.org/library/mencius/.

20 Fenby, *Dragon Throne*, p. 20.

21 Moser, *Chinese Mosaic*, p. 19.

22 Quoted in *China's Millions* (June 1914), p. 76.

23 "Emperor Qianlong: Letter to George III, 1793," University of Southern California, USC US–China Institute.

24 "Emperor Qianlong: Letter to George III, 1793."

25 "Emperor Qianlong: Letter to George III, 1793."
26 It has taken the authorities more than thirty years to excavate one-third of the terracotta warrior pits. They cover a relatively small area and were close to the surface, approximately 10 to 15 feet (3 to 6 meters) deep. The tomb and underground palace of Emperor Qin, however, cover an area thirteen times larger than the warrior pits and are buried about 115 feet (35 meters) below the surface. Initial tests found that the site is extremely fragile, with walls generally made of rammed earth, and that the soil contains high concentrations of mercury which would have a deadly effect on any archaeologists who encountered it. It is unlikely that the secrets of Qin Shihuang's tomb will ever be revealed.
27 Sima Qian quoted in Michael Buckley, et al., *China: A Travel Survival Kit*, 4th ed. (Hawthorn, Australia: Lonely Planet, 1994), pp. 377–78.
28 Chan with Fu, *Faith of Our Fathers*, p. 79.
29 Fenby, *Dragon Throne*, p. 59.
30 Buckley, et al., *China: A Travel Survival Kit*, p. 367.
31 Quoted in Fenby, *Dragon Throne*, p. 123.
32 Construction of the current version of the Xi'an wall commenced during the Ming Dynasty in 1370.
33 Moser, *Chinese Mosaic*, p. 75.

The Bible Revealed in Chinese Writing

1 Jean-Francois Foucquet quoted in Jonathan D. Spence, *The Question of Hu* (New York: Vintage Books, 1989), pp. 44–45.
2 The best book that portrays biblical truth in the Chinese language is probably C. H. Kang and Ethel R. Nelson, *The Discovery of Genesis: How the Truths of Genesis Were Found Hidden in the Chinese Language* (St. Louis, MO: Concordia, 1979).

China's First Christian Influence

1 Samuel Hugh Moffett, *A History of Christianity in Asia, Vol. 1: Beginnings to 1500* (Maryknoll, NY: Orbis, 1998), pp. 13–14.
2 Also known as Liu Gengsheng, Liu Zizheng, and Liu Shang.
3 See "Liu Xin (scholar)," Wikipedia (n.d.), https://en.wikipedia.org/wiki/Liu_Xin_(scholar).
4 Also known as Liu Zijun and Liu Xiu.
5 Quoted in James Hefley and Marti Hefley, *China! Christian Martyrs of the 20th Century: An Excerpt from "By Their Blood"* (Milford, MI: Mott Media, 1978), p. 10.

6 Brent Landau, *Revelation of the Magi: The Lost Tale of the Wise Men's Journey to Bethlehem* (New York: HarperOne, 2010).
7 Brent Landau, in Michelle Healy, "The Story of the 12 Wise Men," *USA Today* (4 December 2010).
8 Landau, *Revelation of the Magi* (2010).
9 Katie Hinman, "Rediscovered Ancient Text Tells a Different Three Wise Men Tale," *ABC News* (23 December 2010).
10 Landau, in Michelle Healy, "The Story of the 12 Wise Men," *USA Today* (4 December 2010).
11 The video "Mystery of the Magi," *ABC News* (24 December 2010) can be viewed on YouTube, https://www.youtube.com/watch?v=R7fggVO37eE.
12 Chan with Fu, *Faith of Our Fathers*, p. 312.
13 Ai was a posthumous name given to this emperor, whose birth name was Liu Xin. "Ai" means "lamentable" and was applied to him because his short reign promised much before failing miserably. He was overthrown after just six years on the throne. Most Chinese historians believe he had a homosexual relationship with a minor official. The tomb of Emperor Ai is located at Xianyang, a few miles west of Xi'an.
14 Chan with Fu, *Faith of Our Fathers*, p. 313.
15 Chan with Fu, *Faith of Our Fathers*, p. 316.
16 *History of the Latter Han Dynasty: Vol. 1, Chronicles of Emperor Guang Wu, 7th Year*, translated by Chan with Fu, *Faith of Our Fathers*, p. 318.
17 Chan with Fu, *Faith of Our Fathers*, p. 318.
18 We-Fan Wang, "Tombstone Carvings from AD 86: Did Christianity Reach China in the First Century?" Lyon Catholic University, *Lettres et Langues* (November 2019). Available online, including pictures of carvings, at https://www.ucly.fr/wp-content/uploads/2019/11/tombstone-carvings-from-ad-86.pdf.
19 Wang Shanshan, "Stones Indicate Earlier Christian Link?" *China Daily* (22 December 2005).
20 Lin Xixiang quoted in Wang, "Stones Indicate."
21 Quoted in John Holzmann (ed.), *The Church of the East: An Edited and Condensed Version of Nestorian Missionary Enterprise* (Littleton, CO: Sonlight Curriculum, 2001), p. 51.

Nestorians in Shaanxi

1 See Paul Hattaway, *Tibet: The Roof of the World*, The China Chronicles Vol. 4 (London: SPCK, 2020), p. 22.
2 Quoted in P. Y. Saeki, *The Nestorian Monument in China* (Tokyo: Maruzen, 1951), pp. 320–21.

3 Martin Luther, *On the Councils and the Church, 1539*, in Eric W. Gritsch, *Church and Ministry III: Luther's Works*, Vol. 41 (Philadelphia: Fortress, 1966), pp. 96–100.
4 See Alopen profile at http://bdcconline.net.
5 Moffett, *History of Christianity in Asia, Vol. 1*, pp. 291–92.
6 Mark Chuanhang Shan, *The History of Christianity in Xinjiang, China: with a General History Background* (Boston: self-published, 2011), p. 20.
7 Martin Palmer, *The Jesus Sutras: Rediscovering the Lost Scrolls of Taoist Christianity* (New York: Ballantine, 2001), p. 18.
8 Martin Palmer, "The Lost Monastery Discoveries of Tang Dynasty Daoist Christianity (Part 1)," an unpublished report seemingly written as a prelude to his book, *The Jesus Sutras*. As the mixed subtitle of his book suggests, Palmer seems to hold a pantheistic faith rather than one with an orthodox biblical foundation. Scholar David Wilmshurst criticizes the book as "new-age fantasy," while the British Christian Tony Lambert says, "Palmer seems to strain every piece of evidence to push his rather New Age agenda to prove that the Nestorians rejoiced in propagating a syncretistic form of Christianity blended with Buddhism and Daoism." Tony Lambert, "The Church of the East," *China Insight* (August–October 2006).
9 If taken literally, this would have meant that there were 358 Nestorian monasteries or churches in China at the time. There is firm evidence for the existence of only eleven. See Moffett, *History of Christianity in Asia, Vol. 1*, p. 293.
10 Moffett, *History of Christianity in Asia, Vol. 1*, p. 294.
11 Fenby, *Dragon Throne*, p. 108.
12 George David Malech, *History of the Syrian Nation and the Old Evangelical-Apostolic Church of the East from Remote Antiquity to the Present Time* (1910, republished Minneapolis, MN: Kessinge, 2010), pp. 245–46.
13 John of Cara, *The Book of the Estate of the Great Kaan, in Henry Yule and Henri Cordier, Cathay and the Way Thither: Being a Collection of Medieval Notices of China, Vol 1* (Tokyo: Kyoyekishosha, 1866), p. 100.
14 Kenneth Scott Latourette, *A History of Christian Missions in China* (New York: Macmillan, 1929), p. 65.
15 Moffett, *History of Christianity in Asia, Vol. 1*, p. 412.
16 James Legge quoted in John Foster, *Church of the T'ang Dynasty* (London: SPCK, 1939), p. 112.
17 Moffett, *History of Christianity in Asia, Vol. 1*, p. 475.

Early Catholics in Shaanxi

1 Moffett, *History of Christianity in Asia, Vol. 1*, p. 475.

2 Latourette, *History of Christian Missions in China*, p. 71.
3 Milton T. Stauffer (ed.), *The Christian Occupation of China* (Shanghai: China Consultation Committee, 1922), p. 458.
4 A. C. Moule, *Christians in China before the Year 1550* (London: SPCK, 1930), p. 9.
5 Schall's full name was Johan Adam Schall von Bell.
6 Luis da Gama, cited in Nicolas Standaert, *Handbook of Christianity in China, Vol. One: 635–1800* (Leiden, Netherlands: Brill, 2001), p. 385.
7 Antoine Thomas, cited in Standaert, *Handbook of Christianity*, p. 385.
8 Antoine Thomas, cited in Standaert, *Handbook of Christianity*, p. 385.
9 Bernward Henry Willeke, *Imperial Government and Catholic Missions in China during the Years 1784–1785* (New York: Franciscan Institute Saint Bonaventure, 1938), p. 93.
10 Willeke, *Imperial Government*, p. 94.
11 Willeke, *Imperial Government*, p. 142.
12 For a profile of Aubin and other Lazarist missionaries in China, see Joseph van den Brandt, *Les Lazaristes en Chine, 1697–1935* (Beijing: Notices Biographiques, 1936).

1870s

1 *Chinese Recorder* (May 1880), p. 194. Just three years earlier in 1870, the number of Catholics was given as 23,000.
2 "Dungan Revolt (1862–1877)," Wikipedia.
3 F. W. Baller, "Pioneer Journey to Shen-si," *China's Millions* (March 1877): p. 35.
4 Baller, "Pioneer Journey to Shen-si," p. 36.
5 Charles Budd, "The Province of Shen-si," *China's Millions* (December 1877): p. 150.
6 James Cameron, "In Journeyings Often, or, Seven Years of Missionary Travel in China and Eastern Thibet," *China's Millions* (May 1884): p. 62.
7 Valerie Griffiths, *Not Less than Everything: The Courageous Women Who Carried the Christian Gospel to China* (Oxford, UK: Monarch, 2004), p. 89.
8 G. F. Easton, "Progress of the Gospel in Han-chung Fu, Shen-si," *Chinese Recorder* (March 1881): pp. 30–31.
9 Easton, "Progress of the Gospel in Han-chung Fu, Shen-si," pp. 31–32.
10 See in the Appendix in "Table 2: All Christians in Shaanxi," p. 241.

1880s

1 Griffiths, *Not Less than Everything*, p. 88. Elizabeth Wilson was not related to Dr. William Wilson who also served at Hanzhong for many years.
2 It is believed Annie Harrison was the first New Zealand missionary to China, arriving in 1891. However, New Zealanders traveled on British passports until 1947, so often their nationality was given as British.
3 Annie Harrison, *China's Millions* (September 1898): p. 174.
4 Wilson married S. Goodman in 1885, who died in 1897. He then married Ely Hanbury in 1898. Note: A different missionary-doctor named William Wilson served in neighboring Shanxi Province.
5 George King, "Work in Han-chung, Shen-si," *China's Millions* (March 1881): p. 32.
6 "Province of Shen-si," *China's Millions* (July 1883): p. 80.
7 George King, "Shen-si Province," *China's Millions* (March 1884): p. 34.
8 Mrs. Easton, "Shen-si Province," *China's Millions* (June 1884): pp. 72–73.
9 Arthur Polhill-Turner, "Good Tidings from Han-chung," *China's Millions* (March 1886): p. 29.
10 "Statistics of the China Inland Mission for January 1888," *China's Millions* (July 1888): p. 92.
11 "Statistics of the China Inland Mission for January 1889," *China's Millions* (July 1889): p. 88.
12 *China's Millions* (August 1897): p. 110.
13 Geraldine Taylor, *Pastor Hsi: A Struggle for Chinese Christianity* (Singapore: OMF Publishing, 1997), p. 218.
14 An extensive chapter on Xi Shengmo's life can be found in the *Shanxi* volume of The China Chronicles.
15 Erik Folke, "The Swedish Mission in China," *China's Millions* (February 1933): p. 24.

1890s

1 Alvyn Austin, *China's Millions: The China Inland Mission and Late Qing Society*, 1832–1905, Studies in the History of Christian Missions (Grand Rapids, MI: Eerdmans, 2007), p. 347.
2 *The Chinese Recorder* (March 1890).
3 These little known pioneer missionaries have never been profiled in English publications, so it is worth noting their brief biographies here. August Berg was born in Sweden in 1861 and was a pharmacist by trade. He arrived in China in 1890 and served a decade before returning to Sweden in 1900 during the Boxer Rebellion. Berg and his wife, Augusta, returned

to Shaanxi in 1903 and then retired to Sweden in 1928, aged 67. August Berg died in 1940.

Axel Hahne was born in Sweden in 1863 and studied at Frederik Fransen's school of evangelism before traveling to China in 1890. After escaping the Boxer troubles in 1900, it was thought his China career had ended, but then he returned in 1921 at the age of 60. He was married to Anna Watz of the Swedish Mission to China until his death in 1935 at the age of 72.

4 Although Fransen (spelled Franson or Fransson in Swedish) died at the young age of 56 in 1906, his legacy continues today. The missions and alliances he founded evolved into today's Evangelical Alliance Mission (TEAM) which has nearly 600 missionaries serving in 35 countries. An excellent biography in English is by O. C. Grauer, *Fredrik Franson: Founder of the Scandinavian Alliance Mission* (Chicago: Scandinavian Alliance Mission, 1939).

5 Austin, *China's Millions*, p. 319.

6 "The Revival in Shensi," *China's Millions* (March 1910): p. 39.

7 According to contacts in Sweden, his name should be spelled Holmen, but all English-language publications at the time spelled his name Holman. Born in Norway, he arrived in China in 1891 at the age of 21, but his career was short-lived, and he died in 1894 or 1895.

8 Taylor, *Pastor Hsi*, p. 221.

9 *China's Millions* (September 1892): p. 118.

10 A good overview of the work of the Baptist Mission in Shaanxi is Richard Glover, *Herbert Stanley Jenkins, Medical Missionary, Shensi, China: With Some Notices of the Work of the Baptist Missionary Society in that Country* (London: Carey Press, 1914).

11 "A Remarkable Movement in Shensi," *Chinese Recorder* (March 1894): p. 150.

12 "English Baptist Mission, Shensi," *Chinese Recorder* (July 1894): p. 317.

13 August Karlsson in "How God Helped — III," *China's Millions* (October 1898): p. 146.

14 An excellent account of Engbring's life can be found in Marion A. Habig, *Pioneering in China: The Story of The Rev Francis Xavier Engbring, OFM, First Native American Priest in China, 1857–1895* (Chicago: Franciscan Herald Press, 1930).

15 Habig, *Pioneering in China*, p. 77.

16 Habig, *Pioneering in China*, pp. 77–78.

17 W. G. Lagerquist, "News from the Si-ngan Plain," *China's Millions* (September 1894): p. 116.

18 From annual statistics listed in *China's Millions* from the start of the decade, *China's Millions* (September 1890): p. 103; and the end of the decade *China's Millions* (December 1900): p. 136.
19 Taken from Austin, *China's Millions*, p. 347.

1900s

1 Bertram Wolferstan, *The Catholic Church in China* (St. Louis: Sands & Co., 1909), p. 451. Shaanxi Province was divided into two administrative regions by the Catholics at the time. Northern Shaanxi, based at Xi'an, contained a total of 24,392 Catholics in 203 churches. Southern Shaanxi, administered from Ku-lu-pa, contained 11,489 Catholic believers in 56 churches.
2 *China's Millions* (November 1905). There were 80 Evangelical missionaries working in Shaanxi in 1904, a slight decrease from 88 in 1900.
3 V. L. Nordlund, *China's Millions* (August 1900): p. 147.
4 George Sherwood Eddy, *Horace Tracy Pitkin: Missionary Advocate and Martyr* (Yale: privately published, 1891), pp. 17–18.
5 Quoted in *Global Chinese Ministries* (November 2000).
6 Latourette, *History of Christian Missions in China*, p. 513.
7 Mary I. Bryson, *Cross and Crown: Stories of the Chinese Martyrs* (London: London Missionary Society, 1904), p. 57.
8 *Chinese Recorder* (September 1900): p. 487.
9 "Sufferings of Native Christians: Extracts from Letter of a Native Christian in Shen-si," *China's Millions* (November 1900): p. 128.
10 For a biography of Crescitelli's life, see Elio Gasparetti, *In God's Hands: The Life of PIME Missionary Blessed Alberic Crescitelli* (Detroit: PIME Missionaries, 1998).
11 Albericus Crescitelli quoted in Mariagrazia Zambon, *Crimson Seeds: Eighteen PIME Martyrs* (Detroit: PIME World Press, 1997), p. 41.
12 Crescitelli quoted in Zambon, *Crimson Seeds*, pp. 43–44.
13 Zambon, *Crimson Seeds*, p. 46.
14 Chinese Regional Bishops' Conference, *The Newly Canonized Martyr-Saints of China* (Taiwan: CRBC, September 8th Editorial Board, 2000), p. 90.
15 "Tidings from the Provinces," *China's Millions* (February 1906): p. 22.

The Xi'an Bloodbath of 1911

1 Kathleen M. Shuttleworth, *In the Hidden Province: The Story of the Baptist*

Missionary Society in Shensi, North China (London: Carey Press, 1937), p. 36.

2 E. R. Beckman, *The Massacre at Sianfu and Other Experiences in Connection with the Scandinavian Alliance Mission of North America* (Chicago: self-published, 1913), p. 118.

3 J. Beckingsale, "The Revolution in Shensi," *Chinese Recorder* (March 1912): p. 180.

4 Richard Beckman was born in Sweden in 1868 and emigrated to the United States when he was 15 years old. After arriving in China in 1891, he married Ida in 1896, and they returned to Shaanxi together. They were in America and Sweden during the Boxer Rebellion, and returned to Xi'an in 1905 to continue their work. After a period of recovery from the traumatic experiences of 1911, Richard and his second wife returned to China 1919, and he worked there until his death in 1923.

5 Beckman, *Massacre at Sianfu*, p. 67.

6 Hefley and Hefley, *China! Christian Martyrs of the 20th Century*, p. 48.

7 Beckman, *Massacre at Sianfu*, p. 70.

8 Beckman, *Massacre at Sianfu*, p. 73.

9 Beckman, *Massacre at Sianfu*, p. 76.

10 Beckman, *Massacre at Sianfu*, pp. 74–79.

11 Mr. Vatne quoted in Beckman, *Massacre at Sianfu*, pp. 84–85.

12 Beckman, *Massacre at Sianfu*, pp. 74–75.

13 Miss M. Anderson, "Kept by the Power of God," *China's Millions* (May 1912): p. 78.

14 O. C. Grauer, *Fifty Wonderful Years: Missionary Service in Foreign Lands, Scandinavian Alliance Mission 1890–1940* (Chicago: Scandinavian Alliance Mission, 1940), p. 44.

15 Beckman, *Massacre at Sianfu*, p. 136.

1910s

1 Annie Olsen, "The Revival in Shensi," *China's Millions* (March 1910): p. 39.

2 "Revival on the Si-ngan Plain, Shensi," *Chinese Recorder* (October 1909): pp. 593–94.

3 J. Darroch, "The Sunday School as an Evangelistic Agency," *Chinese Recorder* (November 1909): p. 609.

4 See in the Appendix in "Table 2: All Christians in Shaanxi."

5 *China's Millions* (December 1914): p. 168.

6 Grauer, *Fifty Wonderful Years*, p. 81.

7 *China's Millions* (August 1917): p. 90.

8 Mrs. C. H. Stevens, "Miss Gregg's Mission in Fengsiangfu, Shensi," *China's Millions* (September 1917): p. 101.
9 *China's Millions* (April 1918): p. 48.
10 In Chinese culture the aged, especially those with grey hair, are treated with respect and honor.
11 Jessie Greg, *China's Millions* (April 1918): p. 48.
12 *China's Millions* (March 1919): p. 32.

1920s

1 Stauffer, *Christian Occupation of China*, Appendix C, p. lvi.
2 Stauffer, *Christian Occupation of China*, p. 213.
3 Grauer, *Fifty Wonderful Years*, p. 82.
4 For a biography on Andrew Young's life, see J. C. Keyte, *Andrew Young of Shensi: Adventure in Medical Missions* (London: Carey Press, 1924).
5 Mrs. Benjamin Broomhall, "General Feng: His Entry into Sianfu, Shensi," *China's Millions* (April 1922): pp. 56–57. Marshall and Florence Broomhall served as missionaries in China for many years.
6 "A Christian Governor in Shensi!" *China's Millions* (November 1921): p. 168.
7 See "History of China," University of Nottingham (n.d.), https://www.chinaeducenter.com/en/whychina/chinesehistory.php.
8 Feng Yuxiang's faith appears to have waned later in life. He was influenced by Communism and died in a ship fire on his way to the Soviet Union in 1948. Many say he was murdered.
9 James and Evelyn Watson quoted in Annie E. Eldridge, "Stories from Rebel-Ruled Shensi," *China's Millions* (January 1920): pp. 12–13.
10 Grauer, *Fifty Wonderful Years*, p. 59.
11 Solomon Bergström quoted in Grauer, *Fifty Wonderful Years*, p. 60.
12 Solomon Bergström, "Hingping in Shensi," *China's Millions* (May 1927): p. 76.
13 Grauer, *Fifty Wonderful Years*, p. 61.
14 Grauer, *Fifty Wonderful Years*, p. 62.
15 See in the Appendix in "Table 2: All Christians in Shaanxi."
16 Shuttleworth, *In the Hidden Province*, p. 64.

1930s and 1940s

1 "From the Front Line," *China's Millions* (June 1933): p. 112.
2 "Arnold Strange," Biographical Dictionary of Chinese Christianity (n.d.), http://bdcconline.net/en/stories/strange-arnold.

3 Alma R. Artibey, "Fengsiang, Shensi," *Friends of Moslems* (January 1934): p. 13.
4 George Young, "Come Over and Help Us," *Friends of Moslems* (October 1941): p. 42.
5 Grauer, *Fifty Wonderful Years*, pp. 84–85.
6 Grauer, *Fifty Wonderful Years*, p. 89.
7 Grauer, *Fifty Wonderful Years*, p. 89.
8 John Sung in Stephen L. Sheng (ed.), *The Diaries of John Sung: An Autobiography* (self-published, 1995), p. 124.
9 J. Edwin Orr, *Evangelical Awakenings in Eastern Asia* (Minneapolis, MN: Bethany House, 1975), p. 75.
10 Andrew Gih, *Bands of Soldiers for War* (London: Marshall, Morgan & Scott, 1941), p. 22.
11 Orr, *Evangelical Awakenings in Eastern Asia*, p. 75.
12 R. J. Begbie, *China's Millions* (April 1935): p. 68.
13 *China's Millions* (April 1935): p. 74.
14 Grauer, *Fifty Wonderful Years*, p. 83.
15 See in the Appendix in "Table 2: All Christians in Shaanxi."
16 J. Oswald Sanders, *Seen and Heard in China* (Melbourne: China Inland Mission, 1948), pp. 38–39.
17 For a comprehensive overview of the Back to Jerusalem movement from its founding to the present time, see the Xinjiang volume (book 6) in this series. Paul Hattaway, *Xinjiang: China's Gateway to the World* (Manchester, UK: Piquant Editions, Asia Harvest, 2022).

Annie Skau

1 Annie Skau quoted in Gene Gleason, *Joy to My Heart* (New York: McGraw-Hill, 1966), p. 36.
2 Gleason, *Joy to My Heart*, p. 37.
3 Gleason, *Joy to My Heart*, p. 37.
4 Gleason, *Joy to My Heart*, p. 52.
5 Gleason, *Joy to My Heart*, p. 61.
6 Gleason, *Joy to My Heart*, p. 62.
7 Annie Skau quoted in Gleason, *Joy to My Heart*, p. 62.
8 Annie Skau quoted in Gleason, *Joy to My Heart*, p. 2.
9 Gleason, *Joy to My Heart*, pp. 74–75.
10 Gleason, *Joy to My Heart*, p. 82.
11 Annie Skau quoted in John D. Woodbridge, *Ambassadors for Christ: Distinguished Representatives of the Message Throughout the World* (Chicago: Moody, 1994), p. 199.

1950s and 1960s

1 Tony Lambert, *China's Christian Millions: The Costly Revival* (London: Monarch, 1999), p. 231.
2 Taken from individual diocese figures published at www.catholic-hierarchy.org.
3 Quoted in K. P. Yohannan, *Revolution in World Missions: One Man's Journey to Change a Generation* (Carrolton, TX: GFA Books, 2004), p. 115.
4 From Andrew Gih, *The Church Behind the Bamboo Curtain* (London: Marshall, Morgan & Scott, 1961), p. 11.

1970s

1 Zhu Chengxin in "Where Two or Three Have Met Together," *Bridge* (September–October 1993): pp. 9–10.
2 Letter to Open Doors, April 1978.
3 Letter to Open Doors, November 1978.
4 Zhang Guanru quoted in Linda Yeung, *The Gentle Pastor with Rock Solid Faith*, Living Faith Series (Hong Kong: Christian Communications, 2006), p. 23.
5 Zhang Guanru quoted in Yeung, *Gentle Pastor with Rock Solid Faith*, p. 25.
6 Zhang Guanru quoted in Yeung, *Gentle Pastor with Rock Solid Faith*, p. 25.
7 Zhang Fengquan quoted in Yeung, *Gentle Pastor with Rock Solid Faith*, p. 33.
8 Yeung, *Gentle Pastor with Rock Solid Faith*, p. 49.
9 See in the Appendix in "Table 2: All Christians in Shaanxi."
10 An unpublished report by Open Doors, late 1970s.
11 An unpublished report by Open Doors, late 1970s.

1980s

1 Jonathan Chao quoted in Leslie T. Lyall, *God Reigns in China* (London: Hodder & Stoughton, 1985), p. 216.
2 Lyall, *God Reigns in China*, p. 174.
3 Lyall, *God Reigns in China*, p. 215.
4 Personal interview with Peter Xu Yongze, October 2003.
5 David Y. P. Wang, *8 Lessons We Can Learn from the Church in China* (Hong Kong: Asian Outreach Publications, n.d.), p. 5.
6 Wang, *8 Lessons We Can Learn*, p. 6.
7 Wang, *8 Lessons We Can Learn*, pp. 6–7.
8 Brother Yun with Paul Hattaway, *The Heavenly Man: The Remarkable*

True Story of Chinese Christian Brother Yun (London: Monarch, 2002), pp. 60–67.
9 Chinese Church Research Center (25 April 1988).
10 See in the Appendix in "Table 2: All Christians in Shaanxi."
11 Danyun, *Lilies Amongst Thorns: Chinese Christians Tell their Story through Blood and Tears* (Tonbridge, UK: Sovereign World, 1991), p. 330.
12 Danyun, *Lilies Amongst Thorns*, p. 331.
13 Allan Anderson and Edmond Tang (eds), *Asian and Pentecostal: The Charismatic Face of Christianity in Asia*, rev. ed., Regnum Studies in Mission (Minneapolis, MN: Fortress, 2019), pp. 364–65.
14 From an unpublished letter sent to Revival Christian Church in Hong Kong.
15 *Bai Shing*, no. 17 (1981).
16 *Tianfeng* (September 1988).
17 *Pray for China* (January–February 1986).
18 *Yi-China Message* (March 1989); and *Tianfeng* (September 1998).
19 Quoted in Tony Lambert, *The Resurrection of the Chinese Church* (Wheaton, IL: Harold Shaw, 1994), p. 170.
20 *Pray for China* (February–March 1989).
21 Quoted in Lambert, *Resurrection of the Chinese Church*, pp. 169–70.

1990s

1 *Compass Direct* (March 21, 1997).
2 *Pray for China* (January–February 1994).
3 *Pray for China* (January–February 1994).
4 "The Challenge of China," Ministry Report of RCMI (August 1999).
5 *China News and Church Report* (7 May 1993).
6 Xu Fang in *China News and Church Report* (14 May 1993).
7 *China News and Church Report* (7 May 1993).
8 Carl Lawrence with David Wang, *The Coming Influence of China* (Sisters, OR: Multnomah, 1996), p. 84.
9 *South China Morning Post* (9 May 1993).
10 UCAN (9 July 1993).
11 *China News and Church Report* (14 May 1993).
12 Xu Fang quoted in *China News and Church Report* (29 October 1993).
13 Unpublished report by Revival Christian Church, Hong Kong.
14 Personal interview with Sister Ling, August 1999.
15 Danyun, *Lilies Amongst Thorns*, p. 332.
16 Danyun, *Lilies Amongst Thorns*, pp. 333–34.
17 Danyun, *Lilies Amongst Thorns*, p. 335.

18 *Yi-China Message* (March 1989); and *Tianfeng* (September 1998).
19 *Amity News Service* (September 1997).
20 *Yi-China Message* (March 1989); and *Tianfeng* (September 1998).
21 In 254 churches "served by four bishops, 84 priests and 193 nuns." *Global Chinese Ministries* (October 2003).
22 Jean Charbonnier, *Guide to the Catholic Church in China 1997* (Singapore: China Catholic Communication, 1997), p. 181.
23 Far East Broadcasting, March 1990.
24 Far East Broadcasting, October 1990.
25 Far East Broadcasting, April 1992.
26 Far East Broadcasting, March 1993.
27 *Pray for China* (May–June 1995).
28 Far East Broadcasting, April 1996.
29 *Compass Direct* (November 1997).
30 Far East Broadcasting, February 1997.
31 Far East Broadcasting, August 1997.
32 Far East Broadcasting, June 1998.
33 Far East Broadcasting, July 1998.
34 Far East Broadcasting, September 1998.
35 Far East Broadcasting, February 1999.
36 Far East Broadcasting, March 1999.
37 Trans World Radio, November 1999.
38 Far East Broadcasting, May 1999.
39 *Global Chinese Ministries* (October 1999).
40 Trans World Radio, November 1999.

2000s

1 "Church Leaders Detained in Shandong and Shaanxi provinces," *Assist News Service* (27 June 2007).
2 "Public trial held for Taochuan Church Leaders detailed in Shaanxi," *China Aid* (8 August 2009). The news report of the pastors' arrest can be viewed on YouTube: "Church Leaders handcuffed on TV in Shanxi Province in China," YouTube (7 August 2009), www.youtube.com/watch?v=HzuoKENo6DQ.
3 See in the Appendix in "Table 2: All Christians in Shaanxi."
4 Brother Luo Ying quoted in Dennis Balcombe, *China's Opening Doors: Incredible Stories of the Holy Spirit at Work in One of the Greatest Revivals in Christianity* (Lake Mary, FL: Charisma House, 2014), p. 154.
5 Balcombe, *China's Opening Doors*, p. 63.
6 *China Harvest* (November–December 2003).

7 *Compass Direct* (February 17, 2006).
8 *Amity News Service* (June 2001).
9 *Amity News Service* (November–December 2004).
10 Patrick Johnstone and Jason Mandryk, *Operation World: 21st Century Edition* (Carlisle, UK: Paternoster Lifestyle, 2001), p. 176.
11 Johnstone and Mandryk, *Operation World: 21st Century Edition*, p. 176.
12 Charbonnier, *Guide to the Catholic Church in China 1997*, p. 181.
13 Far East Broadcasting, January 2000.
14 Far East Broadcasting, October 2000.
15 *Compass Direct* (December 2000).
16 *Global Chinese Ministries* (September 2000).
17 Far East Broadcasting, June 2001.
18 Far East Broadcasting, February 2001.
19 Far East Broadcasting, November 2002.
20 Trans World Radio, March 2002.
21 Far East Broadcasting, August 2002.
22 Far East Broadcasting, August 2002.
23 Far East Broadcasting, December 2002.
24 Far East Broadcasting, May 2003.
25 Far East Broadcasting, March 2003.
26 Far East Broadcasting, February 2006.
27 *Open Doors* (November 2006).

2010s and 2020s

1 Johnstone and Mandryk, *Operation World: 21st Century Edition*, p. 176.
2 Jason Mandryk, *Operation World: The Definitive Prayer Guide to Every Nation* (Colorado Springs, CO: Biblica, 2010), p. 243.
3 Mandryk, *Operation World: The Definitive Prayer Guide*, p. 243. We believe this estimate was too high, as reflected by the lower number for Catholics in Shaanxi in the tables of this book.
4 The Living Martyrs' Fund continues today and has grown to support more than 2,000 Asian Christians. See www.asiaharvest.org for more details.
5 Some China experts believe the one vote against Xi's appointment was cast by Xi himself, in an act of contrition. Certainly if anyone had deliberately voted against him, they would have known they were placing their lives at risk, as thousands of political enemies had already been arrested, "disappeared," or been executed by Xi.
6 "Christian Couple Homeless after Seven-Year Sentence," *China Aid* (25 May 2022).

7 "Christian Detained after Trying to Join Early Rain," *China Aid* (29 June 2022).
8 "Christian Detained."

Researching Christians in China

1 Ye's figure was quoted in numerous publications at the time, including the *2007 Annual Report of the Congressional-Executive Commission on China: One Hundred Tenth Congress*, First Session, October 10, 2007.
2 Ye's figure was quoted in numerous publications at the time, including the *2007 Annual Report of the Congressional-Executive Commission on China: One Hundred Tenth Congress*, First Session, October 10, 2007.

Selected Bibliography

Austin, Alvyn. *China's Millions: The China Inland Mission and Late Qing Society, 1832–1905*. Studies in the History of Christian Missions. Grand Rapids, MI: Eerdmans, 2007.

Balcombe, Dennis. *China's Opening Doors: Incredible Stories of the Holy Spirit at Work in One of the Greatest Revivals in Christianity*. Lake Mary, FL: Charisma House, 2014.

Beckman, E. R. *The Massacre at Sianfu and Other Experiences in Connection with the Scandinavian Alliance Mission of North America*. Chicago: self-published, 1913.

Borst-Smith, Ernest F. *Mandarin and Missionary in Cathay: The Story of Twelve Years' Strenuous Missionary Work During Stirring Times, Mainly Spent in Yenanfu, a Prefectural City of Shensi, North China*. London: Seeley, Service, 1917.

Botham, Mark. *Two Pioneers: Life Sketches of Thomas and Mark Botham*. London: China Inland Mission, 1924.

Broomhall, Marshall. *By Love Compelled: The Call of the China Inland Mission*. London: Hodder & Stoughton, 1936.

_____. *In Quest of God: The Life Story of Pastors Chang and Ch'ü, Buddhist Priest and Chinese Scholar*. London: China Inland Mission, 1921.

Bryson, Mary I. *Cross and Crown: Stories of the Chinese Martyrs*. London: London Missionary Society, 1904.

Burt, E. W. *Fifty Years in China: The Story of the Baptist Mission in Shantung, Shansi and Shensi, 1875–1925*. London: Carey Press, 1925.

Chan Kei Thong with Charlene Fu. *Faith of Our Fathers: Discovering God in Ancient China*. Singapore: Campus Crusade for Christ, 2007.

Chen Hua Yu. *The Path of Life*. Alhambra, CA: Chinese Christian Testimony Ministry, 2001.

Danyun. *Lilies Amongst Thorns: Chinese Christians Tell Their Story through Blood and Tears*. Tonbridge, UK: Sovereign World, 1991.

Davis, George T. B. *China's Christian Army: A Story of Marshal Feng and His Soldiers*. New York: Christian Alliance, 1925.

Eddy, George Sherwood. *Horace Tracy Pitkin: Missionary Advocate and Martyr*. Yale: privately published, 1891.

Foster, John. *Church of the T'ang Dynasty*. London: Society for Promoting Christian Knowledge, 1939.

Gasparetti, Elio. *In God's Hands: The Life of PIME Missionary Blessed Alberic Crescitelli*. Detroit, MI: PIME Missionaries, 1998.

Gih, Andrew. *The Church Behind the Bamboo Curtain*. London: Marshall, Morgan & Scott, 1961.

Gleason, Gene. *Joy to My Heart*. New York: McGraw-Hill, 1966.

Glover, Richard. *Herbert Stanley Jenkins, Medical Missionary, Shensi, China: With Some Notices of the Work of the Baptist Missionary Society in that Country*. London: Carey Press, 1914.

Godwin, R. Todd. *Persian Christians at the Chinese Court: The Xi'an Stele and the Early Medieval Church of the East*. London: I. B. Tauris, Library of Medieval Studies, 2018.

Grauer, O. C. *Fifty Wonderful Years: Missionary Service in Foreign Lands, Scandinavian Alliance Mission 1890–1940*. Chicago: Scandinavian Alliance Mission, 1940.

_____. *Fredrik Franson: Founder of the Scandinavian Alliance Mission*. Chicago: Scandinavian Alliance Mission, 1939.

Griffiths, Valerie. *Not Less than Everything: The Courageous Women Who Carried the Christian Gospel to China*. Oxford, UK: Monarch, 2004.

Holzmann, John, ed. *The Church of the East: An Edited and Condensed Version of Nestorian Missionary Enterprise*. Littleton, CO: Sonlight Curriculum, 2001.

Huc, Evariste Régis. *A Journey Through the Chinese Empire*. 2 vols. New York: Harper, 1855.

_____. *Recollections of a Journey Through Tartary, Thibet and China During the Years 1844, 1845 and 1846*. New York: D. Appleton, 1852.

Huc, L'Abbé. *Christianity in China, Tartary, and Thibet*. 2 vols. London: Longman, Brown, Green, Longmans, & Roberts, 1857.

Kang, C. H., and Ethel R. Nelson. *The Discovery of Genesis: How the Truths of Genesis Were Found Hidden in the Chinese Language*. St. Louis, MO: Concordia, 1979.

Kauffman, Paul E. *Confucius, Mao and Christ*. Hong Kong: Asian Outreach, 1975.

Keyte, J. C. *Andrew Young of Shensi: Adventure in Medical Missions*. London: Carey Press, 1924.

Lambert, Tony. *China's Christian Millions: The Costly Revival*. London: Monarch, 1999.

_____. *The Resurrection of the Chinese Church*. Wheaton, IL: Harold Shaw, 1994.

Latourette, Kenneth Scott. *A History of Christian Missions in China*. New York: Macmillan, 1929.

Lawrence, Carl, with David Wang. *The Coming Influence of China*. Sisters, OR: Multnomah, 1996.

Lyall, Leslie T. *God Reigns in China*. London: Hodder & Stoughton, 1985.

Meyer, F. B. *Memorials of Cecil Robertson of Sianfu, Medical Missionary*. London: Carey Press, 1913.

Mingana, Alphonse. *The Early Spread of Christianity in Central Asia and the Far East: A New Document*. Manchester: University Press, 1925.

Moffett, Samuel Hugh. *A History of Christianity in Asia, Vol. 1: Beginnings to 1500*. Maryknoll, NY: Orbis, 1998.

Moule, Arthur Christopher. *Christians in China Before the Year 1550*. London: Society for Promoting Christian Knowledge, 1930.

_____. *Nestorians in China: Some Corrections and Additions*. London: The China Society, 1940.

Nelson, Ethel R., and Richard E. Broadberry. *Genesis and the Mystery Confucius Couldn't Solve*. St. Louis, MO: Concordia, 1994.

_____. *God's Promise to the Chinese*. Dunlap, TN: Read Books, 1997.

Nichols, Francis H. *Through Hidden Shensi*. New York: Charles Scribner & Sons, 1905.

Orr, J. Edwin. *Evangelical Awakenings in Eastern Asia*. Minneapolis, MN: Bethany House, 1975.

Ross, John. *The Origin of the Chinese People*. Edinburgh: Oliphant, Anderson & Ferrier, 1916.

_____. *The Original Religion of China*. Edinburgh: Oliphant, Anderson & Ferrier, 1909.

Shuttleworth, Kathleen M. *In the Hidden Province: The Story of the Baptist Missionary Society in Shensi, North China*. London: Carey Press, 1937.

Stauffer, Milton T. (ed.). *The Christian Occupation of China*. Shanghai: China Consultation Committee, 1922.

Stewart, John. *Nestorian Missionary Enterprise: The Story of a Church on Fire*. Edinburgh: T&T Clark, 1928.

Taylor, Geraldine. *Pastor Hsi: A Struggle for Chinese Christianity*. Singapore: OMF Publishing, 1997.

Wang, Samuel, and Ethel R. Nelson. *God and the Ancient Chinese*. Dunlap, TN: Read Books, 1998.

Yeung, Linda. *The Gentle Pastor with Rock Solid Faith*. Living Faith Series. Hong Kong: Christian Communications, 2006.

Young, John M. L. *By Foot to China: Mission of The Church of the East, to 1400*. Tokyo: Radiopress, 1984.

Yun, Brother, with Paul Hattaway. *The Heavenly Man: The Remarkable True Story of Chinese Christian Brother Yun*. London: Monarch, 2002.

Zambon, Mariagrazia. *Crimson Seeds: Eighteen PIME Martyrs*. Detroit: PIME World Press, 1997.

Contact Details

Paul Hattaway is the founder and director of Asia Harvest, a non-denominational ministry which serves the church in Asia through various strategic initiatives including Bible printing and supporting Asian missionaries sharing the gospel among unreached peoples.

The author can be reached by email at **office@asiaharvest.org** or by writing to him via any of the addresses listed below.

For more than thirty years Asia Harvest has served the church in Asia through strategic projects that equip the local churches. At the time of going to print, Asia Harvest has successfully printed and delivered more than 420,000 Bibles to house church Christians in Shaanxi, in addition to supporting many evangelists and providing aid to hundreds of persecuted church leaders and their families.

If you would like to receive the free *Asia Harvest* newsletter or to order other volumes in The China Chronicles series or Paul's other books, or if you want to contribute to Paul's ministries to support Chinese Christian workers and their families, please visit **www.asiaharvest.org** or write to the address below nearest you:

Asia Harvest USA & Canada
353 Jonestown Rd #320
Winston-Salem, NC 27104
U.S.A.

Asia Harvest Australia
Mailbox 80, 377 Kent Street
Seabridge House
Sydney, NSW 2000
AUSTRALIA

Asia Harvest New Zealand
PO Box 1757
Queenstown, 9348
NEW ZEALAND

Asia Harvest UK
c/o AsiaLink
31A Main Street
Ballyclare, Co. Antrim
BT39 9AA
UNITED KINGDOM

Asia Harvest Europe
c/o Stiftung SALZ
Moehringer Landstr. 98
70563 Stuttgart
GERMANY